BLOWING
MY OWN
TRUMPET

BLOWING
MY OWN
TRUMPET

AN AUTOBIOGRAPHY
BY KENNY BALL
WITH WILLIAM HALL

JOHN BLAKE

Published by John Blake Publishing Ltd,
3, Bramber Court, 2 Bramber Road,
London W14 9PB, England

www.blake.co.uk

First published in hardback 2004

ISBN 1 904034 83 7

British Library Cataloguing-in-Publication Data:

A catalogue record for this book is available from the British Library.

Design by www.envydesign.co.uk

Printed in Great Britain by CPD, Wales

1 3 5 7 9 10 8 6 4 2

Papers used by John Blake Publishing are natural, recyclable products
made from wood grown in sustainable forests. The manufacturing processes
conform to the environmental regulations of the country of origin.

Every attempt has been made to contact the relevant copyright-holders,
but some were unobtainable. We would be grateful if the appropriate
people could contact us

CONTENTS

'This man is a genius!' – Louis Armstrong

'Kenny's a ham. We're all hams, but Kenny is special. If he was playing in front of that terracotta army buried in China, he'd get them all up whooping and stamping!' – Humphrey Lyttelton, at a Giants of Jazz concert in High Wycombe

'My mission in life is to set people's feet tapping. I love jazz. I'd rather die than not play it' – Kenny Ball, 2004

ACKNOWLEDGEMENTS

I would like to thank everyone who first persuaded me that I should do it, and then helped me to make this book possible: my wife Michelle; all my children – Gillian, Keith, Jane, Sophie and Nicole; my brother Jim; Paul Warren; Alan Freeman; Brian Matthew; and my assistant Heather Lewis.

A special mention must be reserved for the late Lonnie Donegan who gave my career the kick start I needed.

My grateful thanks also to the Jazzmen for jogging my memory on so many of the wonderful, hilarious and often outrageous times we have had together over more than four decades of laughter, fun and music. The two John Bs (Bennett and Benson), Andy, Hugh, Nick, Bill – that's a big one I owe you all.

My particular appreciation goes to William Hall, who has been instrumental (no pun intended) in writing this book with me, travelled with us on our gigs and delved deep into researching the archives. We're thinking of making you an honorary Jazzman, Bill!

Finally, to Phil Hoy, the tireless editor of our fan club newsletter *Jazzette*, who has collected every one of our records (more than 500 at the last count) and whose home outside Leeds is a virtual shrine to us with its posters on the walls and Jazzmen memorabilia. Thanks for all you do, Phil, and to your predecessors Joyce and Reg.

Kenny Ball, Stansted, Essex, 2004

FOREWORD

Camberley, Surrey, south of the M25. The Camberley Theatre on Knoll Road is one of our regular gigs, and the fans turn out in their loyal scores to cheer me on every time I get my silver trumpet out of its case and take to the stage. Close by is the famous Sandhurst Military Academy, and if you feel like a drink there are pubs like the Goose and the Slurping Toad in the High Street.

From outside, the theatre is not the most illustrious of venues: a large purpose-built affair with not a lot of soul but at least with all its vital organs intact, the most important of them being the long bar with its plush carpet and posters of myself and the boys on the walls. This will be the place where we will meet and greet the fans after the show, which I always make a point of doing, however far we have to drive home afterwards.

The theatre has a varied line-up of events, judging by the programme. We're squashed between An Evening with Christine

Hamilton, the Rushmoor Odd Fellows Male Voice Choir and the Magic Mash Show ('Do you believe in the paranormal power of the potato?'). Well, it takes all sorts.

The band room is a riot of pastel shades: pale blue walls, pale mauve door, matched by pale cheeks from the band as they come in one by one from the chilly car park outside. Coffee and sandwiches await us. It's not dripping luxury, but it's comfortable enough.

Anyone who has set foot backstage in any theatre, especially the older buildings around the country, will be familiar with the cramped quarters that pass for dressing rooms: often just a seat, a mirror flanked by naked light bulbs, and a threadbare carpet. This one isn't five star, but it's as good as it gets for a provincial theatre. I get changed, making sure I put my right leg into my trousers first and then my left shoe first. Superstitious? Aren't all performers? But now I'm into my black evening-dress trousers and gleaming white tuxedo, and heading out for the show.

The stage is lined with jet-black screens behind us, so in my tux I'll stand out like a white knight. The audience starts filtering in, bringing their drinks from the bar with them in plastic cups. Plastic, of course, has replaced glass in many public places for security reasons – even Concorde had plastic cutlery in her final months. This does tend to relieve a certain stress factor for performers, particularly stand-up comics and footballers. Have you ever tried hurling a plastic cup at a stage? You'll be lucky to lob it over three rows!

Peeping out from the wings, I spot some familiar faces. Dave and Margaret have followed me for four decades, wearing black fan club sweaters with KENNY BALL inscribed in gold letters. Dave's an electrician, Margaret is a care worker. They get *Jazzette*, our official newsletter, every three months, and follow us round the country. Thanks, folks. I'll have a chat with you later.

XII

A disembodied voice fills the auditorium. 'Ladies and gentlemen, will you please welcome …

'On drums: *Nick Millward*!

'On double bass: *Bill Coleman*!

'On piano: *Hugh Ledigo*!' Hugh, sparky and bearded, has an amazing sixty-eight years behind him, but exudes the energy of a man half his age. He's the guy who actually arranges all the numbers.

The strident voice again: 'On trombone: *John Bennett*!

'On clarinet: *Andy Cooper*!

'On second trumpet: *Ronnie Hughes*!

'And the boss … *Kenny Ball*!'

The boys are all in black suits with white shirts. The boss boasts his dazzling tux. For added impact my shadow appears against a giant spotlight on the back screen, reminding everyone of those opening credits in a James Bond movie when Sean Connery, Roger Moore or Pierce Brosnan walks out with a Walther PPK before turning it on to a would-be assassin drawing a bead down a rifle barrel.

Tonight everyone's safe. The only weapon I'm waving at them is Kenny's trumpet.

We kick off with a lively rendition of 'So Do I', with yours truly adding a few choice words that were never in the original: 'You want a kiss? So do I. Would you like to get pissed? So would I!' Then it's into 'Jeepers Creepers'. Now, a bit of dialogue: 'Hullo, folks. It's nice to be back in … where are we? Oh yes, back in Camberley. It must be a year or two since we were last here.'

A voice from the audience shouts, 'And it don't seem a day too long …' Thank you, sir. Who let him in? The party's warming up. Which is what Kenny Ball and his Jazzmen are all about.

We have several show-stopping numbers in our repertoire.

Every musician in the group is capable of his 'moment of strewth' – that's when the auditorium rises as one and cheers its heart out. Tonight it's Andy's turn, with my world-famous party piece: 'There Ain't Nobody Here But Us Chickens'.

I introduce him. 'This man has a fabulous voice … in a strange sort of way!' Strange is right, as Andy tucks his clarinet under one arm and proceeds to strut around the stage, clucking insanely like a hen that has just laid an oversized egg.

I look around at the boys and give them a grin. I feel a surge of warmth and, indeed, affection. We've been together a long time – and it don't seem a day too long, either! I first formed the Jazzmen back in 1958, and in that first year we performed 370 gigs and concerts all told – and that included a month's holiday to recover. We've been around the world nearly a dozen times, played all over Europe and in countries from America to Australia, via Japan and the Philippines. This year alone we've got more than 100 appearances on our schedule.

But I still love it. We all do. We wouldn't do it otherwise. I'm reminded of something the legendary Humphrey Lyttelton said the other night when we were on the same bill in 'Giants of Jazz', with George Melly up on stage there too. Humph told someone, 'I still find it fun. The day I wake up not looking forward to it is the day I'll stay in bed – for ever!'

I go along with that. Humph is eighty-two. I'm just passing the seventy-three milestone. So that makes me a youngster in this game.

Doesn't it?

CHAPTER ONE

THE MUSICAL BALLS

I was one of nine children. So it's just as well that I'm hot stuff at maths, and have been ever since I was a kid. When my dad, Jim Ball, celebrated his ninetieth birthday, the house in East London was filled with relatives – brothers, sisters, assorted uncles, aunts, nephews, nieces, cousins, all of us gathered to raise a glass and wish him well for the next ten years.

Dad almost made it to the century to receive the Queen's telegram, but in fact dropped off the perch at the age of ninety-eight. Shame, really, but still a great innings. He was a terrific man.

On that ninetieth birthday I totted up the relatives, and do you know how many there were in one room?

Twenty-two!

No kidding. Twenty-two Balls. We could have fielded two soccer teams. There's a joke in there somewhere – like make that twenty-three, counting the round one!

1

Dad had the resilience of an old warhorse. Mum died in 1962, and that was a huge set-back for him, though he eventually got himself a girlfriend – perhaps I should say lady friend, as she was only a few years younger – named Doll. She was a widow, too, and was his partner for years right up to his death. Doll died three years later, and was in her nineties too.

Dad had been born in 1888. He died in hospital of pneumonia in 1986 after two prostate operations, and fought all the way with the courage and tenacity he had shown all his life. He was actually in a coma for seven days. But he woke up halfway through the week, and found Doll at his bedside. She reported back to us later that he woke up, gazed up at her from the pillow, and said, 'How about a fuck then, Doll?' That was our dad – game to the last. They were his last words. He died with a smile on his face, I'm sure. I always said those six words should have been on his headstone.

The whole family came to the funeral. Dad was buried in the City of London Cemetery – he was a Freeman of the City of London, and in fact passed on the honour to me 'by patrimony', as I'm a member of the Worshipful Company of Stationers.

It was the biggest turnout since his ninetieth birthday, and the wake back home in Oakwood Gardens was a joyous affair that went on into the early hours, because that's what Dad would have wanted.

So for a home that was constantly filled with laughter, as ours was, it's ironic that one of the earliest memories I have in life is of my brother Arthur being carried out of the house in a coffin. It was 1934, and he was nineteen years old. I must have been four. I remember standing in the front room with my mum Ethel holding my small hand tight in hers while she fought back tears as four men passed by in the hall, carrying a plain wooden coffin out of the front door.

Peering through the window, I saw them push the oblong box into the back of a shiny black car, which drove slowly away up the street. Neighbours clustered in small groups by their gates, watching silently as it passed out of sight.

Arthur had been in a motorcycle accident, and somehow he got tuberculosis from it. They had no antibiotics in those days that could cure the infection. At least I was spared the funeral, but I remember the dreadfully sad atmosphere in the house for days. It was unusual because we were such a happy family.

We were a musical lot, from Dad downward, and I found out that Arthur had played the banjo. Mum kept his instrument in a wardrobe for years after the boy's death, almost forty years in fact, right up until 1970 when it suddenly disappeared.

Arthur had always been the apple of my mother's eye, but after his death I became her favourite because I looked like him, or so she said. I was the last of seven natural kids – two more were adopted – so maybe that's another reason. Also there was an eight-year gap between me and the last one before me to arrive! I'm told I was quite a shock to everyone. In fact, my elder brother Jim – a full twenty years older than me – summed it up pithily: 'We were disgusted!' Thanks, Jim! More from you later, possibly.

Actually I do have a vague memory of the time before Arthur's death. Arthur slept in the front room when he was very ill so that Mum could look after him. I remember standing by the bed looking down at his pale face, and Arthur shouting from the pillow: 'Get that child out of here! I don't want him near me.'

I was too young to understand any of it, but I did realise that something serious was happening in our lives.

But first things first. I was born at home on 22 May 1930, at 28 Maysbrook Road, Dagenham. The exact time was ten minutes to midnight, so I was informed later, but for the first seven years of my life I was told I'd been born on 23 May, which confused me from an early age.

The family mansion was a two-up, two-down semi-detached on a council estate, and when I came into the world I can at least say that I gave my mum no trouble. As number seven in line, I popped out like a pea from a pod. No pain, no strain. Kenneth Daniel Ball, weighing in at 7lbs 4oz, didn't make a lot of noise, either. I saved that for later. Mum must have been forty-four when I was born, which was regarded as very late in those days. God knows what the neighbours thought, but probably much the same as Jim and the family. 'Christ! Where did he come from?'

Jim has actually told me, sitting by the fireside in his living room, 'When you came along, Kenny, I said out loud, "Good God!" My sisters and I all thought, 'Ere, Mum, it's about time you packed that lark up! That was the attitude in those days. We were all surprised, and Mum was too. She wasn't expecting anything like that. Dad was a year younger, and they broke the news to us when we finally noticed Mum was putting on weight, and realised what was happening. But when you arrived, little Kenny, we forgot all about our original feelings. We all made a fuss of the new baby, and you were spoiled something rotten.'

'Well, that's nice to know, Jim,' I responded. I wasn't so sure about that initial reaction of my cherished brothers and sisters to the result of what had obviously been an incautious gleam in my father's eye.

Dad was in some army camp with the Territorials when I was born. They sent him a telegram. Years later Mum showed me his reply: 'Having a good time. Glad it's a boy. See you next week.' The doctor who was looking after Mum said, 'I'll give him "having a good time". He should be here. Wait till I see him!' And he gave Dad a good tongue-lashing when he got home.

But I have to hand it to brother Jim. 'Listen, Kenny,' he revealed to me. 'I'll tell you something else. I'm the only one of us who ever cleaned your bottom! When Mum went out shopping at weekends I was left with you. I had to change your nappy! I put you on the floor because you wriggled a lot and I didn't want to drop you. I laid you out on a blanket, and changed you. You had a favourite trick: you'd hang on to my ears, and not let go. Proper little devil you were!'

Time for a family roll call, and a head count. Big sister Dorothy was born in 1906 (no kids). Ethel came into the world in 1908 (two daughters). Jim was born in 1910 (one daughter). He is now a proud grandfather (two girls, one boy) and great-grandfather (all boys). The Ball dynasty lives on! Next came Marge in 1912 (three children, four grandchildren), poor Arthur in 1915, and Ted in 1920 (two sons, two grandchildren).

If the Ball family tree is starting to read like a wall map, here comes a twist in the tale. Mum's sister Kathleen married a man who turned out to be a bigamist, and even went to prison for it. We'll draw a veil over that part of the family scene and lock the skeleton back in its cupboard. Suffice to say that in 1923, after a lot of ooh-ing and aah-ing, we adopted Auntie Kitty's two boys, George and Frank, who came to live with us. Mum was the type who wanted people around her, so you couldn't look on it as taking in strays: she brought those two kids up and loved them as her own.

And then, in 1930, along came … me!

With ten years between me and the last brother, Ted, and twenty-four years away from my eldest sister Dorothy, I was virtually an only child. It meant I spent a lot of time with my mother. But many of our extended family – is that the expression? – still hung on in the house.

In fact, Dad had been a World War I war hero, though he kept it quiet, after an extraordinary incident on the field of battle at Cambrai in France, where the first major tank battle of the war took place in November 1917. The battle is all logged at the Imperial War Museum. As for my father's part in it, Corporal James Ball found himself trapped and alone four miles behind enemy lines in the confusion and chaos of the conflict after his commander lost touch with its battalion. The massive 28-ton Mark 4 tank took a direct hit from a shell, killing most of the crew. Despite being wounded and having blood pouring from a head gash, he was handed a Webley by his dying CO and told, 'Get out, Ball! Take my revolver and make your way back to the lines.'

Dad slipped away through the trees. An hour later, resting up in the undergrowth, he spotted four armed Germans coming towards him. When they were close by, he stepped out and shouted, 'Hans hoch!' They all threw down their weapons and put up their hands. Corporal Ball then ordered them to make a stretcher out of their greatcoats, with the sleeves intertwined. Lying on the makeshift hammock, half-conscious and with the gun on his chest and his finger on the trigger, he was carried back to Canadian lines by his four prisoners.

The story came out, as these things do, over a period of years and with little fuss. Most men I ever knew who fought in the 'war to end all wars' seldom, if ever, talked about their experiences – and then only reluctantly. I've met men who were gassed in the trenches, others who went over the top. It was as if they'd shut the memory away into a darkened room and thrown away the key, never wanting to open the door again.

But there was no doubt about it: Dad was a hero. Eventually he revealed a few details about his amazing act of courage and survival, but he never elaborated on it. They gave him a medal, which I found tucked away in the back of a drawer after his death in 1986. I don't think it was the Military Cross or anything as important as that, but it was still something to show for what he did in the Great War.

As for Mum, she was a forceful personality with an uncommonly earthy turn of phrase. In fact, it was sometimes quite shocking. To give you some idea, when at the age of seventeen I first brought my fiancée Betty home (I started young) her relationship with Mum was of the love–hate variety. Betty was a blonde with a fiery temper to match. One day, after a particularly noisy outburst from my beloved, Mum turned on her and shouted, 'You're just like a cab-horse, you are. You shit and stamp in it!' You've seen those cab-horses standing in the cold, stamping their hooves impatiently?

Another descriptive expression she'd use when people were mouthing off too much was 'Stop mucking about. You sound like a fart in a colander!' To which there was no reply that any of us could think of right away. She had lots of little phrases, one of which I still use to this very day: 'Self-praise is no recommendation.'

The world in which I grew up was a hard place. The spring of 1933 was the peak of the Great Depression in Britain, with unemployment standing at three million, which was around twenty per cent of the country's workforce, and dole queues stretching around the blocks. Straggling lines of men in mufflers and cloth caps hunched against the driving rain to get their weekly handouts. From up north the Jarrow shipbuilders were marching on London. Stanley Baldwin was struggling to control the runaway economy, prices were forced down and labour was dirt cheap.

That was the outside world. If the hard times affected us, I was blissfully unaware of it. Somehow Dad was grafting a good living as a bookbinder, and was bringing home a pay packet fat enough to feed those of us still under the family roof. Mum kept the home fires burning. We must have been careful with money, but we never went hungry. She made sure of that.

Everything revolved around the home. There was no TV, and the expression 'couch potato' hadn't been invented. We had to make up our own entertainment, just like thousands of other families across the country. We've all seen photos of a family sitting round a fireside listening to the wireless – pipe-smoking Dad in his cardigan, Mum knitting, the kids playing a game or doing a puzzle. And a dog or a cat stretched out by the fire. Well, it really was like that. Except that the Ball family had music in their blood, and the whole street knew it!

I actually believe people liked to hear us. The sound of a kid rehearsing on the piano, or even a trumpet, meant life was going on. It created a buzz in the air. I'll never forget walking down our street one Christmas Day and seeing every other house with a party going on inside – all of them with a piano in the background. There was a huge community spirit. Everyone was friendly. The neighbours would help each other, and I don't just mean sharing a bowl of sugar or a couple of eggs. I mean *really* help. If there was illness in a family and someone had a transport problem, there'd always be someone willing to give them a lift. When Mum was out she would leave the key hanging on a piece of string inside the letter box, so a neighbour could get in if there was an emergency.

We made up our own games. One that Mum invented was to get us to gather round her chair in the evenings and see how many grey hairs we could pick out of her head! Honest to God! George, Frank, my nephew Terry and myself. Mum had rich black hair.

'Every time you pick eight grey hairs out of my head,' she would say, 'I'll give you a penny!'

We kids turned into a horde of locusts, descending on her and scrabbling around in her hair looking for a tell-tale grey wisp. I used to joke, 'Mum, you'll be bald in ten minutes!' She was in her fifties by then, remember. Dad used to say that her hair had been 'as black as Newgate's Locker' when he first met her – a reference to the old prison cells, presumably. That was his saying. But as time went on, we started to make a bit of pocket money.

We had a dog, Pongo. What else do you call a nondescript mongrel? In fact, he earned his name because he liked to forage around a sewage works down the road! Pongo was a real character, with white fur and a lovely nature. We were inseparable. He followed me everywhere, just like those wonderful stories of Just William and Jumble. When I was four years old, I saw my first Dalmatian. The story has become part of the Ball family folklore. I must have liked the look of this Dalmatian, so much so that I found a tin of black paint and painted our own white dog all over with big black spots. Oh, dear! Poor old Pongo! But he must have forgiven me because years later he would bound exuberantly down the street to follow me when I cycled to school.

When I was about six I took up the mouth organ. Eventually I would graduate to the chromatic harmonica. This has a button on the side which allows you to produce any note, as distinct from the diatonic type that just plays a particular scale. When I was older I could play practically any tune on the harmonica. I used to hear Larry Adler on the radio, and that man was an inspiration to me. I was transfixed by the way he talked about his mouth organ – he never called it a harmonica – and about music in general.

My parents gave me a silver-coloured Hohner, a real beauty. It had wooden strips in between the metal. In those days mouth organs were all the rage – you could get all sorts in different keys. I remember seeing big harmonicas with all kinds of ranges – bass, alto, soprano, you name it.

Most of our family games revolved around music. My brother Ted had built a primitive tea-chest bass with an old broom handle. Sister Ethel played the piano. Sister Marge sang soprano. Dad was on the piccolo, flute and spoons. Junior (that's me) was on the mouth organ. We had a whale of a time.

Even at that age I would play at the drop of a hat. One of my favourites was the old Ovalteenies jingle – Mum and Dad had made me a member of the Ovalteenies Club – which began: 'We are the Ovalteenies, little boys and girls ...' That was one of Junior's showpieces!

Every Sunday afternoon after lunch was concert hour. We always used to have cockles and winkles spread on the table, and occasionally whelks which I never liked because they tasted like rubber. Dad called the shots. Mum used to say he was 'full of beans and tram tickets' – beans because he was always on the move, and tram tickets because of those little machines conductors wore around their necks that shot the tickets out like machine-gun bullets. Dad was like that. Full of piss and vinegar, they'd call it today! While most people relax in an armchair to digest their Sunday lunch, our lot would be allowed no such respite. Immediately after the plates were cleared away, Dad would be on his feet, urging us all to 'get your backsides off the cushions and get the party going!'

He decided on the tunes, and he used to sing them too. His own favourite was 'Old King Cole', and he would imitate the flutes and drums and violins with his mouth. He could make his party piece last about ten minutes. Another favourite was 'There Ain't No Bones in Beer'. Dad liked his beer, and he always insisted there was no such thing as bad beer – just that 'some is better than others'. I'll go along with that. Actually, Dad didn't drink a lot. Towards the end of his life one single whisky would make him tight as a drum. He smoked a lot, though, around sixty a day, which didn't help his vocal chords.

We each had set pieces to play. Dad would go from one of us to the other, waving his arms like a conductor and bringing us in on cue. Sister Marge's regular song, I remember, was 'I'll be Loving You, Always'.

It would turn into one big jam session. 'My Old Man Said Follow the Van' … all the old favourites. Dad encouraged us to do what we wanted: improvise, dance around the table, you name it, anything to keep the party lively and fun. Maybe that turned me into the kind of jazz musician I am today. We could make those old Cockney songs swing like the clappers – you should have heard 'Lily of Laguna'. Years later, now I think about it, many of those tunes had the same heartbeat as jazz, so the transition was easy.

These Sunday sessions normally lasted an hour or so. Then we'd put our instruments away, Dad would switch on the wireless and we'd all sit around listening to the Palm Court Orchestra on the BBC from the Aeolian Hall in Bond Street. How could I ever guess that years later this would be the place where I would get my big break?

The other way we kept ourselves amused was with jigsaws – giant puzzles 3 feet square which the whole family would pore over for hours. The one I remember most vividly was of the 1936 coronation, a colour portrait of King George VI and Queen Elizabeth wearing their crowns and robes, facing each other. That kept us engrossed for a couple of weekends.

You'll have gathered by now that our family tree is very big, and has sprouted in all directions. By and large, longevity runs in the Ball family, which is encouraging for all of us. Older brother Jim did a spot of research and discovered that our ancestors were a seafaring lot. One of my great-uncles was captain of a British warship fighting the Spanish at the battle of Trafalgar, and we even have a silver buckle off one of his shoes to commemorate it. He died before his time, doing his duty for king and country, but those of us who pass on from natural causes seem to last longer than most.

Grandfather Ball on my dad's side – another Jim, incidentally – was a docker, and he survived well into his nineties. The family in-joke is that he worked in Bow Locks. Try saying that fast, and you'll understand why we crease up whenever we recall it.

'Where do you work, sir?'

'Bow Locks!'

'I beg your pardon?'

Dad would last the course until he was ninety-eight, with all his marbles intact. When he retired from his bookbinding work, I joked, 'It must have been all that glue-sniffing. You were probably on a high every day.'

He gave me a paternal cuff around the head. 'Cheeky little monkey. But you could be right. Look at your brother Jim.'

At this point let me introduce you to my older brother, Jim Ball. All of twenty years older, which means he's in his nineties now, he has a spring in his step and a gleam in his eye that are the envy of men half his age. Witness a picture of him with his hands round a couple of lovelies on a recent Fred Olsen cruise.

He followed Dad into the bookbinding business when he was fourteen to learn the trade. Today he is still in the same home in Dagenham where he has lived for the past thirty-six years, in a street with two-up, two-down pebble-dash terraced houses with red tiles on the roof and the walls painted in a surprising variety of pink, yellow and mustard. Jim's own house is ochre-coloured, just to be different. It is a cosy refuge from the world outside. Burgundy curtains and pink wallpaper in the sitting room, and outside a small garden with a shed and a lawn no different from the others on either side all the way up the street. I like to pop round to Jim's and sit with him in front of the fire, listening to him reminisce about the old days.

Jim exudes the optimism that has always been a hallmark of the Ball clan. He may be heading for the Queen's telegram, but he's still as lively as a cricket with a vast reservoir of humour to keep him young.

When he won the pools he broke the news to his wife in typical fashion. Poor Lilian was ill in bed, and Jim records the conversation as follows: 'I went upstairs, sat on the bed, and said to her: "We've had a spot of luck, dear. We've won a bit on the pools. A fair bit."

'She said, "What would you call a fair bit – £10?"

'"Oh, a bit more than that."

'"Twenty pounds?" she asked.

'"A little bit more …"

'At which point she burst out, "Oh, for Christ's sake, let me know how much we've won!"

'"How about £22,000," I said. She made a remarkable recovery on the spot!'

With the money he won on the pools he bought the place outright. Smart move. It's worth a lot more now, though I can't see him ever moving. The sitting room is filled with family portraits, all lovingly framed and polished daily. Jim is a great-grandfather, and the young faces smile out everywhere.

He recalls his own early youth with amazing clarity, as if it was yesterday. 'I was brought up with the smell of glue all round me,' he'll tell you. 'I used to go round to insurance companies to prepare their books for them. In those days we had hot glue, not the synthetic kind like they have today. I used to carry the glue pot in hot water. The first thing you did when you got there was to ask where the kitchen was so that you could heat up the glue.

'But there was one problem. It smelled terrible: a combination of old socks and mouldy cheese and a lot else besides. People would flap their arms around in disgust, and say, "Cor, what a horrible smell! What is it?"

'And I'd tell them: "It's my glue pot. You didn't think it was me, did you?"' Then brother Jim would deliver his own party piece – a stern lecture on glue. He'd tell them: 'Glue is only made out of old bones. Look here, when you wash yourselves in that lovely scented soap I'm sure you use, that's what it's made of. Old bones.

'Now most of those old bones come from India. What happens in India is that scavengers – human scavengers, I mean – collect the bones of the cows that fall dead in the street, the sacred cows, right? And also of the beggars who do likewise. These scavengers are not particular whether they're the bones of cattle or bones of beggars. They sell the bones to the soap factories. So remember, next time you wash your face in that lovely soap – you might be washing yourself in some of our brothers!'

And his rapt audience would chorus: 'Oooh! How horrible!'

According to Jim there used to be a soap factory in Stratford East, and the pungent aroma could be smelled for miles around. I couldn't help noticing the twinkle in his eye as he recalled how he'd go by bus to visit his customers. 'Sitting there with this hot water bucket and a pot of glue on my lap, I wasn't very popular with the other passengers. But I loved the job.'

One high spot of the job was the Book of Remembrance he painstakingly restored, which you can see today in St Sepulchre's

Church in Holborn, central London. Bound in maroon leather from Morocco, it is a true work of art, and Jim is intensely proud of his handiwork.

'It's like the Book of Remembrance in Westminster that's for the whole of the country. This one is for London, and they turn a page over every week. Other times I maybe did a 150-year-old Bible, with the leaves all falling to pieces. You have to take the pages out and resew and patch them. That might take me up to a week, depending on what was required. It's work for which you need huge patience. The one mistake you mustn't make is to hurry.'

Sadly, he lost his Lil three years ago after more than six decades together, and recalls: 'I did think, You're either going to mope around, or pull yourself up and do things. So I decided to do just that.' He has now met a lovely lady named Elsie, and I wish them both luck. He took five different holidays last year alone, which is about four more than I managed. Now he's into cruising – and I'm talking about the kind that happens at sea.

With his typical sense of the ridiculous, Jim tells a story of how he was incarcerated briefly in hospital for tests to his innards. 'They put me in a ward, give me some medicine, and a few hours later I wake up in the middle of the night and find I'm covered from head to foot in shit. I'd completely lost control of my bowels. I get out of bed and call, "Nurse! Pass the glue pot! I've had a mishap."

'The nurse was a young kid from the Philippines. She comes rushing up, takes one look and me and says, "Oh, goodness. Don't do anything. I'll do it all."

'She takes my pyjamas off, and says, "Follow me!" She leads me out to the bathroom and I walk behind her, stark naked and leaving a trail on the floor behind me. I still shudder to think about it! She orders me to stand on a towel and washes me down. I never felt so humiliated in all my life, to be stood to attention by a young girl like that, completely naked and covered in shit, and washed down.

'They put me back in bed. Next morning the doctor comes round early, and you know what he says? "Right, Mr Ball, we need a sample to analyse!"

'I stare up at him from my pillow. "Christ, doctor," I say weakly. "Why couldn't you have been here last night? You could have had a bucketful!"'

That's my brother Jim, a raconteur whose shafts of wit (I think I got that right bearing in mind the last story) always give us something to laugh about.

The last time I visited brother Jim he had a fresh batch of ice lollies in his fridge, supplied by the local Ear, Nose and Throat unit at Ilford. 'What on earth are these for?' I asked him. 'I didn't know you were into lollipops.'

'They're to stop my nosebleeds,' Jim responded.

I thought he was having me on. 'What do you do, stick 'em up your hooter?' I asked, grinning. 'Which flavour is best?'

Like Queen Victoria, brother Jim was not greatly amused.

'Not many people know this, but it works,' he said. 'It's something to do with cooling the inside of your mouth and up through the sinuses. All I know is that it works. A pack of frozen peas stuck over your nose works too – you hold it there like a compress.

'One other thing,' he said, showing me in the direction of the door. 'In case you really are wondering – the flavour doesn't matter.'

Full of surprises, we Balls are.

CHAPTER TWO

BOMBS, BUGLES AND BANDMASTER BAILEY

It nearly all came to a grinding halt for me when I was the tender age of four and my father took me on a day out to Southend. There was just the two of us that day, and it was a real treat for me because I loved being with my dad.

Apart from cockles, winkles and other seaside delicacies, Southend has always been famous for its pier. Built in 1889, it was the longest pleasure pier in the world. It still is, stretching an amazing 1.3 miles out into the North Sea. A couple of bad fires (in 1976 and 1995) did a lot of damage, the last one destroying the bowling alley, but at least the equally famous railway is still running.

In those days the resort also boasted a 30-foot mobile platform beside the pier which ran out along the sand on wheels, and could also float. People would get on this thing to be taken out to where the boats were moored, for a trip around the coast and a spot of sightseeing and birdwatching.

On this particular day little Kenny was scampering around the platform as it trundled out, when he slipped and went right over the side. I must have fallen 10 feet, and plunged into 6 inches of sea water on to the hard sand at the bottom – but the really bad news was that I landed on my head, which did me no good at all.

'Kenny, son! You all right?' Dad's anxious face peered over the rails, a long way above me. I was anything but all right. Actually, I was as close to death then as I have ever been in my life, and I was lucky I hadn't broken my neck.

We took the train home to Chadwell Heath, with me soaking wet and shivering uncontrollably, and Dad trying to comfort me. What he didn't realise was that it wasn't a chill I had caught – it would be diagnosed as meningitis.

There are various forms of this disease. The modern thinking is that it's a viral infection of the membranes that surround your brain and spinal cord. I looked it up in a medical book, so that's how I know. You can even get it from the virus that gives you a common cold or 'flu. All this was happening to me in the early 1930s, remember, when medicine wasn't as advanced as it is today. The doctors told Mum and Dad that you could get meningitis from a blow on the head, as they believed could happen in those days.

Whatever it was, I had a nasty headache and my neck was going stiff – both symptoms of what today is called cerebrospinal fever, and extremely dangerous. Now they just give you antibiotics. In those days little Kenny Ball got the full works.

They rushed me into King George's Hospital in Ilford, where they laid me down on a couch, soothed my pathetic cries as best they could and put me through an X-ray machine. Actually X-rays were in their infancy, rather like I was, and I was told later that I was one of the first guinea pigs. But it worked. They were able to pinpoint the area, and spot a load of fluid going up into my brain.

They must have stuck a needle into me to drain the liquid off the back of my neck, though I don't remember much about it. I have only a hazy recollection of lying in bed in a darkened room and people moving about in white coats.

But it must have been serious, because for the next eighteen months I didn't go to school. I was kept at home by Mum, and spent a lot of time in my bedroom with the curtains drawn while I recovered. Intolerance to bright light is apparently another symptom. But I came through it. And there's been no recurrence, thank God. Sometimes I think to myself, Kenny, you've had seventy years of life which you weren't entitled to. It's a sobering thought. It came into my mind many years later in the sixties when I played a gig on Southend Pier with the band, in the dance hall on the very end of the pier. I could actually pinpoint the spot where I took that headlong plunge.

We moved house a couple of times during my childhood. I don't know why Mum and Dad were so restless, because everyone tells you that moving house is the next most stressful thing to divorce. But they stayed happily married while they shifted the furniture across Chadwell Heath, with all nine of us kids in tow, from Maysbrook Road to a larger house in Roxy Avenue.

Moving home as we did was probably because Dad was going up in the world. In the midst of all the economic doom and gloom he had become a supervisor, earning more of a crust as a bookbinder and in constant demand for his expertise. One day he got an offer he couldn't refuse, to join a firm that was printing the famous Penguin books. Before I knew it the whole family had upped sticks and moved to Worcester, where we would spend the next three years.

By now I was fully recovered, and it meant another school. But that didn't worry me. I was really quite a cheery little chap, able to fit in anywhere and make friends easily. I never had any problems. No sadistic teachers, no bullying – well, one bully, and that was later. My parents put me in the Stanley Road Junior School which was located next to the Worcestershire Sauce factory. I walked past the gates every day. It had a lovely smell, that sauce, which permeated the whole street, and I've been hooked on the stuff ever since!

The only downside to that period in my young life was that I was introduced to the violin. Now this was regarded as a cissy instrument – and that was my nickname as long as I was at that school. 'Cissy! Hey, *Cissy!*' As a young kid of eight I had no choice. Piano was OK – everyone was taught that. But the violin was something else, and I really didn't take to it, or to the insults that flew my way. Apart from being rollocked something rotten, I found it a very hard instrument to play. The sounds I got out of the thing put your average yowling cat to shame.

Luckily my flirtation with the violin remained just that. No lingering love affair, but a blessedly brief encounter. High noon finally came in the playground after only a month, when I was walking home after my music class. Some of the other kids were lying in wait, and I didn't see them until it was too late. There was an ambush, a chase and a tug of war which ended with my violin somehow getting impaled on the school railings, damaged beyond repair. Well, I suppose it could have been me hanging up there.

I made my apologies to the music teacher, who must have realised what was going on because he didn't punish me. And I have never touched another violin to this day – there were no strings attached to young Kenny ever again!

Instead, I would set my sights on another instrument, one that to me exuded passion, power and excitement. The trumpet.

The first real step on my musical journey can be traced back to the day I became a mascot for the local sea cadets, and marched about with them through the streets of Worcester wearing a little sailor suit, complete with cap. I must have been knee-high to a grasshopper, but I loved every minute I was on parade.

The band marched right behind me, deafening me with a cacophony of bugles, tambourines, trombones and drums. This was a brass band, all wind and percussion and not a string in sight. Now *that* was music to my ears, and I was proud as punch to be part of it.

Three years went by before I knew it. The Ball family returned to London just in time for the Blitz – brilliant timing – to hear the dawn chorus of wailing air-raid sirens and the *crump* of bombs exploding down the road.

With unerring foresight, Dad had also found us our new family home right by the goods yards near Kinfauns Road, Goodmayes. This was located at the end of the railway line from the east coast, a line which was visible like a gleaming thread from the air for any eager *Luftwaffe* pilot hell bent on flattening London. The first time I looked out of my parents' bedroom window at the rear, I saw for myself how the view from the back of the house was the shunting yard itself! Prime target. The German bombers would simply follow the line in from Southend just to see where it ended up, and then let everything go. Nice one, Dad!

First off, our local corner shop down the road got it. A direct hit from an oil bomb. This unpleasant piece of Nazi ordnance was a 100-pounder that exploded like a Molotov cocktail and set everything alight when it struck the ground. The whole place went up in seconds.

At the height of the Blitz I actually saw bombs raining down like dark cylinders. First hint was the steady, growing throb of scores of engines in the sky. Then an eerie whistling sound. When she heard that high-pitched howl, Mum would physically throw herself on top of me, protecting her small son until the thing went off with an almighty bang. I'll never forget that shrieking sound. I was ten years old, and images like that stick in your mind for ever.

One time we were in the hall between the kitchen and the front room when that whistle came from nowhere – and next thing I was flat on the carpet with Mum smothering me like a human mattress! Then she calmly got up and went back to preparing my tea, telling me to 'get on with your homework'.

It was the same with the air-raid siren. That warning wail was one of the most ominous sounds in the world, a haunting dirge like a lament for the dead that I can still hear today. And the all clear? Ah … one long note, and what relief! It meant we all felt safe again – until the next raid.

We were probably living on borrowed time, but we never thought of it that way. We just got on with our lives, like so many other East End families in the Blitz whose sheer survival created a kind of myth.

I shared a front bedroom with my brother Ted, next up in the time scale and eight years older than me. It was big enough for both of us not to trip over each other. Our beds were on opposite sides of the room, but there was never anything territorial between us – no dividing line stating 'this is my part, you stay over there'. All in all, it worked out brilliantly.

Ted was a technical wizard, and I looked up to him for his talent with anything mechanical. He could put a bike together in his sleep, which proved particularly useful since we couldn't afford new ones and relied on scrap parts he'd collect and assemble in the back yard. A saddle, pedals, a couple of wheels and a frame, and lo and behold – there it was! One bicycle, ready for the road.

22

When I was old enough, Ted even built a motorbike for me out of bits and pieces from the local junk yard. Maybe he sparked something off in me, because I became fascinated by gadgets and creating something out of nothing. In years to come I would even build myself a car from scratch.

We would share that room together for a few precious months until Ted was called up. At the age of eighteen he became an aircraft engineer. Suddenly he wasn't making bicycles any more. The only handlebars he was mixing with were those on the stiff upper lips of the Flying Officer Kite characters he met on airfields all over southern England.

Ted's attitude to the war could be summed up in a postcard that arrived from somewhere in Kent. He knew we were suffering daily stress from the Blitz, though Mum and Dad did their best to disguise it. The card read, 'Knickers to the Germans! I'm going to get my own back on them!' And he did, by volunteering for the flying corps. He became a flight engineer on Halifax bombers and survived forty trips over Germany, and then a further seventy-five 'operational missions' over hostile territory, which I always thought was pretty incredible. These involved 'spy drops' into Yugoslavia and Italy – Ted was the one who stood by the open door and kicked the guys out into space behind enemy lines. Then it was his job to sling out the guns and grenades and the other gear by parachute, and make sure it all landed in the right place.

Ted, sadly now dead, was also awarded the Croix de Guerre after the war, which was the first we knew that he had also worked with the French Resistance on top of all the other action. The medal arrived through the post – just an envelope with the Cross inside it and a citation. At least he was spared a kiss on both cheeks from General de Gaulle.

To me, Ted was a hero, and always would be.

One close shave was nearly my last. Towards the end of the war, that whole area around Ilford had become a target for the rockets – the V-1, or doodlebug, and later its big brother the V-2, which was a much nastier affair because you never heard or saw it coming. The first you knew of it was a massive bang, and then half the street had gone.

This particular near miss – one of several – happened when I was going to the pictures in Ilford on a number 25 bus. We still went resolutely to the cinema every week, my mates and I, even if the film was frequently interrupted by an air raid and the whole place, including the screen, was plunged into darkness and silence while the audience waited in uneasy anticipation for whatever might be unleashed from the skies.

Life went on. This was V-1 time, the summer of 1944. I was upstairs at the front of the red double-decker with my pal Ron when I heard the familiar drone of a doodlebug from somewhere overhead. We all ignored it, because the thing wasn't dangerous as long as you could hear it. Day after day it had been drummed into us that, when the engine cut out, that was when it would start its glide downwards. Otherwise relax, Kenny, you're going to be OK.

All the windows of the bus had sticking plaster over them to prevent the glass fragmenting – primitive, but apparently it worked. I was searching the sky for the doodlebug with a schoolboy's curiosity, when suddenly the engine cut out. Someone shouted, 'Get down!' Along with every other passenger on that bus I dived for the floor and curled myself up like a worm.

The bus trundled on, and then there was an almighty explosion. I popped my head up to see half a dozen houses ahead of us simply disintegrate in a mass of dust and flying bricks. One moment they were there, with their neat gardens and curtains at the windows, the next they were gone. Later I heard that the doodlebug had knocked out eight houses, though I never discovered what the casualties were.

It was a strange time for a kid, not knowing whether it was an exciting war game or something more serious. Hitler was throwing everything at us with his V-1 and V-2 rockets in a last-ditch attempt to bring England to its knees, and a V-2 nearly had my name on it when it landed down the bottom of our road late in 1944. I had a couple of friends killed in that one. Two of my school mates were in a shelter in their garden, and the rocket actually landed on top of them. Direct hit. Dreadful. Like I say, the difference was that you could see – and hear – the V-1, but you never saw a V-2. The first you knew of it was when a building or an entire street just disappeared.

My nephew Terry had been with me that night. I was fourteen, he was a year younger than me – but still my nephew. This may sound complicated, but he was my older sister Ethel's son. Don't forget I was a late arrival, eight years after the others off the launching pad. We were both asleep in my front bedroom, and the bloody thing blew the whole front of our house out as well as turning a lot of the street into rubble. The wall just fell away. It was a Friday, at about seven o'clock in the morning. I was jolted awake to find the entire wall had disappeared, and there I was staring out from under the blankets with a hazy view of the houses across the road, all of them with broken windows.

I thought, This has to be a bad dream. But it wasn't. Choking plaster dust filled the room, and Terry's grimy face materialised out of the fog. Mum came screaming in through the smoke like a demented ghost. 'Kenny! Terry! Are you all right?' She grabbed us in her arms. Is that a rude awakening, or what? There was dust and glass everywhere, but somehow we escaped without a scratch.

I'd heard a lot of explosions by then, but that was something special. My head was ringing like a hundred alarm bells; I was half deaf and I could hear everything with a dull booming echo, as if through a flannel. But somehow we scrambled into our clothes, and ran out of the house and down the street to my mates to see if we could help. I remember the chilling sight: all that was left of their shelter was a hole 30 feet deep, and no sign of the family. No sign at all. No shoes, no tattered clothes, no blood.

By the following evening the wall was back. Well, sort of a wall. They put plaster and hardboard up, and covered it all over with tarpaulins. Amazing! Don't ask me how they did it. But there was a lot of hammering and shouting and people scurrying around. That night I was back in my own bed, in clean sheets because Mum had washed them, and the room had been scrubbed from floor to ceiling. There's the East End spirit for you.

The odd thing is that I never had a single nightmare. I suppose my attitude was the same as any youngster living through the war night and day: they're not going to kill *me*! Isn't that the attitude of all those young men and women when they were sent off to war, poor beggars? You just go through with it. I never thought of myself as particularly courageous, probably because I wasn't. You always think it's other people who are brave – my dad, for instance, and not just for what he did in World War I. This time he was a firewatcher. He stood on rooftops at night with the shrapnel raining down and reported back to headquarters when something went off nearby. As for Mum, she went through the war supporting all of us, with never a word of complaint.

Actually Terry was a sad case, and even now it upsets me thinking about it. He had a terrible life, poor chap. His father abused him, and made him sleep in a shed at the bottom of their garden. Eventually the boy was sectioned, and ended up in a mental asylum, diagnosed as a schizophrenic. I never saw the bad side of him. But one day Terry turned on his mum with a bread knife, threatening her but without harming her, and that was that. For some reason I was given the job of taking him to the local hospital in Brentwood, just the two of us, where they were expecting him. Strange things happened in those days, things that would never be allowed today. I remember leading him to the reception desk, where he turned to me and said, 'You're coming, aren't you? You're coming in with me as well.'

And I lied. 'Yes, Terry, I'm coming. Don't worry.' But as soon as they got him into the secure ward I left. He was in mental institutions for the next forty years. They were ghastly places. Don't forget there was no cure for schizophrenia in those days: they didn't know what on earth it was. They'd give them a lobotomy, and that was that. Basically they took him away, locked him up and threw the key away. Tragic, it was. Terry had a huge record collection of 78s which they let him keep in his room at the hospital. He would play them over and over again, and sing along with them. I used to visit him, and sometimes I'd sit on the bed and sing along with him, but each time it was a heart-rending experience. Terry died in Goodmayes Mental Hospital in Barley Lane at the age of fifty-five.

Around the age of twelve I joined the local branch of the sea cadets, sixty of us, a full sea cadet corps based at Christchurch School, Ilford. Our instructor was a Lieutenant Bailey, and it was great fun. We met in the evenings to march around the playground, climb up ropes in the gymnasium and do all sorts of physical stuff. Basically being a sea cadet in Ilford meant stomping about on parades and going to sea in a boat on dry land – a mock-up with wooden benches in a local church hall. I learned Morse code and how to semaphore, and can do it to this day, which is handy in a supermarket when signalling the wife.

I stayed with the cadets until the end of the war, and wore

my uniform on the victory parade in Whitehall. What a fantastic day! I managed to climb up a tree near Trafalgar Square without any copper ordering me down, which gave me a marvellous view of the marching bands and the hundreds of troops passing by below. It stirred the blood, and made me feel enormously proud of my country.

But the most important thing that happened to me in the sea cadets was learning the bugle. Actually I'd always wanted to play the trumpet, ever since as a kid I first saw Harry James at the cinema. I remember films like *Springtime in the Rockies* and *Bathing Beauty* – and he always seemed to get the girl. Trumpet meant crumpet, right? Maybe I was naive – but then again, as events proved in years to come, maybe I wasn't.

When Harry actually started his show business career at the age of four in a contortionist act, he was billed as 'the Human Eel'. Maybe that's where he got his success with women – and there, I can't compete. And he did marry Betty Grable, didn't he?

In fact, when I was very small I had an experience that nearly put me off the cinema for life. Our local cinema was the big Odeon on the corner. I was seven years old and Dad took me to see Jack Hulbert in a film about Bulldog Drummond. It was called *Bulldog Jack*, and was supposed to be a comedy thriller about a playboy who poses as Drummond, gets involved with a bunch of thieves and saves the girl.

The heroine was played by Fay Wray, that lovely lady who, as filmgoers will know, ended up in the mighty paw of King Kong. I ended up under the seat!

There was one sequence with a runaway train that had me watching through my fingers, and another where the pair of them had to cross over a bridge that was on fire. That sent me diving for cover – I was scared silly. Much later I found out that the film was actually very highly thought of, and had been acclaimed by the critics. 'As good as anything in screen melodrama,' someone wrote thirty years later, paying tribute to the legendary producer Michael Balcon. *Kine Weekly* praised it for its 'full quota of thrills and laughs'. All I know is that it was five years before I ever set foot in a cinema again, truly! I've never forgotten it.

But if I was put of cinema, my music-making came on by leaps and bounds. First I had to be content with making a start with the bugle. As Lauren Bacall said to Humphrey Bogart, 'You know how to whistle, don't you? All you have to do is purse your lips, and blow!' Well, it's the same with a bugle, roughly speaking.

Our bandmaster taught me how to play it. Lieutenant Bailey was big, burly and an ex-Marine. 'First off, young Kenny, a bugle only has five notes you can play, so you can't go wrong,' he said encouragingly. 'They're called open notes. To squeeze more notes out, you need valves – and that's where the trumpet comes in. For now, we'll stick with the bugle. Imagine an elastic band. The further you stretch it and twang it, the higher it sounds, right?'

'Er, right, sir!' It sounded right enough.

'Good. Same principle with a bugle. The more puff you put into it, the higher the note. OK? Let's hear you!'

And it worked. I blew that bugle for all I was worth and, after a session of strangled cats and constipated chickens, the right sounds started to come out. Next thing I knew I was marching around the parade ground with the band, puffing and blowing like a steam engine in top gear. Bandmaster Bailey nodded his approval. 'All right, Kenny. We'll soon be able to move you up a rung. I'll have to find you a trumpet.'

I still have a bugle in my collection at home, only this one is very special because it came my way on my fiftieth birthday. It was a present from the Jazzmen. The boys had their names engraved on it, one below the other, J. Bennett, R. Bowden, A. Cooper, J. Benson, B. Swift, J. Fenner, with the inscription: 'It's a shame to take your money!' If you've heard me at one of my concerts you'll know this is one of my catchphrases. If I've really enjoyed a particular number, I'll tell the audience, 'I really enjoyed that. It's a shame to take your money!'

The good news about these two instruments is that they're both in B flat. That won't mean a lot to a layman or to someone who's tone deaf, but it meant that I could play the trumpet quite easily. One of the main differences between a trumpet and a bugle is that with a trumpet you can blow higher notes.

For the *cognoscenti* among us, I should add at this point that mouthpieces are important, too: you don't get such a good tone with a shallow mouthpiece. You need one with a bigger bore, like a shotgun. But with a small bore you don't puff so much air into it to make a loud noise.

If I've lost you, don't worry about it. All will become clear.

CHAPTER THREE

MUSICAL
BENT

I should state here and now that, at this point in my burgeoning musical career, I was taught the wrong technique by Bandmaster Bailey, bless his socks. He meant well, but led to me playing most of my early hits the wrong way.

What he actually said was, and I remember his words as if it were yesterday, 'To make a sound come out of a trumpet, my son, you've got to spit into it!' So I did. Over the next twenty years so much saliva went down the tube I could have launched a battleship on it.

The technique in fact is to get your tongue *behind* your teeth. Over the years I was able to teach myself to double-tongue: *ticka-ticka*! But I never managed to triple-tongue: *ticka-ticka-ticka*! Your tongue has to go through your teeth, which sounds impossible until you try it ... and keep trying.

I learned words like 'embouchure' – and how to spell them.

This was one of the first French words I ever learned: it's from *emboucher*, meaning 'to raise one's lips', and before that from the Latin *bucca*, or 'puffed-out cheek'. Actually I have always been totally against this technique that many trumpeters use, which makes them look like Bugs Bunny. You see musicians with their cheeks all puffed out, but it means that there is air in there that you shouldn't have. Dizzy Gillespie, who worked with the Billy Eckstine band from 1944 and was one of the exponents of bebop, used to play like that, and of course he was brilliant. But there is no doubt that playing that way loosens the muscles that control the lips and mouthpiece.

Me, I just steamed in and taught myself.

First things first. To be a trumpeter you need a trumpet of your own. The sea cadets were OK, but I was still on the bugle. By the time I was called up for national service I was already into jazz bands. I actually acquired my first trumpet at the age of thirteen when I spotted an advertisement in *Melody Maker*: 'For sale, one trumpet, price £10'. It belonged to a bloke who lived in Kenton, in the suburbs of north-west London. I phoned first, then took a train next morning, found the house and knocked on the door. A fat bloke with a bandage round his head answered it, and when I introduced myself he said: 'Ah … oh … yes … you'd better come in. There's been an accident.'

I had my £10 in my hand, most of my savings. He said, 'You'd better see the trumpet first.'

He pulled something out from a cupboard, and showed it to me. I stared at it, blinking in disbelief. The trumpet had a nice shine to it — but it was bent sideways in the middle. The whole thing was L-shaped!

'Strewth!' I exclaimed. 'What's happened to it?'

Somewhat hesitantly, the fat bloke began, 'Well, I knew I was selling it today. So last night when I came home from the pub I decided to have one last blow ...' His voice tailed off.

'So?' I said encouragingly.

'Well ... the wife took such umbrage at the noise that she grabbed it from me and hit me over the head with it. This is the result. I'm sorry. You can have it for eight quid if you like ...'

'OK, I'll take it!'

Eight pound notes changed hands. So did the bent trumpet. I shook his hand, took the instrument into the street, waited until I was out of sight behind the hedge, and then – easy does it – I bent my new purchase back into shape over my knee. It didn't crack. In fact it was surprisingly easy. I gave the instrument a few exploratory toots, then danced off down the road blowing my heart out, like the East End's answer to the Pied Piper of Hamelin. It made a marvellous sound.

That was my first trumpet. OK, it was slightly battered, rather like its previous owner. But it never hit a false note. And I used it to start my first jazz band.

I took that trumpet straight down to my mate Ron, who lived at 71 Elmstead Road. I got off the bus, and when I was within earshot of his house I started blowing it again. That brought him to the door and, even though I didn't know any of the notes, we went straight in and had our first jam session in his front room, just the two of us with Ron pounding the piano until his fingers were numb. Luckily his mum was out, and there was no one else home, or it might have been the shortest gig on record.

So here I am, aged thirteen, teaching myself. The first step was to play a note, and then find out how pressing each valve altered that note. I then wrote out which finger played which note, got an exercise book and wrote down all the tunes that I wanted to play. 'Darktown Strutters' Ball' was one of the first. Then, for each tune,

I noted the fingering like this: 1 ... 2 ... 0 ... 1 ... 2 ... 0. Meaning: first ... second ... open the valves ... first ... second ... open!

My mum was wonderful. And patient. I would practise for at least an hour every day. The neighbours were kind, too. They must have been used to it, what with our piano going all the time and the impromptu family concerts on Sundays. Nobody seemed to mind. Just to remind you, these were the days when everyone made their own entertainment, so a singsong in somebody's front room or a kid warming up on a trumpet wasn't something that raised any eyebrows or caused a stir.

Despite the war years and the Blitz and the narrow escapes, I was very lucky to be brought up in a family like ours. We didn't have much in material terms – imagine bringing up nine children in those days. Dad used to give Mum £3 a week out of his wages, and God knows how she managed on that. But we never went hungry, and we were dressed well enough. We shared everything, and learned to look after one another.

Over the years my brothers and sisters left home and went their own way, though we always remained close and stayed in touch. Me, I wouldn't leave home until 1952.

As a very young kid I was never into teddy bears or cuddly toys. They just didn't interest me. The *Queen Mary* was launched when I was six, and my brother George bought me a big cardboard assembly kit for my birthday. I spent hours on that model and, when I had finished, it was almost 3 feet long. That was about the extent of my creative genius.

My favourite toy was a cricket bat my dad gave me when I was about eight. I've always loved cricket, and I must have been good at it because at school I was cricket captain. I used to put insulating tape around the handle to help the grip, and every weekend I would rub the wood with linseed oil to keep it in trim.

My education had begun at Chadwell Heath Infants' School, but now I was at Mayfield Central Junior in Goodmayes, which took pupils from seven to fourteen. I went on to Mayfield Elementary, and that was where I had my best day on the cricket pitch. It's the kind of day that a kid remembers for the rest of his life – taking three wickets against Cheam Grammar! I was a hotshot fast bowler, keen, lean and mean, and I could hurl that ball down like a catapult. It made up for my lack of batting prowess, and on that day I was carried shoulder-high off the field!

There were no uniforms. Everyone called me 'Bally' – pronounced Bawly. It was a nickname that stuck right through my schooldays until I left at fourteen, and certainly beat 'Cissy'. The headmaster was a Mr Steer, a very kind man, your archetypal schoolmaster, rumpled but authoritative. Now I come to think of it, he did once give me six on the hand with a cane for a misdemeanour I'd committed. It was a game we used to play in the toilets – who could pee the highest up against the wall. Show me a boy who can tell you, hand on heart, that he has never been tempted to try his luck on that one! I was winning on this particular day when in walked Mr Steer. That did it. Six of the best for young Bally. By God, it was painful, but I never cried – it was more than your life was worth to be seen as a softie at school.

Corporal punishment never did me any harm, as far as I know. My own view is that it can instil respect – but there is also the danger that there'll be some teachers who are really just sadistic and enjoy beating small boys. So on balance I suppose I am anti it.

I shone at school, but never enough to worry the national grid. I was in the A stream, the best, and in Form 3a I was top in science and mathematics. Science included biology, but all I remember was dissecting frogs and not a word about the birds and the bees. That, I would have to find out for myself. Our science master was Mr

Ivy, and he was a terrific teacher. Under his guidance I became fascinated by the whole subject. He would take us on a journey into the very basics of what makes things tick, and I would sit there at my desk, enthralled. In the science lab I once built a commutator. In simple terms, it's a copper thing that works with alternating currents. In less simple terms, I'll give you the full Monty definition: 'A cylindrical arrangement of insulated metal bars connected to the coils of an electric motor or generator to provide a unidirectional current from the generator or a reversal of current into the coils of the motor.' Amazingly, I got it first time.

To say I was in my element isn't just a bad pun – it's a fact. In my teens I rewired someone's house, and by the time I was in my twenties I could have built a car if I wanted. When I was thirty, that's just what I did.

Another teacher I remember clearly was a lovely lady with a lovely name. Miss Pocock taught English. She had buck teeth, and the kindest nature anyone could be blessed with.

I got on well with most of the lads, and became part of a gang. Five of us, all told, and a right handful of mischief-makers we were, according to my brother Jim. 'You were little villains,' he told me, 'always up to something. You would play games of dare like Knock Down Ginger, where one of you knocks on someone's door and has to get behind the hedge before they come out to see who it is. Or Button Down Jimmy, where you fix a bun on a piece of string, pin it against someone's window and let it tap on the glass without anyone spotting you. That can be quite scary on a dark night.'

I don't recall too much of that. But I do remember one incident which was my first act of vandalism – and I hope my last because I can't remember any others. I went to a building site where there was a large water barrel in one corner. I got a hammer and nails, and started knocking the nails into the barrel. Of course, the water shot out.

But I was clocked. Someone spotted me, my parents were informed and Dad got the local police to come round and interview me. This big copper stood over me in the front room, and said sternly, 'All right, son. You're coming down to the station with us.' It scared me shitless. And it got me over my law-breaking ways on the spot! My punishment? I apologised abjectly, and was kept in for several nights. It's small fry compared to what vandals do today, but it was still a lesson.

As Jim confirmed about our other schoolboy pranks, 'At least it was nothing destructive, like so many kids today with graffiti and scratching cars and the like. I have to say, Kenny, you had a marvellous sunny nature. You were always happy.'

That, I can confirm. My schooldays were truly among the happiest days of my life. For a start, everyone in our gang was musically inclined. We called ourselves the Big Five – after Churchill, Roosevelt and Stalin, who were the Big Three, though not so musical.

Ron played piano, Johnny was on saxophone, Alan on drums, Jim on guitar and myself on trumpet. We were thirteen years old, and it was my first-ever music group. We gave ourselves a name: the Youth Club Stompers. Our debut gig was a dance at Pullman's Road School in Ilford. We used to get lots of girls from a Dr Barnado's home across the road, and it was all jive and fun, the girls whirling around in those bell-like dresses that were all the fashion.

Within the school, of course, it was a different kind of music. As part of the orchestra I played my mouth organ in the school concerts. One song we all sang – 'I'll Take You to a Valley Where the Harebells Grow' – I had never heard before and have never heard since, but I can remember the words *and* the tune. It must have been the school song, because we sang it at every important occasion. What are harebells? None of us had a clue then, but to save you looking it up I can tell you that they're Scottish bluebells.

I was captain of Brook House, and also athletics and cricket captain. I could hurtle 12 feet in the long jump on sports day, run the hundred yards in eleven seconds and never dropped the baton in the 200-yard relay. I was no good at the high jump because I was only a short-arse! And as for football, I hate to admit it, but I was hopeless.

There was one boy who was the school bully. There's always one, isn't there? He was a big lout, much taller than me, and all I knew about him was that his father was a boot repairer. In the summer we used to play cricket after lessons. One day my friends and I were having a game in South Park, Ilford. I must have been about twelve. This bloke came over with two of his mates and nicked our ball.

I was quite incensed, and I was also scared – this thug simply towered over me. But I managed to face up to him, and demanded, 'Will you give us our ball back?'

'No, Bally,' he said, 'I'm keeping it.'

'If you don't give it me, I'll hit you!'

His mates guffawed, and he laughed nastily and said, 'You dare try!'

Well, I did. I thumped him in the chest, because I was too small to reach his jaw. With that he steamed in and beat me black and blue. He almost knocked me out, and left me semi-conscious in the mud.

'Keep your stupid ball,' he called out, striding off with his mates and slinging the ball back at me as I lay on the ground. But he never touched me again, or bothered any of us. Or tried to take our ball.

The bombs were still falling. One time a German bomber dropped a 1,000lb landmine, and it got caught up in telephone wires. It was just dangling there, high up above our heads like an ugly grey metal lump. I stood staring up at it before the police and the ARP boys arrived and moved me on, sharpish. They evacuated everybody from the area, but smoothly, without fuss. They were doing it every day, so they knew the routine. We were led round to the school, and took cover in the cloakroom, sitting on benches with our raincoats over our heads – I suppose to protect us from flying glass.

I heard later that a naval officer turned up with a ladder to defuse it. Now that's what I call a very brave man. He went up the ladder, and started fiddling around with it. All of a sudden there was a shout, and he started coming down very fast and running away. But the mine went off, and he disappeared completely. Blown to bits, they said. I didn't see it, but we all heard the explosion, and afterwards we saw the results of it. That bomb blew the windows out all down the street. We saw at least four houses blown flat, and no sign of the naval officer. You've got to take your hat off to any of the bomb-disposal boys, whether it was 1941 or fifty years later with modern-day terrorism.

Another time the marshalling yards outside the back of our house were dive-bombed. We had an Anderson shelter at the bottom of the garden where we would all take cover when we heard the aircraft coming. One day we had our old Auntie Alice in the upstairs bedroom. When we heard them coming we dived into the shelter, and yelled, 'Come on, Auntie! Get down here! Run!' Auntie ran like mad. We had an apple tree in the garden, and as she ran past it I remember seeing the apples exploding off the branches as the bullets hit them. She was lucky to get away with it, but she was a game old bird and saw the war out with the rest of us.

But, at that stage, as a sparky teenager I had more on my plate than worrying about what Mr Hitler would be sending over next to flatten us into submission. Sex was starting to rear its ugly head!

One girl was Sheila and the other was called Anita. I'm talking about two drop-dead-gorgeous teenagers who took my fancy, and happily seemed willing to show the feeling was mutual. They seemed like young love goddesses. Sheila was blonde, a nice middle-class girl who lived on an estate in Barking and had a well-off father. I'm sure her family thought me beneath her station – I was obviously closer to Chadwell Heath station than Kensington in their books!

Sheila and I were at the same school. I used to write her little love notes and, even though she never wrote back, her actions spoke louder than words.

Anita was a brunette, and she and I used to snog in a nearby bomb site. Mostly it was just kissing and cuddling, but it got a bit serious one evening when we had both reached fourteen. There were four of us in the grass, and Anita and I were divided from the other two by a wall. Anita's friend was with my mate Ron, and he and I had decided we'd try to go all the way.

We put rugs down, but it was pretty uncomfortable with rocks and stones under us. I could hear a lot of scuffling and whispering on the other side of the wall, and I was about to make my own moves when suddenly we heard this other girl squeal: 'I'm not going to …'

Immediately Anita announced, 'All right, well, I won't either.' And that was that! A few kisses, a spot of cuddling, and home early to bed – on my own.

Now I think of it, there was another girl I used to chase, known to all and sundry as 'Bleedin' Brenda'. She achieved that nickname because of her habit of telling the lads where to get off. Her favourite phrase was: 'If you bleedin' think I'm bleedin' going to go all the way with you, you're bleedin' wrong!' Every sentence was peppered with 'bleedin' this or that ...' She ended up marrying a mate of mine, and still talks like that to this day! And I dearly love her.

Me? I had to wait for four years before 'it' finally happened, and that was when I was doing my national service in the Army.

Be patient. You'll find it worth waiting for – even if I didn't.

CHAPTER FOUR

OTHERWISE
ENGAGED

I left school in 1944, at the age of fourteen, when the war had a year to go. There was one place available in a college of further education in south London. I went up for it as one of two contenders to study maths, and the other fellow got it. I still remember his name: Mason. I missed out.

Instead, I headed out into the great wide world and joined the famous advertising firm of J. Walter Thompson. Their offices were in Berkeley Square, Mayfair, where that nightingale sang, and you don't get many addresses posher than that. I would take the number 25 bus all the way from Seven Kings to Bond Street, and it cost me sixpence.

For my first job in life I started as a messenger, taking copy to all the departments, clocking in at nine a.m. and working through until half past five. Actually, I was really just a gopher – go for this, go for that, 'take a cup of tea to the manager', 'here are some letters for the mail room', that kind of thing. But I didn't mind a bit. I was earning the princely sum of two quid a week, lunch in the café round the corner cost me one and ninepence, and the fares were a shilling a day. So I had some spending money at the weekend – and that's where I came into my own because now I was hitting the music trail at last.

My father had wanted me to become a copywriter. After a year with Walter Thompson, I gave up wearing out my shoe leather trotting around the building on errands, and joined Dad's printing firm of Kelly and Kelly. He helped me get the job. But perhaps we both overlooked one thing: the trouble with nepotism is that you have to work twice as hard to live up to the chance you've been given – and you know that everyone is watching you, waiting for you to fail. You can be the chairman's son, the founder's favourite nephew or a youngster brought in with a wink and a nod, as I was. It's all the same in the end. You'll be fighting your own demons to justify the trust someone's put in you.

Which is why I happen to think, even today, that I let my dad down rather badly. I had my chance – but I couldn't keep my mind on the job. There was music in my head, and I couldn't wait to get home and pick up my trumpet to rehearse. It had already become an obsession.

In those days, the youth clubs flourished. Perrymans Farm Youth Club in May Street, Ilford, was where I spent a lot of time, just hanging around. We kids were just coming into drainpipe trousers and brothel creepers, the obligatory clobber of the day. I bought myself a long sports jacket, coloured a sickly greyish-green, single button, double breasted. My first pair of suede shoes, the famous creepers, buoyed me up both physically and mentally in the wishful thinking that the girls would fancy me.

The Ilford Palais was the place I used to go to hear local groups, and specials like Ted Heath and his Band. By now I myself was sitting in with groups at the local St Margaret's Hall in Barking.

They had a band called the Alan Wickham Hot Six, and this actually lit the touch paper that fired my interest in jazz. Alan was brilliant, one of the unsung heroes of the jazz scene, and played a mean trumpet. I'm still in touch with him. A guy called Rags Russell was on trombone, and years later he would die a weird death – he fell off the stage during rehearsals at the Palladium, and broke his neck. I was told he had been at the sauce, but I never knew the full story. But if you've gotta go – what a way to go!

I was playing Friday, Saturday and Sunday nights at youth clubs and dance halls, maybe having a jam session in a cellar. In those days, one important feature of the dance halls, with the kids' ages ranging between fourteen and eighteen, was that there were no bars. If you wanted a drink, you went across the road to the pub, so there was very little trouble. Occasionally, someone would come staggering in stoned out of their head, and try to pick up a bird. Then you'd get a fight. But it didn't happen too often. It was all quite genteel.

I'm quite sure that music helped keep me out of trouble. We'd go to dances and try to pick up girls. Doesn't every teenage boy with fluff on his chin? So that kind of existence didn't lend itself to vandalism. For me, the challenge of jazz beat hanging around the streets or destroying something just for the sake of it.

Jive came with the game. OK, now I can admit that I never learned to jive properly. I suppose I used to jump about a bit, and I can still do a skip and a hop when I'm pushed to it. But my swing seems to stop somewhere beneath my bum. The fact is that my legs wouldn't co-ordinate with my brain or my instincts when it came to being the East End's answer to Fred Astaire.

What kind of a kid was I? Judge for yourselves when I tell you that, the very first time I went out to play professionally as a musician, I was so shy I hid behind the curtain and wouldn't come out! Since the age of thirteen, I had wanted to be a professional trumpet player. I knew it was the only thing I wanted in life. But when I got my big chance I had an attack of stage fright. It was a small group called the Victor Hayes Jazz Band. They played on Saturday nights at an anti-aircraft battery in Wanstead Flats for the personnel based there. They'd be up on a small stage, and there was a small space in front where people would get up and dance.

On my first night with them I was so scared that I actually hid behind the curtain and played my trumpet from there. It's a funny thing, but these moments come back to haunt you when you least expect it. Only just recently two women approached me after one of my concerts and said, 'We remember you. We were at your first gig on the Flats. We remember it because we could hear the trumpet, but we couldn't see it!'

The following weekend Victor persuaded me to come out from behind the curtain so that people could set eyes on me. I think he felt a bit strange with one of his musicians behaving like the invisible man.

So you're getting the picture of young Kenny blossoming in his formative years. Shy with music, and shy with girls? Well, in truth, yes, both. But I disguised it by being cheerful, jokey and feigning confidence. Later that persona would take me over ... and it all became real.

I met my first wife at the age of sixteen when I was playing at a dance at St Margaret's Hall. Betty Tracey. Starting young? I'll say, though we never actually consummated the relationship for six years. I remember thinking she looked like Betty Grable, and when I found she had the same Christian name I was smitten.

My first sighting of her was just like in that old line, across a crowded room. You never forget something like that, do you? She was standing on the stairs, and I fell for her just like that. Hook, line and sinker.

I can't remember my pick-up approach. In later years one or two journalists dared to suggest I had the look of a 'ballroom gigolo'. It must have been the moustache. But at that time, clean-shaven, it was probably something original like, 'Can I see you home?' She had very blonde hair, was wearing a load of lipstick and she had a knee-length frock shaped like a bell tent, the kind Alma Cogan used to wear. Today you'd probably call it the A-line!

We became engaged when I was seventeen and she was only sixteen. Like I say, it was six years before we were married – and she was still a virgin. I'd have been horrified if it was any other way, because in those days it was expected. Sure, there'd be a lot of kissing and cuddling, with the boys trying to 'go the whole way' as I have mentioned already. But most girls just like to flirt. Well, they did where I came from. Dare I say that I more than made up for it later on? Yes, well, I've said it.

My old Auntie Alice, having successfully survived a strafing from the *Luftwaffe*, had been living with us. When she died she left me £19 – and I used £18 of it to buy Betty an engagement ring, a big square stone with a diamond set in the middle. I have to admit I didn't go down on bended knee to propose, or do anything fancy. It was more a case of 'Shall we get married, then?'

And she said, 'Yes, all right.'

I knew that national service would be looming. 'Will you wait for me, Betty?'

'Course I will.'

And that was it.

The printing didn't work out, and by the time I was seventeen I was in another day job closer to home, shifting boxes at our local

Sainsbury's supermarket. The manager was Mr Squires, a skinny man with a bald head and a blue apron, but a good bloke. I was the lowest of the low, just a dogsbody earning two quid a week, but by now I was doing two gigs a week, earning as much in one night as I would in a week at the store.

Part of the job was to deliver bread in the area. One bloke used to come out of his house at nine a.m. to pick up his loaf, and he was always in a dressing gown. I got talking to him, and it turned out he was a piano player in a nightclub. That fascinated me, and added to the mystique of being a musician. I hated getting up in the morning anyway, and I still do. I've always liked to get in a good nine or ten hours sleep, even more as I get older. They say you need less sleep the older you get – with me it's the reverse. But I'm at my best late at night and into the wee small hours, so I'll sleep through until two o'clock in the afternoon, or later. That's what being a jazz musician does to you.

At that time I used to come home in my lunch hour and practise in the front room. I never boarded up the windows with socks like some of the guys do to make them soundproof – the sounds of Kenny's trumpet floated out into the afternoon, and nobody ever seemed to object. So I obviously wasn't regarded as the neighbour from hell.

I took my trumpet with me on holiday too, and practised regularly. I still do. You just can't afford to stop playing for three weeks, or you lose your confidence. It's a fact: if you stop practising, you're bound to go into a decline. I've always said that, as long as you practise, you've got a good chance of getting better. If you don't – down you go.

Fair enough, not everyone appreciates a budding genius. I went on holiday to Majorca, and bumped into this large German who was in the next apartment. I had my mute with me, as I was trying to tone down the decibels as much as possible, and said to him, 'I apologise for any noise if I'm disturbing you. But I need to practise.'

He looked down at me, and said, 'Mein friend, you sound as if you are strangling ze bloody cat!' Then he stalked off with his beach towel to commandeer his lounger by the pool. But at least he made no official complaint, and over the next week the cat happily continued its slow demise until it was time to go home.

CHAPTER FIVE

PRIVATE BALL

National service. For a lot of young lads in the forties and fifties, that meant two years of stultifying boredom, being in the wrong place at the wrong time and a waste of their valuable formative years. The wrong place could be some flea-ridden rat-hole in the Middle East, or as mosquito fodder in the wilds of India where at that time there was unrest over the partition. But it was an invitation which you couldn't refuse, though a lot of the lads tried to duck out of it.

If they were articled clerks in some profession like accountancy or trying for a legal career, they had a chance. If they tried the 'conchie' line – conscientious objectors – they were hauled before a board and asked questions like: 'If a Nazi is threatening to kill your parents with a gun and you've got a rifle handy, would you shoot him?'

If the raw recruit said 'Yes', he was straight into the front line.

If he said, 'No, I don't believe in violence', he was headed for the front line anyway – in the Ambulance Brigade. Tricky lot, the people who sat at those tribunals. Either way, it was a no-win situation. You had to be more subtle. I knew of at least two straight guys who got out of it by pretending to be gay. One lisped to the interviewing officer, 'Is it true that homosexuals are frowned on in the Army?' He was given a '4' rating on the spot, which meant he was out – as well as outed.

Pacifist or homosexual? I suppose I qualify for one out of the two, since I don't like killing anything, but I could never remotely be described as gay. However, it never came to the crunch because, innocent as I was, I rather liked the idea of two years' national service. I figured, You're getting fed, watered and paid, Kenny, even if the money isn't too great.

I realised I might have made a mistake when I reported to the local call-up office in Romford and was immediately grabbed by the testicles and told to cough! Well, almost immediately, after a lot of form-filling and a few preliminary questions. Then I was standing in a line-up of fellow conscripts in another room, stripped down to my Y-fronts, and this bloke wearing a white coat over a brown uniform was walking down the ranks fondling each and every one of us. I wonder how many thousands of young men still have that abiding memory of their first day in Britain's new model army?

I remember thinking, Nobody else has ever held your testicles before, Kenny, apart from yourself. And certainly not a bloke. He'd seemed friendly enough, until he asked my name while he was still hanging in there.

'Ball, sir!' The trouble was, it sounded in the plural. Well, you try saying it fast, when you're more than a little nervous. 'Ball-s-s-sir!'

His eyes squinted dangerously, and his grip tightened. 'Watch it, lad! I said, your name!'

'That is my name, sir.'

'Oh … ah …' He looked at the list on his clipboard. 'So it is. As you were!'

I presumed he was a doctor – at least I hoped he was, or I was going to be in for a rough time in the Army. But I was judged fit enough to fight for king and country for the next two years, wherever that might take me.

You could also learn a trade, if you were clever enough to work your ticket the way you wanted. So, straight up, I asked if I could be a musician … and ended up as an electrician training for the Royal West Kent Regiment, stationed at Hythe. Typical! Despite that, I can say without hesitation that it was terrific. I had a great time – and not a lot of national servicemen say that, do they?

I always was an odd one out, but I thoroughly enjoyed my time in the Army, running around shooting guns of all types. Bren guns, Sten guns, throwing grenades – I loved it. OK, I'd wanted to become a musician, but they said, 'Sorry, no chance.' Actually, I can't remember hearing the word 'sorry'. But at least they let me take my trumpet with me, so I was able to get some music going. In fact they did offer me an option. 'You can be a musician if you sign on for three years,' said the sergeant major at the desk encouragingly.

I smelled a rat. 'Well, I dunno …' Then I perked up. 'Could I join the Airborne?' The idea of parachuting into foreign fields, landing from gliders like my brother Ted had done appealed to me no end. You also got seven shillings a week more pay.

'What do you know about engineering, sonny?'

Second mistake coming up. 'Well, I can start any car that's broken down …' It was out before I could stop it. I could, too, and was mighty proud of my talents in that direction which is probably why I let slip that little nugget of information. We all have our Achilles heel, don't we? But I could strip down a camshaft, wire up a vehicle from battery to back bumper, and generally qualify for a job with the AA or RAC. But right now it was the Army that wanted my services, and there was no joining fee.

Later I would even build my own car from scratch, using spare parts. It was an old Austin Seven with a frame, an entire wiring system, banana exhaust, side valves, carburettors, the lot. I put a white plastic sports-car body on it, added a couple of bucket seats and joined the Austin Special Club. I could get her up to sixty miles per hour. Admittedly, we had to push to start her, and she had no windows and no floor. On my first run with her, of course it had to rain, so my backside was soaked at the end of that little trip. The whole thing cost me £175 to build, and I sold it for the same amount.

But now my fate was being decided for the next two years.

'Start a car? Can you now?' A gleam came into the sergeant major's eye. 'Well now, lad, I think we can find a place for you!' He scribbled a brief note on my file, and grinned triumphantly up at me.

The place was Shorncliffe, an isolated spot on the Kent coast near Folkestone. And the outfit they put me into for my two-year stint to serve the nation was REME, the Royal Electrical and Mechanical Engineers, stalwarts of many a battlefield where they needed to restart a tank in a hurry, or an armoured car that had broken down. The REME boys do a lot more than that, of course, and their expertise goes into all sorts of areas, including explosives.

The pep talk I received on my first day was mighty impressive, I have to say. Along with a dozen other newcomers, I sat open-mouthed at a desk in a large room hung with posters of tanks and weapons as a smooth-talking chappie with captain's pips on his shoulder gave us the military equivalent of the hard sell.

'Now listen carefully,' he began. 'The British Army is a

54

professional, high-tech operation. From rifles and trucks to guided missiles and helicopters, it depends on its equipment being fit and working at maximum effect. We make sure it is. This is a tall order – we confront some of the greatest challenges the Army can offer. You will be at the cutting edge of technology, and trained to the highest standards.

'Remember, the Army operates in a tough and sometimes hostile environment, and inevitably breakdowns and malfunctions do occur. When they do, REME is there in the front line to recover and repair the vehicles, weapons and machinery and get them back into service as quickly as possible. We are in there providing support for every combat unit in the Army.'

Today I know there are REME units in Canada, Belize, Bosnia, Cyprus, the Falklands and the Far East – and that's not counting recent areas of conflict. In those days Palestine and India were the hot spots.

Me, I would get as far as Germany.

First there was what they called 'specialist training': manoeuvres, back-breaking exercise, learning to handle guns and other dangerous bits of military hardware. After that came three months in the workshops, and suddenly you were qualified, not only to kill people, but to injure them with mechanical devices.

Our dormitory was made up of two lines of beds ranged side by side. Before we turned in at night we went through the ritual of 'bulling up' – cleaning our boots by spitting on the toecaps then polishing them with a cloth till they shone like glass. Every night we'd get down to it, packing our gear in the kit bags so we were ready in the morning. It was all part of the discipline, and I must say I've been a pretty tidy person ever since, so that's one legacy from the Army for which I should be grateful.

But I found my true calling on the rifle range, and I was the best shot in the platoon. Bren guns, small Stens, the .303 rifle which had a kick like a mule and nearly broke your shoulder unless you had it tucked in solid and tight: I was top gun in all of them.

We used to run from Hythe back to Shorncliffe along the coast road, carrying a 9lb rifle with 25lb packs on our backs. That was a 3-mile run every day, in full kit, tin helmets on and with ammunition packs and that heavy rifle. I'll never forget it. That thing just got heavier the longer you ran. We'd start off all together, and it would end in chaos. People would bump into each other, fall over out of sheer fatigue, shout and curse – but at the end, by God, we were fit! I must have weighed 10 stone, but I could pull myself up twenty times on the parallel bar and chin it without any trouble at all.

Then there were the grenades. Now grenades are scary things, and rightly so. On my first day of training, a group of us novices were gathered together up to our waists in a line of dugouts behind a trench, while the technique of throwing a grenade was explained to us. The instructor was a corporal, with a voice that on a clear day must have carried all the way across the Channel to France. He pointed at a metal post 20 yards away. 'It's like bowling a cricket ball,' he said. 'Now, who's first? Come on. *Come on!*'

Well, I'd been the Harold Larwood of the school cricket team, hadn't I? And 20 yards is as near as dammit to a cricket pitch. So Private Ball was the only silly sod who put his hand up.

'Good. Come up here and watch closely. The rest of you listen – and get ready to duck.' The corporal handed me a grenade. The first thing I noticed was that it was oval like a rugger ball, not spherical. Hmm … bowling this might not be as easy as I thought. It had a handle on it which he was careful to hold down against the surface.

'Right, this is how you prime it.' The corporal gestured at a tiny cylinder the size of a pin, which I was to put in the side of the grenade. 'Put the pin in, take the pin out … so. Then, as soon as you release that handle, it will hit the primer and the grenade will start to fuse. That's when you get rid of it sharpish – you've got four seconds after throwing it before the grenade explodes.'

The rest of the mob prepared to take cover in their dugouts. The corporal stood poised beside me in the trench. I thought, Sod this. I threw it, and immediately dropped down on my face in the mud. There was a long silence, rather longer than four seconds. Next thing I hear is a voice bellowing from above my head. 'You, Ball, what do you think you are? Stand up! Stand up! Come and look where you've thrown it. You missed. You forgot to prime it.'

I clambered warily to my feet, and peered up at him – just as he shoved the primer in to a second spheroid, let the handle go and tossed the grenade at the post. 'Get down, now!'

My face hit the dirt for the second time inside a minute. The explosion was sharp and deadly, and I heard the *zing* of shrapnel flying overhead. The corporal rose to his feet beside me, brushing himself down.

'Perhaps you'll remember in future,' he said. 'Next man!'

What is it the seasoned old veterans say? 'Never volunteer for nothing. Just keep your back straight, your eyes in front and your mouth shut.' How right they are!

To my pleasant surprise I found the officers extremely tolerant. There's always one, of course, and in this case the corporal was a bit of a tartar. But in the main they realised we were just kids, and treated us firmly but fairly. I had brought my faithful trumpet with me, which I kept in an old sock in a locker by my bed. Sometimes I'd play it to amuse my comrades – although I never played 'The Last Post'! That strictly meant lights out and was sounded by a bugler in the barrack square.

This was the age where a lot of kids get the taste for beer, or something stronger. I didn't. I was never the type to go into the NAAFI and swill the amber liquid. In fact I hardly touched a drop, maybe half of lager just to be sociable. Later, it would be a different story.

Next stop in my military career was Donnington in Shropshire. We lined up on the platform at Paddington, caught the midnight train and arrived at five in the morning, bleary-eyed but curious about our new destination. A sergeant was waiting for us on the forecourt, bellowed us into line and then led a march four miles down a hill to the barracks in time for roll call at seven.

That was my introduction to the next phase of army life: working in 'vehicle and plant' to look after the generators. The problem was that the site was four miles away, and it meant a daily march to get there to report for work at eight o'clock prompt. There must have been a hundred of us, clumping over the hills every day in a long crocodile.

It was all a bit surreal, and later reminded me of the Phil Silvers motor pool, except that ours was a huge sprawling factory with vehicles being serviced and several hard-nosed Sergeant Bilkos to keep us up to scratch. We learned on the job, and to be honest I personally didn't learn that much. Wiring up, turning screwdrivers, changing spark plugs, washing down the motors. I'd been there and done all that before I enlisted. It sounds boring, and it was. But I had my trumpet, and during the day I took my mouthpiece along in a pocket of my tunic and used to toot a few tunes on it. I was secure in the knowledge that no one could hear me above the noise from the workshops, what with all the banging and shouting.

During this time I was promoted from private to craftsman (CFN for short), which we nicknamed 'Craftsman For Now'. My wages were upped to fourteen shillings a week. By then I had formed a trio with two Signals blokes, one on drums, the other on piano. We used to play in the NAAFI and in the officers' mess. The piano in the NAAFI was out of tune, but it didn't matter. The great thing about playing in the evening in the sergeants' mess or the officers' mess was that you were let off parade next morning.

I also played hockey every Saturday afternoon, since there was no cricket team and that was the next best thing. In the Army, hockey was a big thing, and we would play other regiments. I was one of the five forwards. Getting the odd crack on the head was a small price to pay.

Next stops: Düsseldorf and Münster – my first trip to foreign fields. I was seconded to a Light Aid Detachment (LAD), which on paper is a unit commanded by a captain and numbering anything from twenty-five to ninety personnel. We had about thirty in our barracks. As the name suggests, the LAD 'specialises in quick response to the point of failure' (I'm quoting from the Army manual now), which broadly means we carry all the gear to where the excitement is going on. I was pretty excited anyway, like all the LADs in the unit. Coming up to a year in the Army, we felt it was time to spread our wings.

But, when I first saw Düsseldorf, it was the most almighty shock. The place had literally been flattened. This was 1948, and three years after the war there was still nothing standing more than about three feet high, or so it seemed to an eighteen-year-old conscript. Unbelievable. The few buildings standing looked like rotting teeth stuck in a forlorn and wintry landscape. Münster was even worse: at first sight just like a huge heap of rubble stretching for miles.

But all in all, and despite the depressing surroundings, I managed to make the most of my time in Germany. The best thing that happened to me was when they put me in charge of sixteen

German electricians, despite the fact that I couldn't speak any German and didn't know much about what I was supposed to be doing.

One chap in particular, a blonde-haired kid called Hans, could speak a bit of English. He taught me German and I taught him Cockney rhyming slang. As a mechanic he was brilliant – he had been in a tank in the war at the age of fourteen, and knew his stuff.

The first compliment that I can remember anyone ever paying me came from Taffy, who was my closest mate in Germany. Taffy had got hold of a motorbike, and we broke down in the middle of nowhere surrounded by fields and completely lost. For no reason, I started to laugh. He said, 'You know, Bally, it's always fun to go out with you. You always laugh at every situation!' I can hear that Welsh voice today. At that point we were attached to the Signals, looking after the electrical side of their vehicles.

The worst thing that happened to me was having to pull a bloody great fifteen-hundredweight Bedford out of a gorge when it went over a viaduct with two blokes inside. They were due to be demobbed next day, and they had gone into Düsseldorf for one last fling, taking this huge van for transport. The long and the short of it was that they got drunk and drove the Bedford over a viaduct on the way back. I went out with a team to pull the vehicle back on to the road. We had to fix the winch to the van on a long steel cable, and I can still visualise what was left of the bodies inside. I felt physically sick, but someone had to do it.

Another rough moment was when a tank stalled right by a railway line, with its gun pointing over the track. An express train came thundering along, hit the gun barrel and whipped it round, along with the turret. Unfortunately, there was a bloke standing in the turret at the time, and he was actually cut in half. I was one of the team called out to haul the tank away, and I saw him, half in the tank, half on the grass. There was blood everywhere.

Accidents happened like that all the time in the Army. One night we were all on a week of manoeuvres, and it required bivouacking in two-man tents at night in a field. One night, in the early hours, a tank came rumbling along and went right over one of the tents, squashing the occupants flat. I saw the spot where it happened next morning at the end of our row. None of us got much sleep for the rest of that exercise, I can tell you.

Sometimes I used to wonder what would have happened if I'd been put into an infantry outfit. Suppose I'd been ordered to jump out of a trench and go charging off at the enemy with fixed bayonets, shooting at someone else with intent to kill. I don't think there's one soldier who hasn't asked himself, Have I got the guts to do this? I can't let my mates down. I can't show them I'm a coward! I know I asked that question. And I still don't know the answer.

I came close to finding out, because I missed being sent to Korea by just six months. I came out of the Army in 1950, still a CFN, and they were calling up blokes for service in 1951.

In my last year with the Army I entered a talent contest organised through the British Forces Network radio programme: 'Any instrumentalist or comic who wishes to enter, please apply!' They sent me a train ticket to Hamburg and directions to the local barracks, where I made my way to a small studio they had there. I played 'Undecided' on solo trumpet, and passed the audition with flying colours. Sadly, I had to miss the actual talent show because I was out of the Army before they staged it several weeks later.

Hamburg meant the red-light area, that notorious maze of side streets which had a tawdry glamour all its own, with bars and clubs and ladies of the night waiting to pounce on passing strangers from shadowy doorways. The Army handed out free condoms to soldiers whenever they went off for a night on the town. There was a lot of venereal disease around, mainly syphilis or gonorrhoea, with Hamburg a prime contender for the Place Most Likely to Get It. AIDS was a word yet to find its way into the language.

Here we go. My national service did lead to my first sexual experience. Is that the good news? It is not! There's nothing like a bit of romance in life – and this was *nothing* like a bit of romance! It involved a *fräulein* of mature years who practically lived amongst the trees beside the barracks in Hilden near Düsseldorf.

The message had been passed down the line the day that we arrived. 'If you want sexual gratification, you can get it from this lady.' (What they actually said was, 'If you fancy a fuck, there's a hooker out there in the woods!') There she would be, ready and available. Further intelligence reached our eager ears. 'She'll be waiting for you, and you can get it for a packet of cigarettes.' Hormones were running high, and I was the original virgin soldier. So one night I slipped out, bought myself a packet of du Maurier fags – I didn't smoke then, so it meant I had to buy twenty – and headed for the trees.

Apparently this *fräulein* didn't take appointments. She just sat in the bushes and hung around waiting to accost any soldier who came along. When I came upon her, so to speak, I could see why. It was mid-afternoon when I found a figure sitting on a fallen tree by the path, a half-smoked cigarette in her mouth and a half-eaten pear in her hand. She looked old and raddled – but, hey, she was a woman! Her straggly dyed-blonde hair was black at the roots. Maybe she was forty, more like sixty. There was no luxury like a bed, just long grass in the undergrowth.

I can't even remember what she was wearing. But I do remember that my date for the next few minutes, who had been chewing a pear when I arrived, took out her teeth, left them

62

embedded in the pear, placed the fruit carefully on a tree trunk, then gave me oral sex. To this day I can still see those teeth grinning at me.

They say you never forget your first sexual experience. 'I was practically gummed to death, fellers!' I told the eager hordes back in the dormitory that night. OK, she wasn't Marilyn Monroe. She wasn't even Marilyn on a bad day. But I couldn't help feeling smug, and I probably looked it.

At this point I should mention that I told my future wife about all my sexual experiences before we got married, just in case she should meet up with any of my old girlfriends. It seemed the diplomatic thing to do, and I still believe it was right. I would confide similarly in my second wife, too. Some people follow the old saying 'Deny, deny!' But if you've admitted everything before you say 'I do', you've got nothing left to deny, have you? That makes a lot of sense to me. Betty found the whole thing hilarious – or appeared to.

Finally the day came when I hung up my tin helmet and said farewell to the Army. On a grey winter morning I left Hilden barracks to catch the train to Düsseldorf. As a final gesture I took out my trumpet in the NAAFI and blew a long, heartfelt 'The Last Post' to the guys who were tucking in to their sausage and egg breakfasts and counting the days to their own demob. Then I waved goodbye to Germany and the Army and headed back for dear old Blighty. I think there was some regret on both sides. They wanted me to stay in longer. But me, I had a musical career to pursue.

CHAPTER SIX

NOW YOU HAS JAZZ

When I was demobbed, I had enough money to buy a car for £75. That was the first thing I did back in civvy street. I called her Lulu, a 1932 Morris Minor with a soft top, licence number EV 101. The second thing I did was to call on my fiancée.

I had kept in touch with Betty throughout my two years away from home, written sackfuls of letters and managed the odd weekend visit from time to time. As far as I was concerned, we were still engaged. So you can imagine my feelings when I called round to her house in Woodward Road, Dagenham, where she was living with her parents, to find she was – well, I suppose the right term is 'otherwise engaged'. I thought I'd surprise her. Big mistake. The conversation on the doorstep was rather bizarre, and I remember it word for word.

'Hullo, Betty,' I said. 'I'm back! Remember me?'

'Kenny! Oh …' She pulled a small face. 'I'm sorry. But I'm going out with this other bloke.'

'What other bloke?'

'He's inside. He's a boxer.'

That's what is called a brush-off. You could say I was on the ropes. Oddly enough, I wasn't too mortified. After all, I still had my trumpet to help me forget the pangs of being summarily dumped. I started playing at jazz clubs, earning around thirty shillings a night doing three nights a week, and a few weeks later I was going out with a couple of sisters who turned up at the clubs, taking them home on alternate nights for a kiss and a cuddle. Kenny never let the grass grow under his feet!

But a weird thing happened. Betty found out about it and marched round to my house, where she faced my mother and told her, 'Kenny shouldn't be going out with those girls!'

'Does that mean you want to go out with him again?' asks Mum.

Betty's reply: 'Well, if he wants me to.'

Amazing. She didn't tell me – she told my mum! And so it was that I went back to Betty. It turned out that the boxer, despite being light-heavyweight champion of the Southern Region, was a bit of a Narcissus, spending too much time shaping up to himself in the mirror. Did that mean she wanted her bit of rough? Oh, women!

By now I was going up in the world. I could afford a 1931 MG M-type sports car, one of the first MGs ever made. It had an overhead camshaft, which I used to strip down. Now that car was a status symbol, brilliant for picking up birds. The problem was that the battery was always going flat, and the lights kept going out. I had to make do with a couple of oil lamps I'd nicked from the side of the road, a white one for the front and a red one for the back. I'd get the passenger to sit in the back seat and hold the red lamp up to alert following traffic.

I had a few day jobs. I went back to Sainsbury's to work as a shop assistant, probably the worst assistant they ever hired. The jobs included boning sides of bacon and carrying huge slabs of butter up from the cellar to the counter. One time the area manager was due to make an inspection. Mr Squires was still in charge, and that day we were all running about like blue-arsed flies polishing the tiles until you could see your face in them. We were out to make a big impression.

The AM, alias God, duly arrived, and was given the guided tour. At the meat and dairy counter Mr Squires called out, 'Ball! I want 28 pounds of New Zealand butter. Go and get it!'

'Yes, sir!'

I pelted down the stairs to the cellar, heaved a great wodge of butter on to a wooden block, rushed up again, and did a Charlie Chaplin prat fall on the top step! Crash! Over I went, flat on my back. Bang! The wood hit the floor. Wallop! The butter slid off, all over the shiny polished shoes of the area manager. I can still see his face, frozen in disbelief. I didn't know how to pick it up. In panic, my immediate reaction was to stick my fingers in either side of this huge slab and lift it back on the tray. I was lucky I wasn't fired immediately, but I suspect Mr Squires had a soft spot for me because we were the only two at the store who ran a car. Everyone else came by bus.

In all, I lasted six months before moving on to fresh pastures. My next day job was selling for a magazine that didn't exist. All they had was a cover and a few blank pages, allegedly destined for a free local paper. I used to go from door to door trying to get advertisements to put in it, and I would call in at local shops to attempt the big sell.

The system was simple. The customer would hand over £5, and I'd get £3 per insertion for myself. 'This advert will go into a magazine that will be distributed free to 15,000 houses in the area, sir,' I would intone, taking down details in an order book. In theory the 'advertisement manager' would phone to confirm, though whether he did or not I never knew. I was gone long before the magazine came out – or didn't. I had convinced myself that it *was* coming out, so I had a touch of sincerity about my sales pitch.

Other jobs included selling TV sets and washing machines. In Romford I worked for a firm selling vacuum cleaners, doorstepping again. I would also repair televisions, buzzing about in a van with a screwdriver and a load of valves. I didn't have a clue why a TV set would go wrong, but the way I worked it out was to start with the fuse, replace it, then see what happened. If all the valves glowed with a little red light, except for maybe one, that meant this one had gone. So … take out the valve. Ah, that's a VH75, now let's see … I'd look in my little bag for a replacement, and, hey presto, I was your expert TV repair man. Anything more complicated: 'Sorry, madam. I think this one will have to go back to the shop.'

My talents were also called upon to repair refrigerators – or attempt to. Some of the stuff people bought was absolute rubbish, and was always going wrong. One experience I had, I could have done without. I was called to a house at nine o'clock one morning. It was a familiar building because I'd been there three times in three months already. It was the heating element, as usual. I replaced it, and couldn't help noticing how agitated the lady of the house had become.

'Oh dear, I've waited in for you, and now I'm late for an appointment. What can I do?'

'Tell you what,' I said, always willing to please. 'I'm going back to Romford. If you don't mind sitting up front with me in the van I'll give you a lift.'

'Oh, will you?' she said. 'That's very kind.'

'Hop in!' I drove off, and suddenly noticed she had gone very quiet. Glancing sideways I caught my breath. Christ! She's collapsed! I knew a local doctor's surgery was nearby, put my foot down and had her there in three minutes. A nurse hurried out, took one look at the figure slumped in the passenger seat and snapped, 'Get her to a hospital! We don't have the facilities here.'

I got her to Old Church Hospital, and watched as two attendants carried my erstwhile customer in on a mobile stretcher. Then I drove off, relieved that she was in good hands. A week later I recognised her husband in the street. 'How's the wife?' I asked.

'She's dead,' he replied. 'Someone took her to hospital, and she was dead on arrival.'

It just goes to show the stress a little thing like a fridge going wrong can cause. It didn't stop me being a salesman, but it made me think. As long as I was selling something that was quality, I was fine. I fact, I like to think I was a pretty good salesman. If I had something good to sell, I could sell it. My approach? Sincerity. I believed in what I was doing. For instance, with TVs, I knew I was OK selling a Bush. They were the best. You knew if you sold a Bush you'd never have any trouble with it. Some of the other rubbish was hard to believe in.

That little episode rather put me off fridges, and I joined an outfit called ExpelAir, which did just what its name suggested and was one of the original extractor fans. I had the whole of north-east London as my beat, a very large area. They gave me an old Ford for an office car, the salary was £15 a week, free petrol and three quid per machine you sold. In 1952 that was a good salary.

I took a model with me wherever I went to demonstrate to potential buyers. The thing had two toggles on it which pulled down a shutter and switched on an electric motor. All the customer had to do was cut a hole in the window. They were selling for £15 apiece.

My first call was to a chemical factory in Stoke Newington, a place with no air vents, and I sold them half a dozen on the spot. My second was to a Chinese restaurant close by, where I sold them one for their kitchen, and for a joke wrote my report in pidgin English! I still go past the place sometimes, and cringe when I see it.

I went into a chicken farm on the Southend Road, a nursery with battery hens. Mr Sincerity goes in with these electric things. I convince the owners that they'll save twenty-five per cent on electricity. 'And you can get two lots of eggs laid a day. Switch them on at five in the morning, and those chicken will start laying.' I never went back to find out – but they're still in business, so I must have done something right.

Betty and I tied the knot in 1952. The wedding was fantastic. It took place at St Andrew's Church, Goodmayes, on 14 June, and the entire Charlie Galbraith jazz band turned out in the churchyard to get the mood warmed up with clarinets and trumpets and trombones. I'd been playing second trumpet with Charlie at the time, and that day he did me proud. We left it to the organist inside to do the honours with the 'Wedding March', but afterwards the reception at my parents' house in Oakwood Gardens was a right old knees-up. We had a jam session with me on trumpet and Dad on piano. The whole family joined in – even aged Auntie Alice who was still living with us there at the time.

We borrowed my dad's old 1934 Vauxhall to get to Weston-super-Mare for our honeymoon, and spent a week there in a bed and breakfast where you could just glimpse the sea from our bedroom. It was nothing fancy, but the honeymoon night went off all right. I did what a man's gotta do, and tried not to think of a set of dentures buried in a pear grinning at me from a tree trunk.

I was twenty-two years old, far too young by today's standards, and absolutely boracic (boracic lint – skint, right!). We shacked up in a room in my sister Ethel's house in Seven Kings – very sweet of her, of course, and we were duly grateful, but it was hardly the ideal way to start married life. So there I was, newly wed Kenny, scratching a living, earning a crust by day, and trying to follow his true star at night in Soho jazz cellars for an occasional fee and a few pints of beer.

At that time Betty was a typist in a nearby office. We started house-hunting – well, she did – and eventually spotted a big old house at the end of a terrace in Goodmayes. It was right next door to a field where they kept two huge dray horses which used to pull coal trucks around. The house had been built around 1900, solid as a rock, and they wanted £1,175 for it. To get a mortgage off the Woolwich I had to raise £350. I never had that sort of money sloshing about, but the bloke who wanted to sell it was a really nice feller.

'You get £175, and I'll let you pay off the rest at six quid a month,' he said. Dad lent me the money – and I bought my first house! The last DIY job I ever did was to knock a wall down between two ground-floor rooms to make one huge area, a lounge with a dining alcove, and I've never lifted a hammer since.

So that was the start of my personal roller coaster of a marriage. Betty would give birth to our first daughter Gillian in 1955, when I was with the Sid Phillips band. My son Keith didn't come along until 1960 when I had my own outfit. Jane was the final little ace in the Ball pack, and was born in 1963.

Now. Let's talk about the other love of my life: music.

The history of jazz is a saga in itself. In the early part of the last century a new and recognisably different form of music developed in the New Orleans area of America. At first without a name, around 1914 it became known as jazz. After 1918 it began to spread throughout the States, largely in speakeasies and clip joints.

Historians have pointed out how the years after World War I were restless and reckless, and a time of release from old-style conventions. Now people simply lived for kicks. The new music flourished, with its spontaneity, its freshness, energy, excitement and earthiness, played by mainly black brass bands in the streets of New Orleans for weddings, funerals and elections. It was the genuine music of the people – the untutored, underprivileged folk of the Deep South, who knew nothing of notation or scales but simply sang and played as they felt.

The vibrant intensity of jazz was felt in the distinctive dance music originating in the saloons and clubs of Storyville, where it sprouted like wildfire. This was the notorious red-light area by the rail track, where streets with names like Liberty, Franklin and Basin Street come leaping out of the pages for anyone as fascinated by that whole era as I was.

Storyville, named after the Alderman who drew up its ordinance in 1897, actually had a guide to the brothels and bars published for any eager stranger in town looking for action. The pages listed 200 'houses', plus the names and addresses of all the prostitutes, and the entertainers as well. Now there's an address book to be reckoned with!

Jazz grew into a vast canvas of diverse strands with different names, all with their own followers. Originally, it was almost exclusively the territory of black bands, with a few notable white exceptions, like the New Orleans Rhythm Kings. Dixieland was derived from this, with a two-beat style, and was a speciality of Brown's Band and the Original Dixieland Jazz Band.

Chicago style? Now you're talking my kind of music. Remember Kenny and the Chicagoans? This was almost exclusively the domain of white bands, and originated in the Windy City. This time the emphasis was on the two and four beats, where we could expand into solos, breaks and what are known as 'chase choruses', where the whole front line solos at the same time. To the untrained ear, it might sometimes sound as if the whole thing is about to run out of control, but this in fact is the art form: each of us knows exactly what we're doing.

As for trad, this is the word that describes any jazz played either in New Orleans, Chicago or New York styles, as opposed to mainstream or modern jazz. It began with the New Orleans revival in the forties and fifties, and mushroomed from there.

The 1947 film *New Orleans*, starring Louis Armstrong and his All Stars, Billie Holiday and Woody Herman, tells the birth of the blues and all that went with it just like it was. In the words of the song, 'Now you has jazz ...'

I was truly in love with jazz. Fresh out of the Army with all my faculties intact, I went on a Bohemian kick with three other young musicians: Lennie Conway on tenor sax, Vic Ash on clarinet and a third guy named David Heneker, a guitar player who became a famous writer and eventually wrote *Expresso Bongo*.

I still had my original trumpet, the one I called my 'bent instrument' – which always got a laugh ('Let me show you my bent instrument. Careful now ...'), but I was moving up the scale. In that summer of 1951 we used to hitch-hike down to the coast, where we would stay the weekend, playing jazz on the beach and sleeping in open-air beach huts. Littlehampton ... Worthing ... Bognor ... 'One day, all this will be mine!' I used to joke, staring out at the theatres on the end of the pier and imagining myself facing an audience of cheering holidaymakers.

But not just yet. I started on the bottom rung of the ladder, which did me no harm at all, sitting in with other groups, and getting to know faces and the names that went with them. I played second trumpet with a local group called Freddy Randall and his Band, who had occasional gigs in Edmonton, and had a blow or two with the Eric Delaney band, still in its infancy but destined for great things.

More important, I was being accepted as part of the clan, that itinerant bunch of musicians who drift from gig to gig, for whom the term 'one-night stand' meant just that, with no sexual connotation. Ah, the days of innocence! We were a nomadic tribe, setting up our tents in a Soho cellar to sweat and drink and sweat some more, and play the music we loved, before heading out into the small hours to catch the last train home. If we missed it, someone would have a room somewhere where we could crash out on a sofa.

Closer to home, in Essex, I found myself with a group of pals who were all chasing the same dream. Dave Jones was a salesman by day, a musician by night. Dave had his clarinet, Charlie Galbraith his trombone. Pat Mason was a gifted young pianist who ran his own electrical business to pay the bills. Dave Wood, a bass player, was in insurance, and Johnny Hollingsworth was an interior designer.

One day I said to them, 'Gather round, fellers. I want to form a group – our group. That means you! What do you say?' I wouldn't have taken no for an answer, but I didn't have to. I hauled my mate Charlie Galbraith in, along with his trombone, and on that day in 1954 the Chicagoans were born. I aimed for the relaxed Chicago style of jazz which was sweeping the country, and it seemed to go down well with the crowds when we finally put our noses over the parapet for a public performance.

I'd bumped into a guy named John Potter. He was a bank clerk, though you'd never believe it if you saw him strumming his banjo like a young George Formby. This man was mad on jazz, so mad that he had opened the South Essex Rhythm Club at the Greyhound pub in Chadwell Heath a few months earlier, starring with his own group, the Rhythm Ramblers. John ran it at a loss for weeks, but putting his money where his faith was he kept at it, and, by the time I dropped in at his invitation to blow a few notes, the membership was up to 600, and rising.

Eighty bodies a night perspiring on the dance floor or watching from the bar was a good number, though we both knew there were thousands more kids out there if we could only ensnare them. On the spot he asked me if I would make it my own venue, and overnight Kenny Ball and the Chicagoans had their own base camp. I've always said there's no place like home.

We actually gave our first interview, to the *Ilford Recorder*, and I was both delighted and relieved to read, 'This group should meet with increasing success. They are all modest, serious young men, and their enthusiasm comes through to the listener like a breath of fresh air on a rush-hour tube train.'

The headline read BOY WITH A BUGLE LEADS NEW GROUP, but at that budding stage of my career it didn't worry me overmuch. Bugle? Trumpet? *Boy* ...? Any publicity was good publicity. Thank you, Mr Alan Massam, if you are around to read this. That's a drink I still owe you. It lifted our hearts and our spirits, and increased our determination to succeed.

Finally my name came to the attention of Sid Phillips, who in every sense was one of the big noises in town with his Dixieland band and that raw, thumping beat. I first met him when he was running a free jazz club with Charlie Galbraith upstairs at the Duke of Hamilton pub in Hampstead, North London. Free meant free and easy. No charge to the customers, who just sat around drinking and tapping their fingers to the beat.

The great thing about the place was the atmosphere – the word was out, and musicians would drop in from nowhere to have a blow just for the fun of it. Chris Barber was one big name who would come and play purely for pleasure. The audience were true jazz aficionados, and sometimes you could hear a pin drop at the end of a number before the applause broke out.

I heard about this mini-Mecca for jazz lovers, and turned up out of the blue one day on an old Norton 300cc motorbike, clutching my trumpet.

'Any chance of a blow, Sid?' I hadn't been there before, and it was polite to ask the first time.

He had vaguely heard of me, but treated me like a new-found friend. 'Of course,' he said. 'Kenny, is that what you said your name was?'

A few weeks later, the phone rang and Sid's voice came on the line. He was offering me a place in his band at the then handsome salary of £30 a week. Did I want the job? Has the Pope got a balcony? Yes, I wanted the job.

So I took it.

CHAPTER SEVEN

CRUMPET VOLUNTARY

The dawn of the fifties heralded a great era for my kind of music, and the sixties even more so. Let me paint the picture for you. London was the Mecca for every wannabe actor, social climber and C-list celebrity. Musicians, too, and for us London meant Soho – the ultimate magnet as it was then, still is now and always will be.

Soho in those days has been described as a 'glorious decadent square mile with a split personality. Like a scarlet lady who is both duchess and tart, she is everything to all men.' A village by day, bustling with activity, it had its own bakery, dairy, fruit-and-veg market, laundry and newsagent.

By night it was something else. The narrow streets and back alleys offered tantalising glimpses through open doors of peeling wallpaper, threadbare carpets and creaking stairs leading up to forbidden fruits on the upper floors. As someone once remarked: the streets were paved with gold-diggers, and all human life was there.

Above ground, the image of this colourful *mélange* was one of pimps, prostitutes and people of an unsavoury disposition. But there were also Bohemians, poets and more congenial figures who adorned the pubs and coffee bars. Gangland legends like the Kray twins, the Richardsons and Jack 'Spot' Comer would turn up in clubs with their entourage of large men in double-breasted suits with padded shoulders, and help foster the myth.

There were razor fights that left blood swilling across the pavements, and ladies of the night – like Russian Dora, Black Rita and Ginger Raye – who met a gruesome end before their time.

In those heady days, London was a strange place of glamour and danger. There were places like the Blue Angel, where the walls were strung with fishermen's nets, with a dance floor the size of a fish tank, and the place full of hard-looking men who stayed at the bar and drank Scotch; the Jack of Clubs below Isow's, a glitzy restaurant in Brewer Street; the legendary Churchill's, where the chorus girls could be tempted to sit with customers after the show and quaff champagne with them – at £20 a glass. And these were the fifties, my friends, so God knows what that would be costing the punter today.

My present pianist and musical director Hugh Ledigo, who joined the band a mere sixteen years ago and seems to have passed his apprenticeship, has a vivid memory of those early days when we eager beavers were trying to climb the greasy pole. Hugh found himself on a two-year stint at an East End club called the Regency, owned by a notorious pair of villains who used to hang out with the Krays.

'It could be a rough place,' Hugh recalls. 'But as far as musicians were concerned everyone was fine. We never had any trouble, and we didn't go looking for it. But we'd watch from the stage when trouble erupted, saw the fights and the nasty brawls, the broken bottles and the tables and chairs hurtling past. And we tried to be professional under fire. The club boss said, "Keep playing until it gets too close for comfort. Then grab your instruments and duck out of it." What he meant was, Don't shoot the musician, he's doing his best!

'I witnessed one particularly unpleasant episode at the Regency when a big thug thought he'd been insulted. He took umbrage and flattened this other bloke, then proceeded to smash several chairs over the unconscious figure on the floor right in front of us. He got to the point where he couldn't stop. You see that kind of thing when people get drink inside them, or maybe they're just vicious psychopaths. But when it all goes off, it's nasty and very upsetting.

'What did we do? Like the man said, we just kept playing ...'

Another time Hugh was at the Regency having a drink at the bar before the show, and got talking to one of the customers. 'Suddenly the phone rang. One of the owners came down, took the call and then announced to the whole bar, "We've just got a tip-off from the local nick. There'll be a raid here in five minutes."

'This guy with me went absolutely green. "I'm in trouble," he pleaded, his voice all choked up. "You've got to get me out of here, fast!" At that moment the police moved in, the door crashed open and the room was full of uniforms and dogs.

'I looked at the bloke with us. As far as I was concerned these people were just customers. I wasn't interested in their life, what they'd done or if they had just been guests of Her Majesty. In those places you mind your own business and they mind theirs.

'But now I said quickly, "Do you play the bass?"

'He stared at me. "No ... no ..."

'"Well, you do now!" And with that I shoved him up on the

stage, pushed the double bass across to him, and he started playing. That was the one place the police didn't look.

'Finally they left. My new-found friend stopped playing, and his fingers were literally dripping blood, he'd been strumming those strings so hard. But he gave me a big thank you and bought us all a drink before moving on. I never did catch his name.'

Yes, they were lively times. In fact, ninety per cent of the vice in Soho was controlled by Greeks, Maltese and Cypriots, though the general public scarcely ever got a whiff of it. And on the whole tourists were safe. The violence was usually meted out by the ungodly to their own kind, either for gain or revenge. As Hugh says, they never touched musicians. We seemed to lead a charmed life, possibly because we never troubled anyone and just wanted to get on with our music. Show business and the underworld have rubbed shoulders since time immemorial – witness the roaring twenties and the gangsters with their molls in the US. But inevitably there has always been a certain glamour attached to music which villains have found irresistible.

Below ground was another world. Here you would find most of the jazz clubs located in small cellars, some candlelit, others with low-key lighting. The sounds that filtered through to the street would take you down a flight of battered wooden stairs and through a door into a place where time stood still. Some of the clubs had tiny stages, others just a space to squeeze in a trio or a quartet.

Each club had its own character and identity, but even Humphrey Lyttelton's legendary 100 Club in Oxford Street had its flight of stairs down from the street into the cavernous interior. This was the place that achieved a certain reputation for its graffiti in the Gents. People would make a special trip there, and come back chuckling. There were a lot of graffiti merchants around

Soho in the early days before it expanded to railway carriages and freshly painted white walls. Whether you think they should be given an art exhibition or locked up, some of them were always good for a laugh.

One I liked at Humph's was where someone had written, 'I like Grils'.

Below that someone else had scrawled, 'Surely you mean Girls?'

And below that, a third offering: 'What about us Grils?' Silly, but that kind of thing sticks in your mind.

Another one I recall was, 'It's no good standing on the seat. The crabs in this loo jump sixteen feet!'

And (look away, ladies):

> This is the story of Jack McGrew,
> who had a penis with a left-hand screw.
> He spent his life in one long hunt,
> looking for a girl with a left-hand smile.

But the most priceless one that I encountered at that time was in the Leicester Square Gents. I remember standing there pointing Percy at the porcelain – and right in front on the tiles was a small square, with the single world 'HELLO!' in it and an arrow pointing upwards. Naturally, I followed the line to another square, which said, 'FOLLOW ME!'

The line went on, up and up. The next square said, 'DON'T GO AWAY'. By now, of course, I was hooked. The line went right up to the top, and then back along the ceiling, so, still standing there, I had to crane my head to follow it. One more square: 'STILL WITH ME?' And then the final one, as you're almost breaking your neck to read it. 'YOU ARE NOW PIDDLING IN YOUR BOOTS!' And, yes, maybe some poor saps were. Was I one of them? I'm not telling. Now that's what I call a humorist. Unless he was ten feet tall he must have used a stepladder, and I had to admire his initiative for completing the job without getting caught.

Most were informal clubs, aimed not just for purists but for those who wanted a good night out and had a love of jazz. Two other leading venues were Cy Laurie's basement club in Windmill Street, and Ronnie Scott's, opened in 1959 by Ronnie himself in partnership with fellow tenor sax player Pete King. Along Old Compton Street the coffee bars had their skiffle groups, with Lonnie Donegan the acknowledged king of the castle and a young fair-haired kid named Tommy Steele about to be discovered at the Two I's.

Jazz, of course, had spread all over Europe, as I would soon discover for myself. There was one jazz hot spot in Paris situated off the Champs-Elysées which always fascinated me, because the only applause allowed was the snapping of fingers. Imagine fifty people all doing that in unison after a number. Spooky. The thought crossed my mind that I should open one in Soho and call it the Clickety-Click Club, but I never got round to it. I was too busy trying to carve out my own niche.

Talking of Paris reminds me that the first small jazz band recording I ever heard was the Hot Club of France Quintet, led by the legendary Stephane Grappelli, whose name sounded Italian but who was actually French. What a lovely guy he was – he could make his violin sit up and beg! Sadly he died in 1997, in his eighties. But that first record turned me on to the idea of forming my own group, so I owe it all to him.

I told him as much once, when out of the blue I had a jam with him. Sometimes fate is smiling your way, and you've got to take advantage of it because you may only get one chance. This happened for me at a concert in London, when Diz Disley, who

Top: My parents – Ethel and Jim Ball.

Bottom: Back row and second from the left – Ted, my elder brother, who was a hero in the Second World War.

Top: Taken whilst on my National Service. I'm in the middle of the back row, leaning forward.

Left: Dapper and on the road to success in 1955.

Top: With Lonnie Donegan in 1983. Lonnie helped me get my first break with Pye Records.

Bottom: Comparing notes with Humphrey Lyttleton, with whom I continue to tour today.

Top: The Jazzmen in action at the London Palladium.

Bottom: Money! Money! Money! *Back row*, Ron Weatherburn, Vic Pitt, John Bennett, Clinton Ford, Bill Dixon. *Front row*: Dave Jones, Kenny Ball, Ron Bowden.

Inset: Our brick in the wall of the Cavern Club in Liverpool.

Top left: Jack it up! A publicity still around the time of our million selling hit 'Midnight in Moscow'.

Top right: Blowing my own crumpet! A publicity shot for our No 1 record 'March of the Siamese Children'.

In 1963 I got Honorary Citizenship of New Orleans in recognition of my services to jazz. *Bottom*: Examining Bix Beiderbecke's horn. *Inset*: I am pictured here with the band in Basin Street outside the Jazz Museum there.

A very proud moment indeed. Louis Armstrong presenting me with a gold disc for 'Midnight in Moscow' which sold over a million copies.

Louis and the Ball band close the Odeon Hammersmith show

WHAT A WONDERFUL NIGHT FOR SATCHMO

Kenny Ball's Jazzmen were going all out in their last number at the Odeon, Hammersmith, when, in the wings, I caught a glimpse of Louis Armstrong, a wide beam of appreciation stretching from ear to ear.

Altogether a pleasing session which the Kenny Ball band got going very well. Like Louis they know that to get Jazz going these days you've got to be entertaining with it.

IN RENO . . . July 26 - August 12

Louis Armstrong and his All Stars

HAROLDS

Later, me and the Jazzmen toured with Armstrong when he was over in England. Back in the states he sent me this postcard from Reno, USA.

KENNY BALL

Exclusive **P Y E** Recording Artiste

KENNY BALL AND HIS JAZZ BAND

Exclusive **P Y E** Recording Artistes

Top: Pye publicity stills for the band.

Bottom: Relaxing on the beach with some real legends. From left, me, Micky Ashman, Acker Bilk (with his hat on), Ken Colyer and Ken Sums.

later played banjo and guitar with the Jazzmen, was Stephane's regular rhythm guitar player and soloist. He introduced me to Monsieur Stephane in the great man's dressing room. By luck (or fate), I had my trumpet with me. Diz brought out his guitar, Stephane produced his violin from its case and there and then we had a jam session! When it comes from nowhere like that, it's like a surreal dream.

People often ask me how you know when it's your turn to come in on an improvised jam session, and not interrupt the bloke who's playing. Good question. We seem to do it naturally. But in fact the guy playing just nods when he's about to wind up, and then you take over. With the Jazzmen, during my last four bars I simply turn to whoever is going to play and give him the thumbs-up. You can get a slight overlap, but it doesn't matter. When he's had enough, he'll turn back to you, and you take it from there. If he's going strong and producing amazing ideas and swinging like Tarzan, I'll call, 'One more, one more!'

Count Basie did that to me once when we performed 'April in Paris' together, calling out 'One more time' in that gravel voice. At the end, people from the audience were echoing the Count's words: 'One more time!'

But sometimes that 'one more time' gets to you. I thought, Why not? Let's do it again. And I did. I went into some scat singing, making words up as I went along. You can also do that when you forget the actual words, but don't tell anyone.

Louis Armstrong is actually credited with the start of scat singing, ad-libbing once when he was recording and hadn't got any words to sing. If Satchmo could do it, people figured, then that made it legitimate, and soon scores of other jazz aficionados had caught the bug and followed suit. And no, the word does not come from 'scatological', I hasten to add. The dictionary definition is:

'The improvisation and repetition of meaningless syllables sung to a melody.' So you can sing nonsense as well as talk it!

Sid Phillips kept me busy. His BBC radio show was obligatory listening to his army of Dixieland fans across the country and, since they were paying just twenty shillings a year for the licence fee, I reckon they were getting value for money. There had been no hard feelings from Charlie Galbraith when I told him I wanted to move on, and it was then that I realised just how much the shifting sands of opportunity applied to musicians the world over. We remained great mates – after all, he'd seen me say 'I do' and had taken a major part in the celebrations. I had some great months with him and the boys, mainly one-night stands or functions.

I would experience the same situation myself when I formed my groups. You hire someone, they stay a while and suddenly they feel the time has come to try another band. So it would be a huge compliment when I finally formed the Jazzmen in 1958 to have some of the gang stay up to forty years with me!

Sid Phillips was not only hailed as Britain's best clarinettist of the time, he was also a renowned musical arranger, and composer of both light and serious music. One of four brothers, all of them musically inclined, he taught himself the saxophone and clarinet, but also studied opera, and even travelled to Milan to attend the funeral of Puccini in 1924. Now that's what I call an enthusiast. For the record, the band at that time consisted of Norman Cave (trombone), Cyril Glover (alto sax), Frank Freeman (tenor sax), Arthur Fall (piano), Ron Fallon (bass), Mike Nicholson (drums), with the vocalist being the delightful Kay McKinley.

Sid had made his name on radio with his weekly late-night show live from the 'Rhubarb Room' in 1948, but by the time I joined this elite throng he had moved on to *Every Sunday Afternoon*, which achieved some of the highest ratings of the weekend and helped write his name into musical folklore. As one critic wrote, 'This eagerly awaited show has only one fault – it goes too quickly.'

Now I knew what it was like to be out on the road. A sample two months in the autumn of 1957 took the band to Skegness, Grimsby, Banbury, Porthcawl, Swansea, Torquay, Rugby, Birkenhead, Southport, Wolverhampton, Herne Bay, Colchester, Widnes, Manchester … and a few other venues besides.

I came across an old copy of the *Sid Phillips Magazine* for March 1954 the other day, and found that 'Kenny follows association football and supports both Arsenal and West Ham' – though it failed to explain what happened when they played each other.

Another collector's item from those days is an LP from a group calling themselves Dixielanders Anonymous, recorded in London in February 1957. Would-be purchasers were tempted by the promise of 'Tunes you have hummed, played in the New Orleans manner', which included golden oldies like 'I'm Gonna Sit Right Down and Write Myself a Letter', 'Stairway to Paradise' and 'Muskrat Ramble'.

Teasingly, the cover photograph shows a stage with all the instruments in place – drum kit, double bass, piano and so on – but with no players. Welcome to the Invisible Seven! On the sleeve the list of 'The Musicians' describes what they do but not who they are. I was credited only as: 'Trumpet is a Beiderbecke fan in his twenties. He started work in the electrical business, but decided to make music his career.' Yes, that was me, for the more perceptive jazz student. Much later Sid Phillips confessed it was indeed his group, but that he couldn't be credited as he was under contract to HMV at the time.

One of the notches on Sid's career ladder was the royal family's Christmas staff party at Windsor Castle in 1954. Norman Wisdom, then at a peak of his career as Britain's highest-paid performer, was the star turn. They were all there: the Queen, Prince Philip, the Queen Mum, Princess Margaret, plus an audience of staff and their friends.

The Waterloo Chamber was hung with decorations. The Queen danced a succession of quicksteps and tangos with her footmen and other members of the staff. Sid played a waltz, after which the Queen approached the stage. 'Can you do something a little more lively?' she asked.

Sid went straight into 'Darktown Strutters' Ball'. 'That's much better,' said Her Majesty, twirling off into a trendy jive.

That was the famous night when Norman Wisdom finished his act to resounding applause, and managed to fall backwards into the flower arrangement on the stage, breaking a vase with an almighty crash as he rolled around on the floor. Good old Norm! He picked himself up, dusted himself down, looked the Queen straight in the face and said, 'Don't worry, Your Majesty. I'll pay!' The Queen led the laughter, and Norman escaped with his head.

Sid Phillips actually had a reputation for being a bully, but he never came down hard on me when I worked for him. I thought he was terrific. Short, bald and stoutish, he could be intimidating, particularly if you played a bum note. Then he would just point his clarinet at you like a rifle, and fix you with his famous 'death look'. It was enough.

One saxophonist I knew stayed with his band for twenty years – and he could never look Sid in the eye. It wasn't because he was terrified. It was because he hated Sid's guts and couldn't bear to look at him! He just sat there with his saxophone, staring straight ahead. I couldn't understand it. One day I asked him, 'If you're not enjoying yourself, how can you put your heart and soul into the music?'

He simply looked at me with that deadpan stare, and said, 'The money's good!'

During that phase of my yet-to-be-burgeoning career, I joined the Eric Delaney Band for a brief spell. Every night on the road I counted as good experience, and on some of those experiences I could dine out long afterwards. On one occasion, we were playing the Empire, Liverpool, and one of the tunes in the programme was the 'Sailor's Hornpipe', with all that diddle-diddle-diddle stuff. The brass section had five trumpets and five saxophones. At the rear of the stage, two whacking great guns used to emerge from the backdrop of a ship, right over their heads. Behind the curtains they had maroons that went off at a certain point, and a puff of smoke would come out from the gun muzzles. To make it extra loud, the roadies put these maroons in dustbins.

One night we were playing away: diddle-diddle-diddle … bang! The left gun went off. The audience jumped in their seats. It was *loud*. We were giving it all we'd got, as it's a very lively song that everyone knows, but even I was startled as the smoke blew out over our heads. One gun gone, one to go. Diddle-diddle-diddle … nothing! The right gun failed to fire. We finished the tune. 'Must have been a dud,' I said to the bloke next to me.

'Yeah, you're right,' he replied, and we thought no more about it as we finished the set and bowed our way out.

Next, a female singer comes on and starts to sing a love song, quiet and romantic. Then – bang! The second gun goes off with a massive explosion and a huge puff of smoke, the loudest we'd ever heard. That brought the show to a grinding halt as the place erupted in hysterics.

On that same show, we used to play 'Roamin' in the Gloamin'', another popular standard – 'with a lassie by my side …' The special-effects boys were having a field day. They had erected a screen of the Scottish Highlands, with heather and moorland, clouds scudding from left to right, and rain sleeting down.

The theatre had direct current – DC as it was called. If you put the plug in the wrong way, you'd get negative instead of positive. We started off with our usual gusto, then wondered why the audience was convulsed with laughter. I looked round. Oh, no! The roadie had put the plug in wrong, and now the clouds were rushing from right to left, and the rain was going *up*! That put paid to our roamin' on that little number.

It was around this time that I got my first real taste of what became known as the 'groupie scene'. The word actually entered the language officially in 1967, when *Webster's Dictionary* solemnly described the groupie as 'a fan, usually a woman, who follows pop bands from concert to concert with the possible aim of having sex with the musicians.' The *Reader's Digest Universal Dictionary* put it more discreetly: '… usually in the hope of having personal contact with them'. Personal contact? What a nice way of putting it! But the phenomenon goes a long way further back than that.

A groupie was once described thus: 'She's young, she's beautiful, she's got loose morals and looser clothing. Music gets her hot and musicians get her hotter. In America her name could be Bebe, Pamela, Sable or Stephanie. In Britain she could be Jenny or Patti, Patsy or Paula.' If this sweeping generalisation seems a trifle unfair on the Pamelas and Paulas of the world, there's certainly something about musicians that sends girls wild. In my younger days I had a ball – no pun intended, but that's the only way to describe it.

We used to give these crazy chicks nicknames. One young woman in particular we called Bradford Alice. As the name implies, she was a Yorkshire lass who lived 'oop north'. She had lank black hair and too much lipstick, and I first encountered her in this busy year with the Sid Phillips outfit. Apart from being a jazz lover, she also happened to be a raving nymphomaniac, wild and wanton – wanton it all the time, as we used to say among ourselves.

Alice was without shame. She went through whole bands more than once, whoever had a gig in that part of the world, and included the roadies and anyone who happened to have anything to do with the groups. Mention Bradford Alice to any musician of that era and a certain look will come into his eyes, slightly glazed and a little moist. Call it nostalgia. Call it what you like – but we never forgot her.

I met her with more than one group over the years, including the Jazzmen when I finally formed them. Alice would turn up to see the show, and be waiting in the hotel afterwards for us to come back. In those days we were pretty wild ourselves, and after a gig we'd be firing on all cylinders, adrenaline running like hot lava, looking for action and getting the drinks going to get the party warmed up.

This particular night after a gig we were having a right old orgy in one of the suites, with Alice in fine form. She was going round us one by one to 'pleasure' the band, as they say, any way we wanted it. On the sofa, on the bed, under the bed …

Someone produced a camera, and started taking photos of her doing what she did best, but making sure that our faces weren't in the pictures. Very clever – although we were past caring anyway – and when they were printed the pictures were a hoot. I suppose we were lucky that no one reported us to the authorities, but these were the days before political correctness became a phrase in the nation's vocabulary, and anything went. That's what we did in the fifties and the swinging sixties – we swung!

The photos were produced a week later in the back of our band bus on the way to another gig, and we crowded round with howls of laughter and appreciative comments. We'd been so smashed we couldn't remember half of what we'd been doing, but the photos showed it all. Thank God our heads were missing, so even if *we* knew who we were, no one else would.

Until someone spotted something.

'Look there!' One of the blokes had a big hairy mole on the back of his hand – and it showed up bright and clear so everyone knew who it was. That photo did the rounds of the bus until it reached the particular individual, a roadie as I recall, whereupon it was promptly torn into shreds!

Another girl we knew only as Kate, and promptly dubbed her ForniKate after she offered her services to the entire band. She was a wild one. It didn't take long to excite her, and when she was aroused she would sink her nails deep into your back. Comparing notes in the coach afterwards on our way to the next gig, the general consensus was that we'd all have to wear T-shirts getting into bed back at home with the missus.

The mass of pulchritude that engulfed us lusty lads in those halcyon days now all tends to blur into one dreamlike image of flesh and fantasy. I was always aware that it was purely trophy hunting, so that the women could go back to their friends and boast they'd had the entire band. But, if the sweets are on offer, who are we to decline?

One particular face in the crowd was a delightful little thing named Crystal. We became very close. So close that I used to tell her, 'You do realise, don't you, darlin', that if we ever get married you'll be Crystal Ball?' I think that probably stopped either of us taking it any further, even if we'd seriously wanted to.

Another time with another band we were having the usual after-show party in one of the hotel suites, and I was dragged off to the bedroom by an eager young groupie for a spot of what I used to refer to as 'crumpet voluntary'. When she had finished having her wicked way with me, she insisted I call in all the other band members. She was probably on drugs, or maybe she just liked sex. Whatever was turning her on, she issued a challenge from the rumpled sheets. 'Right, I want every one of you to make love to me.' (Possibly she used another word for it.) 'Come on. Don't be shy. Who's up for it?'

Well, the banjo player thought he'd try his luck. And as the rest of us crowded round the bed egging him on, only one thing was wrong. He couldn't do it. After a lot of panting and sweating, he finally gave up. And you know what? The same thing happened to every one of the other guys. In private – no problem. In public – no chance! The only bedfellows that night were loss of libido and loss of face.

Today? Times have changed. Not just because we've all grown older, but it seems today's groupies have all grown younger. As Robbie Williams put it when asked about the sexual antics of his fans at the height of the Take That mania, 'A quick snog is about as wild as it gets. They're just too young, and even if we wanted to we wouldn't be allowed. It's too much of a risk.'

And as Pamela Des Barres, one of the more notorious groupies from California, summed it up succinctly in a book she wrote about her experiences, 'No one had heard of AIDS, no one knew how bad drugs could be, everyone just wanted to have fun.'

And the band played on. At Herne Bay, the local paper recorded, 'There was deafening applause as trumpeter Kenny Ball finished his rendering of "Blue Suede Shoes". The crowd called repeatedly for more.' That one went straight into my clippings book, which at that time was still in its infancy. But not for long, I vowed. Not for long.

I always say that the hardest part in your first steps in learning the trumpet is acquiring one. For a kid with no money, it isn't easy. First of all, the cost: the least you can expect to pay for a trumpet today is £200, and that's a real cheapo. For a decent instrument you're looking at £400 minimum.

To give you an idea of the way prices vary: I was once offered a double-bell trumpet made in Oregon for £10,000. My answer to that was that if I'm offered a trumpet for ten thousand quid it would have to play itself! That's way out of line and way out of sight.

I once played a trumpet worth £2,000 and found it was too weighty for me. If you have to hold a trumpet for an hour or more, it gets heavy. They're made of brass, don't forget. Or they might be silver plated or 'nut-gold' plated, which is brass with lacquer over it, which will still make your arm muscles ache.

In the whole of my career I would say I must have played thirty trumpets, give or take the odd blast. Today I've got thirteen in my personal collection tucked away in cupboards, including one called a Silver Flair, a lovely piece of work.

I did have a favourite, but I gave it away. It was a King Cornet, a beautiful instrument. It happened like this: in the 1950s I was being paid £30 a week playing with Sid's band. But I was free to have a toot elsewhere, and one evening I headed for the bright lights of Soho to sit in on an all-night Ken Colyer session, playing my King Cornet. What a lovely sound that thing made, pure magic.

The night grew lively, as these things did, with musicians coming out of the audience to jam with us, then disappear into the gloom again. Some young fellow came on stage and blew his heart out with a battered old trumpet, worth about a fiver, which reminded me of my old bent treasure. He played pretty well, and I'd had a few drinks. You can guess the upshot. 'Here,' I called him over. 'Take this! You can have this one.' And I handed over my beloved King Cornet.

The lad stared down at it in disbelief, and stuttered his thanks. Stupid, or what? When I sobered up next morning I comforted myself with the thought that the only gift that matters is something you value for yourself. That same day I went out and bought a Convicta, one of the best on the market.

The best advice I can give is to follow the obvious rule: the more you pay, the less likely you are to get a dud one. You'll be unlikely to get a £200 trumpet which will play better than a £1,000 one. Sorry if you're skint, but that's the way it is. One mistake I once made was to buy a Constellation, a large-bore, big-band instrument, and I was playing with a small band at the time. With a big bore you use more air. I took the thing to Margate Ballroom for a gig without trying it out properly, and at the end of the first half I was absolutely shattered. However experienced you are, you have to break yourself in gently with a different-size instrument. I mean, you don't jump out of an Austin Seven and into a Ferrari and put your foot down without a bit of practice, do you?

So what's so special about a trumpet? For me, I can express myself more emotionally with a trumpet than I think I could with any other instrument. More than with a clarinet, a tenor sax or a flute, for example. There's something sensual and sexy about a trumpet. It can convey such emotion. It can convey happiness: it can be bright, bouncy and cheerful. And it can convey darker, more profound feelings.

The older and the more experienced you get, the more feeling you get out of it. There are exceptions to the rule, I'm sure, but I think that to convey emotions you have to have lived them. Divorce, death, tragedy – I put that into my playing the way playwrights tackle a script. And I'll let you into a secret: I've noticed that my playing has become happier since I became married to my second wife.

My contract with Sid Phillips allowed me to freelance as a 'dep', meaning that I could sit in to deputise for another musician if a band needed one. Often a panic call would come in for a gig the same day. 'Kenny, you free tonight?' And I would do my best to oblige. After all, that's where I wanted to be – up on a stage somewhere, blowing hot and strong.

I sat in on a few gigs with the Terry Lightfoot band, and finally left Sid Phillips to join Terry full time – albeit briefly. Terry, an accomplished clarinettist, had tried both mainstream and Dixieland for a time, but finally reverted to New Orleans. 'I feel this is the best jazz I can play. Neither of the other two was suitable for my interpretation,' he said at the time.

I couldn't go along with that, so I told him I was quitting. No hard feelings, though I have to say Terry wasn't too happy when two more of the band went with me – John Bennett on trombone and pianist Colin Bates.

He was even less pleased when he learned we had set up our own band, the Kenny Ball Dixielanders, but that's the name of the game. I brought in Dave Jones on clarinet, Colin Purbrook on bass, John Potter (from those Rhythm Ramblers days at the Greyhound) to strum his banjo and guitar, and Tony Budd on drums.

You'll notice the way names pop out of the woodwork, then disappear, only to pop up again. A minestrone of musicians! That's what I mean about the shifting sands of the business, and the way the restless tides of style and ambition can take you. But now I had come to a crossroads in my life, and the path I took stabilised that situation for ever. Say hello to the King Canute of jazz, as I held the tide and turned it back, creating a group whose name would last for close to half a century – and is still going strong today.

The year was 1958. In that year a number of other things happened.

For many it will be remembered for the terrible Munich air crash, in which eight Manchester United players – the famous 'Busby Babes' – died. The team still reached the cup final three months later, going down 2–0 to Bolton Wanderers, but the aftermath of that wintry February day would cast a shadow over football for years to come.

Elsewhere, Charles de Gaulle was elected the first president of France. Elvis Presley caused young girls to weep in the streets when he joined the US Army for two years, pocketing a pay packet of $78 a month. The first leg of the Ml, an eight-mile stretch of the Preston bypass, was opened by the prime minister Harold Macmillan. *The Bridge on the River Kwai* won three Oscars, including one for Alec Guinness as best actor. Donald Campbell hit a new water-speed record of 248.62 miles per hour. The phenomenal Sugar Ray Robinson became world middleweight boxing champion for the fifth time.

For me, it was the year I formed the Jazzmen.

CHAPTER EIGHT

ENTER THE JAZZMEN

Calling my band Kenny Ball and his Jazzmen was no great flash of inspiration. No one shouted 'Eureka!' The name just came from nowhere. It could have been the Kenny Ball Stompers, or Ravers, but we kept it simple. It actually began as Kenny Ball and his Jazz Band, just to make sure I turned up in person for every gig. Then, within weeks, it evolved into the Jazzmen.

Branching out on my own, I was looking for musicians who felt the same as I did about jazz. Instinct comes into it when you're building up a band. For some reason, unlike other band leaders, I never put any of them on probation to see if they fitted in. You could say I took a chance, but I just took them on face value, and it worked. Well, mostly.

Occasionally I made a mistake. I once took on a chap called Colin Bates, a good lad who played his double bass with zest and humour. I used to pull his leg. 'So, Colin, your parents were Mr and Mrs Bates. That makes you master …'

'Thank you, Kenny,' he would reply wearily. 'I wonder why I haven't heard that one before?'

But on one of our German tours, when we were staying in a hotel in Hamburg one night, Colin locked the door in the bathroom, climbed out of the window on to the roof and disappeared! We never saw him again. Admittedly, he had been drinking heavily – or to put it another way, he was pissed out of his brain. Presumably he sobered up some time, but he never came back. Musicians are like that – unpredictable. Or maybe that joke finally got to him.

Choosing the first Jazzmen went like clockwork. Everything and everyone just seemed to fall into place. The line-up was listed in the music industry's top magazine *Melody Maker* as follows:

John Bennett (trombone). Names his favourite trombonists as Lou McGarity and Abe Lincoln. He has been with the bands of Trevor Williams and Terry Lightfoot. He is a keen photographer.

Dave Jones (clarinet). He is Somerset born, and started playing eight years ago with Charlie Galbraith. Choice clarinettist: Benny Goodman.

Ron Weatherburn (piano): Led his own band in Germany for nine months. Ron has also been with 'Eggy' Ley and Cy Laurie, and toured the East End pubs as a soloist. Favourites: Scott Joplin, Jelly Roll Morton.

Ron was with us a number of years, a real humorist who curiously wore horn-rimmed spectacles which only had one lens. He was able to perform the feat of rubbing his right eye without taking his glasses off, and did it frequently.

Sadly, Ron died suddenly in 1995 of a heart attack while he was in Canada on tour with the Ken Sims band. He was only sixty-one. Ron had been a great favourite with our followers, and enjoyed his own mentions in *Jazzette*, our fan magazine, one of which read: 'Apart from playing with his rattle, Ron did not enter the music world until he was six years old and began taking piano lessons ...' Is that a late starter, or what? John Bennett paid a warm tribute to him in the magazine: 'British traditional jazz has lost one of its great characters. As a pianist, Ron was in a class of his own.'

How true that was. His speciality was ragtime, and I can still see him sitting with long legs entwined round his stool, thumping out Jelly Roll Morton's knuckle-bruising opus 'Fingerbuster', and making it sound like three piano rolls being played at once.

Bill Dixon (banjo): A twenty-year-old who formerly played with Dick Charlesworth's City Gents.

Vic Pitt (bass): Now eighteen, he started playing at fifteen with the City Ramblers Skiffle Group. Favourite bassist: Ray Brown.

Ron Bowden (drums): Began playing in 1948 with the famed Crane River Band. Later played with Ken Colyer and Chris Barber. Favourite musician: Louis Armstrong.

Clinton Ford (vocals): Was with Liverpool's Merseysippi Jazz Band for three years. His choice singer is Mel Torme. Before turning to singing he toured the music halls, playing in revues.

So now I'm twenty-seven years old, and I've formed my first band: Kenny Ball and his Jazzmen, aiming for the big time. So the first thing is to get ourselves a band van: a big moment in any musician's career. The one I settled on was a Dormobile, not spanking new, but an old beaten-up green van that I came across in south London. At that time I had a Triumph Mayflower, one of those two-door, square-bodied vehicles, which I bought for £500. I sold the car for the same price, and went looking for a van.

The one I found at a garage near the Elephant and Castle was going for £100, a ten-year-old green Dormobile which had been used by the PDSA, the People's Dispensary for Sick Animals, and had seen better days. It seemed to work well enough as I tested it around the side streets off the Old Kent Road, so I took it. We put a roof rack on it, and then we had to wash it out about twenty times with Jeyes Fluid to get rid of the stains.

Obviously we had to get something to sit on before we could all set off on the road. There were two battered seats in the front, and our instruments packed into the rear, but I had to find something across the back behind the driver for the group. I went nosing around the scrapyards in Romford, and spotted a big American car that had been written off in a crash. It had a bench seat, just what I was looking for. I talked the dealer in to letting me have it for two quid. Who else would want it, anyway?

I unscrewed the seat, took it home, and then spotted a large brown stain on the back. I started to wash the stain off, and it turned bright red. Blood! I never told anyone in the band, because I didn't want to upset them.

That van became part of our life. We thought we should give her a nickname, but it took us ages to decide on a final one, mainly because we were too busy calling her lots of names, none of them particularly affectionate, when she broke down. In the end we simply referred to her as our Green Goddess.

She didn't have any windows in the back, and the end doors weren't up to much. In fact, now I think of it, none of the doors were that good – one of the sliding front doors fell off in the

Mersey Tunnel once, and made a heck of a noise. A few weeks later down in London we were heading for Bromley in Kent to do a gig, and we were circling the roundabout by Waterloo Station heading south for the Elephant when I saw a wheel overtaking us. I was driving, and John Bennett sitting beside me in the passenger seat spotted it. 'Look at that,' he said. 'Someone must have lost a wheel!'

'Oh, yeah!' I responded with interest, then felt the van swerve and dip. There was a dreadful scraping sound, like a thousand cats screeching. 'It's us!' And it was. One of the rear wheels had come loose, and had spun merrily past. The axle dug into the road, and sparks were flying like a firework display.

Somehow I kept the van on the road, steered it into the side, and managed to stop. We leaped out, ran back to retrieve the nuts and bolts scattered along the road, jacked her up and replaced the wheel. Then we went on our way, chortling with relief.

Another time the exhaust pipe fell off. We were up in the wilds of Yorkshire and stopped in a lay-by for what is euphemistically known as a 'comfort break'. Our roadie went to open the rear doors, and the whole pipe and silencer fell off and clattered into the road. We threw it in the back until we could get to a garage and have it fitted back where it belonged.

But our Green Goddess did us proud. She would even get us to Germany on our first foreign date, albeit in a cloud of black fumes.

Confession time. The general idea was to get women into the back. At the end of a gig when everyone was in the bar, one of us would hope to take a girl out to the van for a session.

One of the group whose libido was particularly active – that's a polite way of saying he tried to shag everything in a skirt – was Dave Jones, our clarinet player who was then aged twenty-six and at the height of his bird-pulling prowess. Once, up north, I was sharing a room with him in a one-star hotel. The deal always was that you had to pretend to be asleep if the other guy in your room brought a girl back. Well, Dave did, and surreptitiously opening one eye I could make out in the mirror that she was Japanese.

If you've ever been in that situation where you're lying there like a lemon while your pal is having the time of his life, you'll know how utterly frustrating it is. You can't help thinking: Why not me? That nagging thought just won't go away as you hear the bed springs creaking and the gasps emanating from a few feet away. But this time, something weird happened. After it was over, and Madam Butterfly was on the way out, she planted a dainty kiss on my head, thinking I was asleep. I managed to stay absolutely still, but inside I was fuming as ungenerous thoughts filled my brain, like: Lucky for some!

We started getting regular work, because by now we all had our track records and had been making serious waves on the jazz scene. The big thing in the early days, of course, is to get yourself noticed. As someone once succinctly put it: 'If you don't toot your own whistle, no one else is going to do it for you.' We went out on the road, touring from club to club, and getting home to our loved ones whenever we could. I have to tell you that being on the road isn't always as romantic and glamorous as it might sound.

We criss-crossed the country as if we were charting an ordnance survey map of the UK, often travelling throughout the night after a gig, dozing in our seats in the band bus to snatch what sleep we could before the next engagement. Looking at some of those early dates, I'm amazed at our stamina. But you know something? We're still doing over a hundred gigs a year.

A sample month, November 1961, gives you an idea of our gruelling schedule. Are you ready?

Friday 1 .... November: Doncaster

Saturday 2 .... November: Spennymoor (south of Durham)

Sunday 3 .... November: Liverpool Empire

Monday 4 .... November: Leicester Rondo Ballroom

Thursday 7 .... November: Bedford Corn Exchange

Friday 8 .... November: Cambridge, Rex Ballroom

Saturday 9 .... November: Southampton Park Ballroom

Sunday 10 .... November: Bournemouth Pavilion

Monday 11 .... November: Hitchin, Hermitage Hall

Tuesday 12 .... November: Aylesbury Town Hall

Wednesday 13... November: High Wycombe Town Hall

Friday 15 .... November: Northwich (east of Chester)
 Memorial Hall

Saturday 16 ...... November: Buxton Pavilion

Sunday 17 .... November: Portsmouth Guildhall

Monday 18 .... November: Ipswich Baths

Tuesday 19 .... November: Berkhamsted, Kings Hall

Thursday 21 ..... November: Lewisham Town Hall

Friday 22 .... November – Wednesday 27
 November: London, various venues

Friday 29 .... November: Swindon, McIlroys Ballroom

Saturday 30 .... November: Kingston, Surrey, Baths

Sunday 31 .... November: Jazzhouse, London

Phew!

One of the places where we slept was a truckers' stop on the A5 near Whitchurch. It was ten shillings a night to stay there, in a great big dormitory. I lay down on my bed alongside the others, and I could smell feet. Not mine or theirs. Phew again! It was a horrible smell right under my nose. When I took the blanket off, then located the bottom sheet and turned it over, I found out why. The people who ran the place just turned the sheet around after each person. They didn't even bother to wash it!

The first place the Jazzmen really tooted their whistle and were heard throughout the entire country was on the BBC radio show *Easy Beat*, with the legendary broadcaster Brian Matthew presenting. It was Brian's idea to have a jazz band on, and we were invited to become the resident group. Now *that's* what you call a milestone. The show was hugely popular. It was recorded in front of an audience in the Playhouse Theatre by the Thames Embankment on a Wednesday, and went out the following Sunday morning.

We wore sparkly houndstooth check jackets with gold braid running through them, and black trousers. And always bow ties. On more casual gigs we'd wear ordinary ties, but still made sure we looked smart. No riff-raff on *this* jazz scene!

Brian was an amiable soul with a diffident manner that contrasted sharply with his on-air quick-fire delivery, friendly manner and breathless enthusiasm that won him a listening audience of nearly three million at his peak. We met in 1958, when his taste was for 'quality popular music – good melodies with good lyrics', and hit it off immediately. He was two years older than me, and began his career as a disc jockey for Radio Luxembourg before becoming a BBC announcer. His career continued for more than thirty years as he went on to host *Easy Beat, Saturday Club* and *Round Midnight* on radio, and *Thank Your Lucky Stars* for ITV. Brian described his image as 'like being the man you meet in the pub', adding that his number one rule was: 'Never talk down to your audience. Treat them as friends.' My sentiments exactly.

When I started getting broadcasting work for my band, we used to be given a little sheet from the producer asking us what we were going to play. Instead of just sending it back in the post, I used to take it personally to Aeolian Hall to meet the guy, and talk about it. The personal touch. It was also a form of networking, helping to set up future jobs. To this day, whenever I get a gig, I'll phone up the organisers and ask if they need any publicity, or if there's any way I can help the show along. It's not only good manners, it's a smart move! That way you get noticed.

Funny things happen on radio. I was on a programme with Geraldo and his Orchestra doing a late-night show from the BBC's Paris Studios in the West End. His real name was Gerald Bright, and he was something of a legend in the BBC. Eventually he became Sir Gerald Bright, but he had a right Cockney accent and used to do his own announcing on live radio on Saturday nights. The night in question he went up to the mike, and in broadest Cockney announced, 'I would now like to play you the latest British hit.' Unfortunately, the last two words sort of ran into each other, which reduced the rest of us, and presumably the great British public, to hysterics.

Lonnie Donegan put us further on the road to success. Next stop for the Jazzmen was obviously television, and I spent hours, days and weeks trying to get my foot in the door, any door, and my face and trumpet to follow it. Fat chance. All the programmes seemed to be planned way ahead, and no one seemed prepared to give us an audition, let alone a booking. We had made an appearance on a talent show called *New Faces*, which was the forerunner to a similar programme of the same name years later and, of course, shows like *Opportunity Knocks* and *Pop Idol* which will always be popular whatever name they go by. But, unfortunately, not a great deal came of it.

Finally, in 1960, I got us an audition with the BBC for a spot on a late-night talk show. The Aeolian Hall in Bond Street, in the heart of fashion-conscious Mayfair, was the unlikely venue, but we arrived full of hope and gave it our best shot. Lonnie Donegan, at that point several rungs ahead of us on the ladder belting out his wonderful skiffle numbers, happened to be in a neighbouring studio rehearsing his own TV show.

He put his head round the door of the control room and took a look at us. We had met a few times jamming at clubs, but it had always been very casual and informal. At the end he came up to me for a word. The conversation went like this:

Lonnie: 'What are you doing here?'

Kenny: 'We're doing an audition for TV.'

Lonnie: 'So you want to be on TV?'

Kenny: 'You bet I do.'

Lonnie: 'OK, you're on my show.'

Just like that! Then he enquired: 'By the way, have you got a record contract?'

'Er, no.'

'Do you want one?' Did I? I nodded dumbly. 'Well,' said Lonnie. 'You've got one. Leave it to me.' And he arranged it through Pye Records. We had been knocking on every door for weeks without any luck, and suddenly we were at a turning point in our lives.

Thanks to Lonnie's influence, we recorded our first album for Pye, *Welcome to the Ball*, in 1960. The subsequent single, 'The Teddy Bears' Picnic', went down like a lead balloon. I fear it was several sandwiches short. But our second one hit the jackpot – I'm talking about 'Samantha', of course. We were always looking for something different, and in fact I got the idea to give this beautiful and haunting song a completely new sound during a gig in a club in Liverpool. We had just come off stage and were packing up our gear to go home, when suddenly we heard a piano player hammering the tune out.

As one man we stopped what we were doing and stared at each other. I shook my head in a sudden daze. I could only just make out the original song that Bing Crosby sang so movingly, but there was something in the arrangement that sent a shiver down my spine.

'That's the way we're going to do it – ragtime!'

Back in town I called the boys together at the studio, and tossed the idea at them. 'What do you think?' I looked at Bill Dixon, the banjo player and said, 'Give it some rug-a-dug-a-dug-a!' That changed the whole sound on the spot.

Shortly after we'd put down the record of 'Samantha', we decided to treat the public to our version on *Easy Beat*. It was a risk, I knew. When you have such an old favourite ingrained into the public psyche it's dangerous to play games. But the audience went potty. They kept clapping and cheering for so long that the BBC had to cut a minute of applause off the final recording. After that we never looked back.

'Samantha' was a total surprise. She came from nowhere, and suddenly she was way up at the top of the charts. And my love affair with that lady has lasted to this day.

Lonnie's faith in me was justified. I owe all that to Lonnie Donegan, and you can imagine how I felt when he died in 2003.

Another equally legendary name gave us a huge boost where it counted, in print. Steve Race, then writing his column 'Round the Clubs' for the influential *Melody Maker*, paid us this extraordinary accolade in May that same year:

> Let's put it in a sentence: the Kenny Ball Jazzmen
> constitute one of the most exciting things on the
> current traditionalist scene. Throughout the whole of
> an evening the band never stops swinging. And its

standard both in jazz and instrumental ability is startlingly high.

There is no weak link anywhere in the group. Trumpeter Kenny himself blows a strong, toneful lead, and is a likeable leader. Trombonist John Bennett plays with the fire of Trummy Young, laced with flashes of Teagarden's technical facility, though his style is very much his own. Dave Jones on clarinet produces driving sound without sacrificing the tone of his instrument.

The three of them comprise a swinging, sympathetic frontline which would make exciting listening even without such a good rhythm section. Along the back row sit Colin Bates (piano), Vic Pitt (bass), Dickie Bishop (banjo) and Tony Budd (drums), working genuinely as a team, and sometimes driving the band to a pitch of excitement which has to be felt to be believed.

Yes, this is a rave notice for a band which disproves all the modernists' pet theories about trad musicians. They play the tunes, they know the chords. What's more, they listen intently and appreciatively to each other's solos.

I raise my straw boater to them!

I couldn't have put it better myself!

'Are you sure you didn't write this for him?' John Bennett asked me, folding the paper into his briefcase for his files. John kept a diary of the Jazzmen from day one, and this would be a rather special cutting for the future, whatever kind of future we had. Looking back now, it's part of posterity.

As for the rest of us, we walked on air for a week.

CHAPTER NINE

THE MAGNIFICENT
SEVEN

The Jazzmen's first trip abroad was to Germany in April 1959, when we were invited out to do a gig in a jazz club in Frankfurt, and then go on to Hamburg for another booking. We took the Green Goddess, which amazingly was still roadworthy, even if the springs on the sofa were wearing out quicker than the camshaft, and we kept the old girl well oiled as we motored down the autobahns.

We knew we were in for a challenge at Frankfurt when we found we had to play seven (yes, seven!) hours a night, with matinees on Saturdays. We played twenty-minute sessions, then we were allowed a short break, and it meant we had to stay on our feet from nine in the evening until four in the morning. But we were young, we were fit, we were in the groove and we didn't care.

At Hamburg the story was the same. In the New Orleans Club we played six sets from eight right the way through to four. Dickie

Bishop, our banjo player, was a bit of a right-elbow expert, if you get my meaning, and the beer in Germany tends to be rather strong. He was a short, dumpy little fellow with a goatee beard who used to get tired at about three in the morning, especially after imbibing a few pints. We'd actually watch it happen – his hand playing the banjo got slower and slower, and finally stopped altogether when he went to sleep! Luckily the banjo was tied round his neck with a cord, so it didn't clatter to the stage when Dickie dropped off.

One night in the New Orleans Club he fell asleep as per his custom, and the rest of us carried on playing to conclude the number. As we finished and took our bow, Dickie woke up, and in a panic started strumming that banjo for all he was worth – but all by himself! Everyone else had stopped. That cost him a round in the bar afterwards, and a great deal of ribbing too.

That tour was fine, but the next trip to Deutschland nine months later wasn't so funny. We still had some way to go to make it to the five-star circuit, and this time we found ourselves in one of the worst hotels ever – and, believe me, we've had some rough ones. This particular hostelry was located on the road between Frankfurt and Düsseldorf. It was midwinter, blistering cold with leaden skies, there was snow on the fields and the roads were icy.

We rolled up in our battered van around three in the morning, knowing that we had to be up again and out at six. We had booked ahead but, when the sleepy concierge gave us the keys and gestured upstairs with a thumb, I had a feeling this wasn't going to be the Ritz.

I was right. In my room the window was wide open, with cold air coming in – and it wouldn't close. The bed had so many lumps it felt as if there were stones in the mattress. The only way to get warm, I thought, was to have a hot bath, so at half past five, I turned on the taps and put a toe in. Ice-cold water! There was no shower, so I had to set off again in the bus and drive all day without a shower, hardly any sleep and no breakfast.

The rest of the band had found much the same in their rooms. But what can you do? It happens. No need to make a crisis out of a drama.

To get through moments like that, you can only fall back on one vital asset: your sense of humour. My favourite jokes are shaggy-dog stories. For one thing they help pass the time on long journeys, so the further you can string out a story, the better to alleviate the boredom.

One that tickles me is about the fellow who had a stomach ache. He goes to the doctor, moaning and groaning. The doctor can find out what's wrong. He passes him on to a specialist, but he can't help either.

Then he hears about a witch doctor visiting Britain from Africa, and goes to him. 'Can you help me?' he asks.

'I think I can,' replies the witch doctor. He gets out a leather thong, and ties seven knots in it. 'I want you to eat one of these knots every day for a week, then come back and see me.'

The fellow, startled, says, 'Are you sure? It sounds highly unusual to me.'

'Trust me,' says the witch doctor. 'This should do the trick.'

So the chap goes away and religiously does as he's told. But it doesn't get rid of the stomach ache, and when he goes back to the witch doctor he's fuming. 'I've done all you said, and I've still got this terrible pain.'

'Ah,' says the witch doctor. 'That means only one thing.'

'What's that?'

'The thong has ended, but the malady lingers on.'

That's when everybody groans. Loudly.

On that trip something else happened that has gone down in the annals of the Jazzmen. One night we found ourselves forced to stay in a hostel. It was virtually a dormitory with a dozen beds, all of them occupied. We came in late after our gig and a few drinks, and rolled into bed. I was just dozing off when I heard a strange slapping noise. The sound came from our banjo man, Dickie.

The rest of us stirred in our beds. A few mutters broke the embarrassed silence. Slap, slap, slap! What else could he be doing but having a wank? It kept going on … and on. I thought, Blimey, he's having a long one! Finally I had to turn the lights on, and found Dickie was smoking in bed and was so drunk he kept setting light to himself. He was slapping the sparks out on his shirt!

It was one of those rare times when I had steeled myself to sleep in the dark. Usually, whenever I stay in a hotel, I must have the light on. All night long. Normally I can never go to sleep in a completely darkened bedroom. It stems from when I was a kid in Worcester, and one night my Auntie Alice – remember her? – tucked me up in bed and closed the door. I can remember that bedroom now, down to every piece of furniture. For some reason I panicked when the room went completely black. I didn't cry out, but I cowered under the bedclothes, thinking there might be spiders or mice on the loose. So today in any hotel room I always keep the bathroom light on and the door ajar. Just a little bit of light, even from a window, is all I need.

Three nights later we found ourselves in Düsseldorf, this time in a grotty hotel in the suburbs where we rented two rooms for a week. The landlady was a large, humourless *hausfrau* who had preserved a portrait of her dead husband in German uniform on the wall. When she wasn't around we amused ourselves by using it as a dartboard. By the time we left there were so many pockmarks in his cheeks he looked as if he'd died of smallpox. Somehow she never noticed it.

She would put her head round the door and say, 'Herr Ball! Vot is all this noise I can hear?' But we had heard her heavy tread on the landing, and were sitting around innocently reading books.

'Herr Ball? I thought that was something that got stuck in a cat's throat,' said Dickie.

'Or up its arse!' added John.

'Fun-nee,' I said.

For the rest of that trip I became Hairball.

Talking of hair reminds me how at last I got my own back on Dickie, the prime joker in the pack, and his goatee beard. 'Did you hear the story about the sex-starved wife who was fed up with her boozy husband?' I asked him as we rumbled down the autobahn.

'Go on,' says Dickie.

'Well, every night he comes in drunk, and falls asleep straight away. It comes to the point where the poor woman hasn't had intimacy for a year, and is considering divorce.

'After he's away another night in the pub, she decides to confront him when he gets home. But her man staggers through the front door and, before she can give him an earful, he says, "Baby, get upstairs to the bedroom!" She can't believe it. At last he's going to pay her a bit of attention.

'They get to the bedroom, and he orders her to take her clothes off. She's only too willing to comply. "Now, darling, do a handstand against the full-length mirror on the wall."

'Wow, she thinks. Kinky ... I like it! She does an athletic handstand, then suddenly her hubby pulls her legs apart and puts his chin between them.

'"The boys down the pub were right," he says. "A goatee *would* suit me!"'

One up to me, as I listen to the laughter in the back of the van.

It was in Düsseldorf that we found ourselves playing in a cellar that was shaped like a railway carriage, and not much bigger. We were squashed between the bar and the toilet, and it was so narrow that John Bennett couldn't play the trombone properly unless he was sideways on to the wall. What with people pushing past to get to the loo, and pouring beer over our shoes when they bumped into us, that was one club I wasn't anxious to visit again.

Back home in Blighty, we were starting to roll. I'd say rock 'n' roll, except that our music was trad jazz. 'Samantha' was up in the top ten, and stayed there for weeks. It meant we were regulars on *Top of the Pops*, and doing gigs round the country at the rate of four a week. Now *that's* motoring!

We'd been playing at Dundee and it was two o'clock in the morning in the middle of a Scottish winter. The Green Goddess was out of action with engine trouble, so the seven of us were in a VW Camper, with our drummer Ron Bowden driving us after a gig. We were singing the band song, which goes like this:

> Knickers, knickers, those are the things to have,
> You put them on in the bedroom, you take them off
> in the lav.
> Knickers, knickers, those are the things to wear,
> So you must buy a pair of knickers, if you don't want
> your bum all bare!

We were singing our little ditty for the third time when suddenly we hit black ice on a left-hand bend and ran out of road. The Camper overturned and skidded along on its side, with glass shattering and all our luggage and instruments being flung about inside, along with us. I ended up lying between the seats with John Bennett's face buried in my lap. In the sudden silence that often falls after a disaster, all I could think of to say was, 'Don't tell anybody, John, and I won't!'

The windscreen and several windows were broken, but we managed to climb out through the doors and heave the bus upright. Somehow nobody was hurt, apart from the driver who suffered a sprained shoulder. We were dead lucky – that is, lucky not to be dead.

I thought we were all out of the bus, when I heard a weak voice calling out, 'Help me! Help me!' It was the banjo player Paddy Lightfoot stuck under a pile of luggage at the back. We got him out, and drove on thirty miles to Ayr, with no windscreen and a freezing draught blasting through the windows.

A major charity we were involved with was Stars for Spastics, and one night we were playing Wembley Arena, opening the second half. Cliff Richard was topping the bill with the Shadows. I looked down the list, and noticed that a little-known group called the Beatles was finishing the first half. My dressing room had a door which opened out so that you could see part of the stage.

I was shrugging myself into my sparkly jacket when there was a knock on the door. Cliff put his head round. The Shadows, led by the bespectacled Hank Marvin, were bunched behind him. 'Kenny, do you mind if we watch from your dressing room?' Cliff asked. 'We don't want to block the gangway.'

'Sure you can.' I let them crowd in.

'We've heard about these kids,' said Cliff. 'We just thought we'd have a look at them.' In fact I had been on *Easy Beat* with the Beatles, but I'd never actually played with them and never did, not even a casual jam session. After all, we were completely different styles.

Cliff made sure no one could see him as the Beatles took to the stage. It was still the first half, remember. And with every number, the crowd went wild. We could hardly hear ourselves above the din. In my dressing room that night, we all sensed we were seeing something special, the shape of things to come. It was just a taster, but the dressing room went quiet, and the group took on a sudden hangdog air. Cliff looked at me. He knew the score, and he was sportsman enough to acknowledge it.

'How are we going to follow *that*?' he asked.

In March 1961, Dickie Bishop bowed out, and was replaced by Diz Disley who had been leading the Soho String Quintet, the only group in Britain to style itself on the original Hot Club of France. Bill Dixon moved on to join the Mac Duncan band, and I brought in Paddy Lightfoot, who left his brother Terry's outfit.

Dave Jones took his clarinet elsewhere for a few months, and I found Alan Cater as a replacement before Dave came back to stay until 1966. On drums, Tony Budd was followed by Jim Garforth, who in turn relinquished the sticks to Ron Bowden – he would stay with me from 1960 until 1992.

It was in those marvellous heady days of the sixties that someone in musical circles dubbed us 'The Magnificent Seven', and the name stuck. I wasn't arguing. The boys were great, and we started producing hits as if they were coming off a conveyor belt. The Jazzmen were on a drum roll, and showed no signs of flagging.

We had struck pay dirt with 'Samantha', and even the traditionally staid BBC radio programme *Housewives' Choice* was getting regular requests for her. But it takes more than one hit record for a singer or a musician to stay at the top of the tree, and now I was about to have a pair of beauties. 'Midnight in Moscow' overtook our lucky lady to reach number two, and remained up there in the top ten for an amazing twenty-one weeks. The song was derived from 'Moscow Nights', which was originally 'St Petersburg Nights'. It was OK to play it in Russia, but not in places like Lithuania – we soon learned the diplomacy of not playing it in certain countries.

It was with 'Midnight in Moscow' that Kenny and the Jazzmen sold a million copies, earning me a coveted gold disc to frame and put on my wall, with miniature gold discs for each of the band. It was also the first record on which I ever conveyed personal emotion, and I have a theory about that. I've touched on it already, but to be more specific: in order to make a record emotionally acceptable to those who listen to it, you have to put something of yourself into it. Does that make sense? It does to me. Once they find it, they say, 'I like it'. And they don't know why. With 'Midnight in Moscow', they found something of themselves, and I put it there. It touches a chord. That chord is hidden in them, and I bring it alive.

It's a talent that has to be there to start with, but you need to have learned a lot and loved a lot before you can develop it. There are some brilliant musicians who can play wonderful stuff on their instruments, but can't use that ability to convey emotion. There are sounds that can make you weep – haven't we all shed tears after hearing some music? (I suppose people have cried at mine for the wrong reasons, like, How can he be so bloody awful? Just joking – I hope ...)

In 1962 we recorded 'The March of the Siamese Children', which made it to number four, and hung on in the top twenty for a gratifying thirteen weeks, later to be overtaken by 'The Green Leaves of Summer' from the epic film *The Alamo*, which did the business for fourteen weeks and touched the number seven spot.

The *New Musical Express* gave us further cause to celebrate by reporting: '"Midnight in Moscow" is nicely settled at number one in Australia, Canada, Sweden and Japan, and is riding high at number two in the US.' The record was now being referred to simply as 'M in M' by the literati and glitterati, and everyone seemed to be humming it.

Headlines in the music press, and even the nationals, spoke of a 'trad jazz bonanza', and they weren't far wrong. Names like Bob Wallis, Monty Sunshine, Chris Barber and Acker Bilk seemed to fill the pages, along with other hot groups of the day such as Ian Menzies and his Clyde Valley Stompers. Looking back in my files, I find I had moved up from getting £20 a night for the band to earning us £120, a goodly sum if not quite a small fortune in those days.

From 1958 to 1962 I experimented with featured vocalists: Jackie Lynn, Jeannie Lambe and Clinton Ford were up there on the mike, and Gary Miller, Lonnie Donegan and even Max Bygraves have all recorded with us. But now we do the job ourselves. I may not be Pavarotti – but, then again, I don't have to be.

To prove our growing status, we chalked up two London Palladium firsts. In May 1961 we became the first trad jazz band ever to tread the hallowed boards of that Mecca of show business, with a two-week stint on a bill topped by Frankie Vaughan. And the following month we were the first trad band to appear in the hit ATV show *Sunday Night at the London Palladium*, which in its day boasted the biggest TV viewing figures of them all.

I was meeting some wonderful characters. Chet Baker was a fine trumpeter and vocalist with a trio which was world renowned and had classics like 'Tea for Two' and 'Stella by Starlight' on his albums. He was much in demand at festivals where other musicians would sit in, such as Newport where he played with Dave Brubeck and Gerry Mulligan. In his youth he was a handsome kid who reminded me of a mixture of James Dean and Montgomery Clift.

Now Chet was a great guy, but I have to say that he was not the brightest lamp in the chandelier. At one of the festivals the piano player was Mussolini's grandson, hardly out of his teens but a kid who knew what he was doing. They came off after playing the first set. The clarinet player, a mate of mine, asked Chet, 'Do you know who that is with us on piano?'

'No, I don't,' said Chet.

'He's Mussolini's grandson.'

'Yeah? Who's Mussolini?'

My mate told him. 'Mussolini was the dictator of Italy in World War II, and at the end of the war they strung him up by his heels from a lamp post with his girlfriend.'

'Really, man?' Chet said, impressed. Before they went out again for the second half, Chet went up to the kid and said, 'Hey, son, sorry to hear about your granddad!'

'Samantha' had sold 175,000 copies when I recorded a new song for Pye specially aimed at the US market, which went out on their Jamie label. It was a bouncy ditty about eighteen girls, with the title 'I Still Love You All' and was actually a jazzed-up version of a song called 'Padam Padam' recorded by Vera Lynn nine years earlier, though I suspect the words must have been changed. Eighteen girls? Vera herself was very generous. She said, 'The jazzing up of the song doesn't surprise me at all. It's a lovely tune.' I've always agreed that there's nothing like a dame, and there's certainly no one like Dame Vera for a place in our hearts, and nor will there ever be.

The song itself did well enough, making it into the top thirty for six weeks. But now I was fired with a new ambition. We were hot. It was time to break the American market. 'Get your visas, boys,' I ordered. 'We're heading west!'

First stop, New Orleans. Which means Bourbon Street – and all that jazz! Middle-aged men in striped shirts and red braces played wonderful smoky rhythms in bars that ran the length of the street. You bought your drink in one bar, drank it as you wandered along the pavement, and dived into a bar across the road for a refill. We were part of British Week, and went around the city in a London double-decker bus, playing for all we were worth. I'm glad to say the Americans loved us.

We were guests of the New Orleans Jazz Society, and gave them a show that knocked their socks off. So much so that the leading jazz critic, one Charles Dawn, reported in the *Chicago American*: 'These Londoners play Dixieland on a par with the best of all America's groups.'

High praise indeed, and I was reading all about it as I took a cab to visit the grave of Bix Beiderbecke, the legendary white jazz trumpeter who died too young at the age of twenty-nine. I had always been a fan – he was my hero as a kid – and I promised myself I would make this pilgrimage one day. But I never thought I'd be a VIP when I got there.

The icing on the cake was when 'Midnight in Moscow' was placed in their Museum Archives, and I was made an honorary citizen of New Orleans, the cradle of jazz.

One thing did upset me about that first experience of the Deep South: the segregation, if not degradation, that was apparent everywhere – right down to the separate toilets for coloureds and whites. I found it deeply depressing. Don't forget that I learned so much of my jazz off black musicians like Louis Armstrong and King Oliver, to name but two.

We saw it for ourselves as the tour took us to Baton Rouge and on through Louisiana, bringing the Kenny Ball sound to jazz clubs and country and western bars. Everywhere we made a big hit. One local paper reported, 'This band is positively therapeutic. They cured one old lady's arthritis because she was snapping her fingers and jerking her shoulders around so much!'

With an accolade like that, how could we fail? The Jazzmen came back to the UK glowing with pride.

CHAPTER TEN

INTRODUCING
THE BAND

Time to strike up the band, and meet the boys. These are the current Jazzmen, and I'm proud of each and every one of them. Let's start with (drum roll) ... on trombone, *John Bennett*!

John is a true friend. We've been together through good times and bad, for richer and poorer. Sounds like we've taken our vows, doesn't it – and in a sense we did. Yes, to music and to the band we are wed! When I first set eyes on John, my immediate thought was that he looked a bit like Elvis Presley, in other words a handsome devil and a real ladykiller. The women used to flock around him.

John and I would talk music until the sun came up. We were trying to capture a sound, a special sound that would touch a chord in people. Chris Barber, George Melly, Cy Laurie, Humph and Ken Colyer were all leading figures of the time, but we were trying to get a different sound.

'Listen, John,' I would say. 'The sound the band gets is achieved by the trumpet playing with a mute, and the trombone playing mute, with the clarinet weaving in and out of those harmonies in the lower and upper register. That, basically, is the key to it.'

'OK.' He nodded slowly. 'That sounds good.'

The plain fact is that there's no copyright on sound. People can try and emulate a band, and they do. But as they always said about people who tried to copy Glenn Miller, they could never get it quite right. God knows how many people have been influenced by Louis Armstrong, but they still can't get it. There's a saying about imitators in the business: it's morally wrong and physically impossible! No way could you ever get it. Louis was a genius. So was Miller. And as for the Jazzmen, others can play the songs, but they can't get it the way we do.

Now I'm going to get technical, but only for a moment. The way we get the Kenny Ball sound, is from these few 'basic' principles: you take the major scale, the natural seventh chord, and the minor seventh chord which leads you to another key. The augmented chord, the ninth chord, is one note above the octave. Like a D on the octave above C. You can get a flattened fifth. You play the major chord like C, E and G, then instead of playing the G you flatten the fifth, so you play G flat. It's a semitone below the actual note that would in theory be there if you are playing a simple major triad. The fifth note of the major chord is flattened. There's one note out of sync along the top. Got it? No? Well, don't worry.

John and I compared the subtleties of trumpet and trombone till we were, well, breathless. A trombone and a trumpet have got a lot in common from a technical point of view – and musicians tend to spit into them, even if I later wished I hadn't! The trombone has a bigger mouthpiece, but the amount of wind and air passing through it doesn't make a lot of difference.

John's turn: 'Where they part company is that you've got valves on a trumpet and a slide on a trombone, though some trombones do have valves too. The idea is pretty easy, like a bugle. A bugle plays a chord. That's all it can do. No notes in between. But, if you think of seven bugles, you've got yourself a trombone.'

'I reckon you have, John.' He had himself a trombone.

Now to the comedian of the outfit (more drums) ... on clarinet, *Andy Cooper*!

Andy came into my life at the Lord Mayor's Show in 1967, and you could say he never left the procession. He has stayed with me ever since, for more than thirty-five years. Marvellous! Tall, craggy, with a nose that inspired Concorde – his words, not mine – this man is a laugh a minute, and we hit it off straight away. Over six feet tall, he used to have a beard and long hair, and was always getting mistaken for Billy Connolly, until he opened his mouth. Apart from being a natural comic and extrovert, Andy is one of the most talented clarinet players around. Thirty-five years on he still hasn't lost his puff, and he's still got his own hair. Whenever he does his 'chicken act', complete with gestures, he brings the house down.

Andy is the one for practical jokes, particularly on anyone who arrives late. They're likely to find the sleeves of their tuxedos have been sewn up, and you can imagine the struggling and the swearing as they try to get their arms through!

How did we meet? Let Andy tell it his way.

'It was in the Lord Mayor's Show, of all places. I'd never met Kenny before. Terry Lightfoot had left, and I got an urgent phone call. They were short of a clarinet, could I make it? Why not! That cold November day in London the entire band was up for it, and so was I. They had lined up seven Mini-Mokes, with a small platform built on the back where each of the Jazzmen could sit or stand, starting off from London Wall and touring the City.

'That's where I met Kenny. We shook hands, then he slung a blue sweater at me with the band's logo on it and said, "Get that on you, cock, or you'll bloody well freeze!" That was my introduction to the Jazzmen. And off we went.

'I should perhaps add that there was a Miss World contender perched on each float to add glamour to the scene. With a future Miss World in full national costume rustling up against you, it's enough to put anyone off his pizzicato, but I'll say this for the boys – they did their best to keep their minds on the music.

'The problem with being surrounded by such pulchritude, as some of the boys found when they tried to chat up theirs, is that they may be global beauties, but too often they don't speak our language, apart from the odd phrase that has been drummed into them by their chaperones. As for us, "Please … thank you … fancy a beer?" doesn't get you very far in any language, does it? And you can only send so many messages with your eyes, especially when you're blasting out "Midnight in Moscow" on the back of an open Mini in near sub-zero temperatures.

'At one point, when the procession came to a dead stop in Fleet Street, I did hop down off my Moke and head into the pub – but only because I saw the other guys doing it. I like this bunch, I thought. They've got their priorities right! The old George Inn it was, down an alleyway by the Law Courts. Quick snort, and back on the float. Nobody noticed.

'In fact, I was dead lucky. I had Miss Australia and Miss Canada on my Moke, two for the price of one, and at a time when Kenny and the Jazzmen were well into the hit records. It was quite surreal: sometimes the small cars were chugging along side by side, other times they were in a long line like something out of *The Italian Job*. But we could still hear each other, pick up the cues from Kenny at the front and make sure the whole street could hear us coming!

Kenny would yell out something and expect you to know it. He took no prisoners.

'I wasn't given any material to learn. I just went straight in, no time for rehearsals. But that happens all the time. When you're a jazz musician of a certain standard, you know the songs even if you don't necessarily know the arrangements. You pick it up pretty quick.

'At the end of the morning, all the toffs went off to the Mansion House for a slap-up lunch. Kenny took us for a quick Chinese, then I found myself zooming up the M1 to Nottingham for a gig that night. Somewhere along the line Kenny invited me to join the band. I must have said yes, because I ended up at the Flying Horse Hotel in Nottingham in an all-night drinking session. That was my inauguration – and I've never looked back. Next morning, Kenny said, "Welcome to the gang." I was in.'

Andy had been with the Alan Elsdon band, and, coming to us at the age of twenty-five, he was our youngest new recruit. But he played like a veteran. This young man had been around.

In those days, Archer Street near Tottenham Court Road was the legendary hang-out for musicians looking for work. Close to Denmark Street, better known as Tin Pan Alley, you could find four hundred, repeat four *hundred*, hopefuls standing around waiting to be picked in the early morning as the sun came up over the City to the east. Some of the boys were even in their DJs with their instruments after coming straight from a gig, ready to get session work.

There had been a surge of unemployed musicians and performers demobbed from ENSA after the war, and the ripples lasted for a long time afterwards. Somebody would arrive with a board, announcing work, and hold it up. 'I need a bass, I need two trumpet players.' The crowd would surge forward. It was like being on the docks waiting for work in a scene from *On the Waterfront*. You'd raise your hand and try to catch the man's eye.

Andy likened his new position as one of the Jazzmen to acting. 'In the theatre you spend all your time out in the provinces or doing revues, and all of a sudden you're in the West End or on Broadway. Big time! Joining Kenny was that big a jump for me. I was lucky. I never had to hang around Archer Street waiting for a call.'

In his first year with us, Andy found out the hard way what being part of a hit band meant in practical and logistical terms. 'In those twelve months we did 370 shows, and that included four weeks' holiday. We were sometimes doing two concerts a night in two different venues.' Not long married, Andy would for ever after remind me that, after the day he joined us on that Lord Mayor's float, he didn't see his first-born kid for the next five weeks.

Ask Andy to define the band, and he gives you his usual subtle riposte: 'It's an up-your-arse band! Straight between the eyes. You can never call us laid back – we're a fire band! You can detect the Kenny Ball sound a mile away.'

OK, Andy, I'll go along with that.

Next, please welcome the King of the Ivories (drums again) ... on piano, *Hugh Ledigo*!

Hugh is our brilliant pianist, composer, arranger and all-round good guy. A true blue. Physical description: on the short side, has follicle trouble (i.e. thinning hair) and used to sport a ponytail until he got too old for it. One of the stalwarts of the band, he has a terrific sense of humour – and needs every bit of it.

I think his name originates from Spain, though I never stumbled across a Spaniard who knew it. *Le Digo*, maybe? Which actually means, 'I say!' Hugh's father was a watchmaker, and he still wears the old wind-up watch his dad gave him when he was kid.

Hugh's musical influence was his brother John, ten years older, who started life on drums and ended up as a regular bass player. Born in 1934 in Bromley, Kent, Hugh always intended to play classical music, and it shows today when he lets loose with 'Für Elise', another on our 'most wanted' list when it comes to audience requests.

He had his first piano lesson when he was seven, but once told me how his first public performance was actually at the age of six, in a pantomime in a local church hall. Apparently all the kids were invited on stage to do a party piece, and Hugh sang 'Coming Home on a Wing and a Prayer' – highly emotive at that time, because it was during the Battle of Britain.

'I reduced everyone to tears,' he assured me. 'And at the end I was bombarded with money. So you could say it was my first paid gig.'

'You're still doing both, my friend,' I replied.

By an odd coincidence, Hugh went straight from school into advertising, just as John and I had done. It was a City firm, a big agency in which he specialised in lettering and designing. That was his day job, to pay the bills. Hugh's problem arose when he started to fall asleep all the time, because, like us, he spent his nights in clubs playing jazz until four in the morning. Hugh showed his early gift for improvisation by sneaking off to the office loo, putting the seat down in a cubicle, and snatching ten minutes' kip. 'Cat napping became my speciality,' he confirms. 'Eventually I was able to time it so that I slept for ten minutes, got up, pulled the chain, and came out whistling! Nobody ever cottoned on, though they might have wondered about my bowels and bladder.'

Hugh took the familiar route through the clubs, then gravitated into hotels. Those were the days of tea dances at the Café de Paris and the Ritz, usually with a trio – piano, bass and drums – slipping occasional Gershwin, Shearing and Nat King Cole jazz into the traditional afternoon waltzes and foxtrots. The Dorchester, the Savoy, Claridge's, the Mayfair. You name it, he played there. He became musical director at the Showboat in Lyons Corner House, then joined the Pasadena Roof Orchestra, and toured the Continent with them.

Hugh joined me through the grapevine. I was looking for a pianist, and I knew his name; I had heard he was available and rang him. He remembers my opening words: 'Christ, you're bloody hard to get hold of!' I like to get straight to the point. That was seven years ago, and he has been with me ever since.

Hugh knew all the tunes, which helped. Like so many others in our game he was thrown straight into the deep end on his first gig with us. 'Luckily,' he says, 'I'd played with a million bands and was comfortable with every kind of music from rock 'n' roll to South American music, and jazz of course. You name it, I'd played it. So I knew all the tunes. The fact the band didn't carry dots around with them didn't faze me.' Dots being our jargon for sheet music.

Hugh remembers how we drove to Wales on that first gig, ending up in a huge barn in a waterlogged field, with a flock of sheep staring at us through the hedge. He got an idea of the band's humour when someone spotted them and piped up, 'What do you call a sheep tethered on a Welsh village green?'

Shaking of heads all round.

'A leisure centre!'

Thank you and goodnight. Don't call us, we'll call you. We kept that one out of the script, along with, 'What do you call a Welshman with a sheep under each arm? Bisexual.'

The place was packed to the rafters; we were given a huge ovation and our new arrival was off to a good start with the Jazzmen.

Hugh has his own ground rules about his job. 'The pianist sits at the side, and as long as he has a grin on his face from time to time that's all he has to do. He can't really move about much, or jump up and do a tap dance. But the one thing you can't do with *this* band is fall asleep.'

Some pianists have a large finger-span, which obviously makes it easier for them to cover the keyboard. It's hard to believe from the way he works that piano, but Hugh in fact has very small hands. He describes it: 'I play a nine, counting from C to the D in the next octave. Rachmaninov spanned twelve! Oscar Peterson was eleven, I'm told. Which gives you some idea of how hard it is for me to dance my hands over the keyboard in leaps, jumping like a flea. It matters not. I get what I need out of it.'

But there's a price to pay. One problem a pianist can get is impacted bones in the wrist, caused by too much jumping about on the keyboard. The first sign is pains and stiffness, like tennis elbow in the wrist. Hugh suffered from this for a time, without knowing why the pain was so excruciating. Then he found out. 'It wasn't tendons, it was tension. The muscles had contracted under the ongoing tension as I played, and impacted the bones in the wrist by pulling them together. No wonder I was in such pain. But, once I realised the cause, I did a few exercises, and in no time at all it was cured.'

Hugh and I have tried experimenting with all sorts of ideas, letting our imagination run riot and then seeing if it's practical. We even came up with a concept to try my trumpet out against a string orchestra. As I may have mentioned before, the Kenny Ball band has no strings attached. Hugh suggests that this particular flight of fancy came up towards closing time somewhere. We couldn't afford a string section, so we did it with a synthesiser. Bass and drums, Hugh on the keyboard, and we went straight through it at one sitting. We played tunes like

'Stranger on the Shore' (I know it's your territory, Acker), and songs associated with Frank Sinatra.

It worked. In fact it worked so well that it was put out on an album under the title *Strings and Things*. Moral: we can always do the impossible. Miracles take a little longer.

Hugh has virtually cornered the market in jazz arrangements of classical pieces. He is not the first. He tells me of a thirties band led by one John Kirby, essentially a jazz group. 'He did phenomenal things like setting Chopin's "Minute Waltz" to jazz,' says Hugh. 'Some classical purists might object, but it's amazing how few people know the original, and so this is their first introduction to the piece. Sometimes when I play it, people come up to me and say, "I used to play that when I was young – but never like that!" What they usually mean is that they couldn't play it as fast.'

Soon after joining me, Hugh was invited by a record company to create an album based on themes by Tchaikovsky, Beethoven, Mozart and Bach. We called the CD *Jazzical Class*. It was quite a challenge. As he explains, 'First you look for the harmonic structure, how it moves from one chord to another. You find a theme you want to adapt – maybe just five minutes maximum – and improvise on that.' And he adds modestly, 'Judging by my royalty cheques it's done rather well.' Glad to hear it, Hugh.

To relax he plays chess with John Bennett. The oddball fact is that neither of them has any idea how good they actually are because they never play anyone else. Hugh's wife even bought them a silver cup, for which they compete annually. John has won it a dozen times, Hugh just four, which would seem to give Mr Bennett the edge. Once a year they hold a championship of five sets, on the lines of tennis, with each set having twenty-five games. So a championship can last six months! I leave them to it.

I must mention a notable gag the boys played on another of our pianists — no, not on Hugh, I hasten to add. Just before a major concert, they managed to run a piece of transparent tape along the length of the keyboard without him seeing it. When he hit the first chord of the opening number that night every single key on the piano came crashing down! Talk about discordant. I've always suspected Andy was the arch conspirator on that one, though nobody ever owned up to it.

Now stand up and take a bow (drums? He's playing 'em!) … *Nick Millward!*

Our drummer Nick is the baby of the outfit. Well, he's actually forty-two, but he's still the youngest of the group. He joined me in 1998, though I had actually first met him when he was sixteen years old. Nick is a terrific enthusiast and a wonderful drummer, one of the best in the whole country, and swings like the clappers.

He lives near Birmingham, the son of an engineer whose intriguing job was to build the original clay models to test Austin cars back in the fifties. Well, that was his day job. By night, Clive Millward was an accomplished drummer, and played with numerous backing bands around the country at clubs and jazz festivals. Quite how he managed to fit in both jobs in the twenty-four hours available on any given day is beyond me, but he did.

As far as I'm concerned the two best things Clive ever did were to give his son a drum kit when the lad was just five years old, and to introduce him to me when Nick was an eager-beaver teenager who played snare drums with the Scouts and was hell-bent on turning it into a major career move.

I was at a gig in Stourport-on-Severn, amid the beautiful hills and valleys of Gloucestershire close to the Welsh border. Railway enthusiasts like myself probably know that this is the town that has a famous railway line with a historic train that runs up and down a small-gauge track, stopping at the station which has been tarted up to be used for those Agatha Christie-style thrillers you see on TV.

Nick was sixteen, and his parents brought him along to hear the Jazzmen at the civic hall. His father was standing in for my own drummer that night, who was indisposed, and during the interval Clive brought the lad backstage and introduced him.

I remember how he said, 'Mr Ball, this is the band I want to play with one day.'

I looked at his dad and raised an eyebrow. 'Well, son,' I said. 'There's no time like the present. Come on!'

And with that I led young Nick out on to the stage, sat him down at his father's drum kit and told him to have a go. I tell you, he went at it as if he was putting out a fire with his bare hands! Hugh Ledigo gave him some backing on the piano, and I blew a few blasts on my trumpet – but he was off the leash and running!

'Tell you what, Clive,' I said, in front of the boy. 'I wish my own son could swing like your kid.' I meant it.

Nick had natural rhythm, and he knew exactly what he was doing. Twenty years later when he finally joined me, he told me he had never forgotten those words. 'It spurred me on,' he said. 'I missed school next day because I was so tired I couldn't get out of bed – but it was the best thing I could have heard!' I've always said it pays to encourage 'em when they're young, whatever the neighbours say.

Nick left school and thought of a career in catering. But music was in his blood – literally, I think. And, although he serves up a mean spaghetti bolognaise, he thankfully followed his star and stuck with the drums.

He kept his original set until he was fourteen, by which time he had joined the Scouts and learned how to read and write music, and was a stalwart of the local St Chad's troop. He teamed up with some local Birmingham punk rockers who called themselves Vortex, then took his first big professional step with a comedy show band called Dizzy Heights, playing in USAF bases around Europe. 'I got a chance to sing and even do gags,' he recalls. Well, he's still doing them!

In 1991 Nick married his childhood sweetheart Kay. They were at school together, and have known each other since he was fourteen. They have three kids: Christie, thirteen, Joel, nine, and Elijah, aged five and looking for his first drum kit. Kay comes with him on the big world tours – in Australia, for instance, and maybe if we're spending time on a European visit.

Nick had played with well-known groups like the Pete Allen band and Terry Lightfoot before I snapped him up six years ago. He's actually something of a bebop enthusiast, he tells me, 'though I play across the spectrum'. He does, too, and his solos can set an audience alight. They last anything up to seven minutes, and Nick brings every one of his instruments into play.

I've always felt that the drums are the staple building block of a band. Of course, you need a piano and a bass but, when the curtains go back and audiences see those gleaming percussion instruments waiting to explode into life, they know they're in for the full Monty. Listen to Nick describe his Yamaha collection as if they're the family jewels. 'They're all plywood, which creates a better resonance. There's the big bass drum, snare drum, three tom-toms – ten-inch high tom, twelve-inch middle tom and sixteen-inch floor tom.' (Nick is talking about the diameter of the skins.)

'Then I've got the hi-hat and a selection of other cymbals. When I get into overdrive, I play them all at once.' When Nick does get going, it's hypnotic. He starts quietly, rises through the decibel scale and increases tension and pressure as the sticks move faster. 'I try to give 100 per cent each time. It's hard to explain, but sometimes you know you've only achieved ninety-seven per cent and the audience know it. Other times I hit 120 per cent, and the whole place erupts. It just happens. You get those nights where it goes out of your control.'

I know what he means. One recent gig where we all hit 120 per cent happened at the Mill Theatre at Sonning, in the Thames Valley. Weeks later, the band still remember it vividly and people who were there still talk about it. Only 220 seats, but the place was humming. The good folk who turned up by car and coach had a three-course dinner first to get them in the mood, then filed into the small theatre for the show. I don't know what they put in the food that night – officially roast lamb and a buffet – but whatever it was, I'd like the recipe!

Nick again: 'Sometimes it just catches fire. That's what you hope for. My solo is in four sections, and every part is different, building up into one continuous sound, like a giant wave gathering, building the tension, before exploding on the shore. I start off with the brushes on the snares, build up a pattern, then switch to the African sound with my palms and fingers beating on the tom-toms, making the skins change tone. I pick up the sticks, and build it from there with the cymbals and bass drum, getting bigger and bigger until I'm doing quadruple rolls and then it's one continuous sound. Then I stop suddenly, and the audience goes bananas. I hope!'

Most nights Nick comes off the stage soaked in sweat, and reckons he loses two pounds every gig. 'I enjoy my drum solos,' he says. And so do we, Nick.

Finally (last drum roll) … on bass, *Bill Coleman*!

Bill plucks an impressive twang or two on the big double bass, and has an equally impressive track record. He used to be with the Barron Knights, and went on to become Helen Shapiro's musical director, piano player and arranger. The notes he plucks from his instrument are pure magic. I've never heard another bass player like it. He is also a tremendous wit, and is currently collecting jokes for a book he plans to publish shortly.

Over the years, we haven't been too lucky with basses. Vic Pitt used to strap them on to the roof rack when we travelled around the country. On one occasion he hadn't tied the big feller down properly, and we were buzzing merrily along the M4 when we heard a funny scraping sound from above our heads. There was a large lorry behind us, and we watched helplessly from the back windows as the double bass slid off the roof and into the road … then scrunch! Oh, dear. The lorry churned it into matchsticks.

Another incident with a bass involved Colin Purbrook, who used to keep his in a van parked outside his house. When he came out one morning, the van was empty. We called in the police, and started scouring the area. Later that morning a woman rang up the police station, and said, 'There's something in my garden!' They eventually found the bass embedded in her lawn on its spike. The old dear thought it was something from outer space, and wouldn't go out of her front door. It's amazing what vandals will do to get a kick out of their pathetic lives.

Of my original Jazzmen, Dave Jones was my brilliant clarinet player for ten years. A tall, dark-haired guy who had once been a tile salesman, he sadly has since died. I'd known him since 1949. When he left me in 1968, I needed a clarinet player in a hurry. I called up Terry Lightfoot, who by then was running a pub in Enfield, and asked him to help out.

He agreed, adding: 'If you want me to join you permanently, I'll give up the pub!' And he did. He stayed with me a year. 'You've learned how a proper jazz band should be run,' I used to joke with him, before he went off and started up his own outfit. He's still got them, and they're terrific.

Another long-standing friend who turned to drink when he left us was John Benson, who played the double bass with the Jazzmen for twenty-five years. Now that's what I call an innings. He bought a pub in 1999 and turned it into a smashing little guest house, the 200-year-old Branston Dog near the coastal town of Southwold on the Suffolk coast. There are three rooms for six guests, named Collie, Spaniel and Labrador – the rooms, that is, not the customers. I always knew John would end up with a hair of the Dog! His photographs are all around the walls, and his double bass takes up a fair amount of space by the piano in the breakfast room.

That's his day job. John is a great exponent on the strings, still has his fair share of gigs with different groups, and I was sorry when he moved on in 2002. Before he joined me in 1977, John had been a familiar figure in London's East End, playing in famous watering holes and tourist spots like The Prospect of Whitby, The Waterman's Arms, The City Arms and The Londoner. He was fabulous, and so was Ron Weatherburn on the piano, a ragtime exponent with the style of Jelly Roll Morton. Our drummer Tony Budd died of cancer and Ron Bowden joined me, and stayed for forty years on the sticks. Paddy Lightfoot was on banjo, for a time – he was Terry's brother. What made them all brilliant was their technique and their swing.

In the business we call it bollocks, for want of a better word. 'That guy's got bollocks!' you'll hear someone say, which means they gave it everything they'd got. All the above lads had bollocks.

It's a compliment, so please don't get the hump if you hear me say it in your vicinity!

CHAPTER ELEVEN

GOING GLOBAL

The year 1962 saw us turn truly international. We had done Europe and Russia. Now the Jazzmen went globetrotting with a vengeance. Our first US tour had been in the spring, and Australia loomed in the autumn.

The summer was filled with gigs across the country, which included our spell on *Sunday Night at the London Palladium* with Bruce Forsyth in charge. Well, he said he was – just another of his catchphrases, remember? And yes, Bruce, it was nice to see you … to see you, nice!

For this hugely popular ATV show, aware that we were being watched by millions, we invested in smart new uniforms: crisp blue blazers and grey trousers, and a badge on the breast pocket showing the initials KB against a background of the globe with a chirpy Cockney sparrow sitting on it – top of the world, ma! And guess what the little fellow is playing? A trumpet, what else?

We also cut the records of 'So Do I', which is the number we use to barnstorm on stage at our concerts, and 'The Pay Off', both of which sold well. And by now I had my very own KBAS – the Kenny Ball Appreciation Society – which even had its own magazine. It all put me in danger of having to order a new hat size. It was hugely gratifying, and I vowed I would do my best to live up to it.

The magazine began as a monthly newsletter called *Jazzette*, run by a delightful lady named Joyce Harp. It gave details of our future engagements and was full of news, gossip and letters from my supporters. For the past seven years it has been run by Phil Hoy, an ebullient Yorkshireman who lives outside Leeds. His house is practically a shrine to myself and the Jazzmen, with posters on the walls and my entire record collection in his sideboard – all 500 plus of them! Phil first heard me at the age of fourteen, when he invested his pocket money in 'The Teddy Bears' Picnic', which proves that somebody bought it.

'I started buying the records, and over the years it just grew from there,' he tells anyone who asks. 'I went berserk, collecting every single record Kenny ever made.' Finally Phil caught up with me at one of our concerts, and I couldn't believe how knowledgeable he was about the band and every single member who had ever played in it. He took over in 1997, and now sends out *Jazzette* four times a year. What a guy!

But, away from the microphones, the mixing decks and the massive home-grown support we found everywhere we played, we were building up for our biggest adventure yet. On 20 October, lift-off! We were up, up and away to the southern hemisphere for a four-week tour that would take us to the other side of the world. It started in Perth, and we flew across to Adelaide, Sydney, Melbourne, and various spots in between, ending up with seven days in New Zealand.

During the twenty-four-hour flight, I warned the band on two counts. 'Do not be smart-ass with the customs boys in Australia, or they'll send you right back home again. They will ask you if you have a criminal record. Do not on any account reply, "Why, is it mandatory?"'

'And when we get to New Zealand, do not crack the BA joke.' We were flying British Airways, as we always tried to do to show the flag.

'What's that, boss?' enquired Bill Dixon, radiating innocence.

I sighed inwardly. When Bill called me boss I knew I could be in for trouble.

'It's the one where a BA captain announces, "Ladies and gentlemen, we are about to land in Auckland. Will you please put your clocks and watches back fifteen years!" Kiwis do *not* like that joke.'

'Right, boss.' And to his credit I never heard Bill tell it. Or, if he did, he chose his moment carefully. Me, I love Kiwis.

Remembering that long, long flight, I'm reminded of a remark the Prince of Wales made to me on a later tour when we met during one of his royal walkabouts in Sydney. Charles asked me, 'How long have you chaps been out here?'

'We just got here,' I explained.

And when I added that because of delays we had been taken straight to the stadium from the airport as soon as we got off the flight, he exclaimed, 'Good God, after that journey? You must be suffering from lip lag!'

Whatever you've read about him, let me assure you that our potential future monarch has a great sense of humour. Well, he was a fan of the Goons, wasn't he?

But, on that first trip to Australia, I almost didn't get to blow a single toot on my trumpet, because what happens to us on the first-ever British jazz tour to go down under? We run straight into a nationwide strike, that's what happens.

You can plan a tour down to the tiniest detail, leaving nothing to chance, or so you think. But you can always be caught out. For this, a major concert tour of Australia, everything was set down to the last kangaroo hop. Or so we thought. We knew the towns, the venues, the hotels. Then what happened? Just after we landed in Perth for our first gig, there was an internal airline strike. Christ! We were about to fly thousands of miles all over the continent – and Australia is a very big place!

We touched down in Perth, no problem. In fact we had no hint of airline trouble until after we landed, and a worried-looking local agent broke the bad news on the way to our hotel. We would have to rely on coaches. But we played a sell-out gig to a gratifying response, then had to get ourselves a few hundred miles south-east – on the road. That would be a twenty-six-hour trip we were facing. The coach was a massive vehicle, two drivers, with a compartment at the back so that they could take it in shifts to sleep.

We finished our gig, and were about to head for the coach when we learned that the local jazz appreciation society had laid on a special celebration for us – a huge buffet, drinks, the lot.

We could hardly tell them, 'Sorry, we're off.' So it was at least midnight before we got away, nipped back to our hotel for a quick shower and headed out into the car park where the coach was waiting. Everyone had been told to take a pillow from the hotel for the ride. I thought we were stealing them, but it turned out it was by arrangement with the hotel, and the pillows were returned a few days later.

So this is what it means being on the road, I thought, staring wearily through the window at the starlit night, with the Southern Cross sparkling like a diamond necklace against the black velvet sky. The stillness and space of Australia is so vast it is mind-numbing, and at night out in the endless scrub and desert the silence is almost tangible.

That first trip down under we did the entire continent, crossing it from Perth to Adelaide, and on to Melbourne and Sydney. In the end, somehow, we lost only three gigs. But we were all keenly aware that a crisis like that, totally beyond our control, still meant hundreds of disappointed fans, money returned, and impresarios hitting the roof. The climax to the trip was playing in the Sydney Stadium, a huge indoor arena with a revolving stage that could turn 180 degrees. It was often used for boxing events and could hold up to 6,000 people. It was just like *Sunday Night at the London Palladium*, so we felt it was a home from home. The place was jam-packed, and we were given a huge reception.

We had to walk down the aisle the way boxers do, with people clapping us on the back and wishing us luck – it was incredible. I'd never had an entry like it before. The seven of us got to the stage and clambered up. We played our hearts out, and the place erupted. Yes, I decided, I like Oz and I like Aussies. They're friendly, they like their Sheilas and they enjoy a drink. What more can you ask?

But it's a funny thing: every time we went down under it seemed that the Poms were getting pulverised, especially at cricket. I couldn't help noticing that people were wearing 'Punch a Pom a day' T-shirts, and they really took the mickey out of the Brits. Luckily, no one actually swung a punch at us, though once or twice it was a close call.

Australia is notorious for insects, so I think I've been lucky to get away with only a few minor scares during all our tours. The worst thing that happened was spotting a funnel-web spider on the patio outside my hotel room in Adelaide. Nasty big beggars, which are highly poisonous and apparently can jump a foot or more in the air. I spotted the large funnel-shaped web in the far corner of the terrace as I was about to sit down for breakfast, and then saw the thing itself, rearing up on its legs and waving its front mandibles in the air like a boxer. It didn't look as if it was giving me a round of applause, and I wasn't going to risk its wrath if I started a spot of trumpet practice. I killed it with my shoe.

My most bizarre adventure had to be an encounter with the self-styled 'oldest groupie in the world'. Let me elaborate. This lady is a veteran Australian swinger named Jeannie, who cornered me at the stage door of the stadium in Sydney, flashed a huge smile, and said, 'The party's at my place on Bondi Beach. Come on by. I want to show you my matchbox collection!'

She was attractive, in a ballsy Aussie way, vivacious and funny, but not my type. Having heard about this lady, I made sure I had some of the boys with me when I headed for the beach. Jeannie lived in a bungalow overlooking the ocean, and it made a wonderful vista that night with the crashing surf throwing creamy trails of phosphorus high into the air and making a sound like thunder. The party was in full swing on the porch, and I recognised some familiar faces in the crowd, mainly from the jazz circuit.

Jeannie put on one of our records to mark our arrival, then beckoned me with an imperious finger into the living room. 'Look, Kenny!' She slid aside the glass window of a large cabinet that ran along one wall, and gestured inside.

'What?' I asked, bewildered. All I could see was row upon row of matchboxes stacked in neat piles on the shelves.

'My trophy cupboard,' she said proudly. Looking closer I saw that each box was labelled with names from bands like Louis Armstrong's All Stars, the Duke Ellington Orchestra, the Lionel Hampton Band, the Count Basie Orchestra and numerous others.

And inside … I recoiled as she took one out and opened it.

'Is that what I think it is?' I looked down in disbelief.

'Sure,' she said, with the pride of the true collector. Each time Jeannie had made love to her conquests, she collected a pubic hair and put it in a matchbox, with a note identifying the owner, his instrument (so to speak) and the date.

'Good God,' I said faintly. 'I think I need a drink.'

Jeannie had been through every band that played in Sydney, and was a legend among the music establishment. I was in the presence of Australia's answer to Eskimo Nell. Legend has it that they even wrote a song about her, though I can only imagine how it went. Possibly to the tune of 'The Girl from Ipanema' ('Short and curly, and dark and handsome, the boy from …') And the title? It's got to be 'I Dream of Jeannie with the Light Brown Hairs'!

I must tell you that today Jeannie is a game old bird, now in her seventies, a real character with a wonderful sense of humour, a naughty twinkle in her eye and a nostalgic smile on her lips. We keep in touch, and if I add that I even introduced her to my wife on my last tour, you will know that the only time I had to ask for a matchbox from her was to light a cigarette. Won't you?

Times have changed in Australia. When we first went there in the sixties the men were total chauvinists, while the women were docile and knew their place, which was back in the home with most of the time spent in the kitchen. For visitors, it was enough for any man who happened to behave like a gentleman and pay them a compliment to find the ladies more than receptive. To put it bluntly, they were there for the taking. So we did the decent thing: we took 'em! As we used to say in the band, 'We will take advantage of their hospitality!' No wonder we looked forward to our Aussie tours.

Now all that is history. Men are less macho, women are more confident, even dominant. You can see it in the films, and in the soaps they pour out on TV. It's not like that everywhere, of course – Australia is a vast continent – but you can't help seeing it in the cities.

You've still got to hand it to the Aussies for repartee. Nobody does it better. Last time we were there the Test series was on – or maybe it was World War III, I tend to get confused. It meant that a whole lot of sledging was going on around the wicket, with insults freely exchanged.

Shane Warne was reportedly taunted by an English batsman when they almost collided in the middle of the pitch, 'Hey, you fat bastard, how come you're so overweight?'

Shane replied, as quick as a flash, 'Because every time I screw your wife, mate, she gives me a biscuit!'

That story became part of cricketing folklore, though I don't think it will ever appear in *Wisden*. The nearest we ever got to anything like that level of wit was during our 1972 tour of Australia. We were playing at the St George's League Club, a vast concert hall in Sydney. As usual we arrived an hour before we were due on stage, and found our dressing room was neatly situated bang next to an enormous male-only bar, full of noise, chattering fruit machines and cork hats. A real cash bar, as it's known, full of large blokes downing the amber liquid as if their lives depended on how many pints they could sink.

We were all smartly clad in our lilac suits for the show, wearing our hair shoulder length as was the fashion, and felt like a tipple or two to get ourselves in the mood. Perhaps that was our first mistake. The second was for Johnny Parker, our extrovert pianist at the time, to take up a position at the bar to order his round, right next to the kind of archetypal Aussie they used to feature in cartoons: belly hanging out of his shorts and a crack in his ass you could park a bike in. He was knocking it back like a fish.

His eyes fell on Johnny. 'Jesus Christ!' he exclaimed with the full accent. 'What the fuck do you look like? Why don't you get your hair cut, you fucking poofie ponce?'

Johnny eyed him haughtily. 'Jolly good,' he drawled in his plummiest English tones. 'Just goes to show that once a jolly swagman, always a jolly swagman!' We then made a smartish exit left, and had someone bring our libation into the dressing room.

Our other piano player Ron Weatherburn, that brilliant ragtime exponent, was a little more direct in his approach. More accurately, he would occasionally go way over the top. He had become epileptic, poor chap, and used to take phenobarbitone tablets. Unfortunately, if you have alcohol on top of the pills, you're flying three feet off the ground. Ron was a real character who came across as happily nuts.

One of his more choice gags was to cross and uncross his legs at the stool as he was playing – while picking his nose and pretending to flick the greenies at the audience! Oddly enough, no one ever led a stampede for the exit.

During a tour of New Zealand, we were playing at the Majestic Theatre, Christchurch, to a capacity crowd, when Ron had an attack – fortunately backstage in our dressing room during the interval. He recovered enough to stagger out to the piano, high on drugs and beer, and tried to light a cigarette with a box of Swan Vesta matches. He opened the box, and dropped the lot into the piano keys. He spent the whole of that second half trying to pick out the matches, because the piano wouldn't play properly.

The audience gave him a huge amount of stick, shouting, 'Come on! Why aren't you playing?'

In the end Ron just turned round to face them and bellowed back, 'And why don't you lot fuck off?'

That was our Ron. Always ready with the witty riposte. But nobody out there worried, because they all like characters. And

147

what would the world be without characters? The way I see it is like this. Do you want a bland outfit standing up like soldiers on parade, or do you want a bunch of guys who are fiery one minute, maybe a little subdued the next, but always ready with a joke and a laugh, and always able to deliver one hell of a solo when called on? Virtuosos one minute, off into the wings for a quiet fag the next. I think I know the answer. Eccentricity is part of the make-up of any jazz group. I've seen Ron Weatherburn lift a complete concert with one solo. In East Berlin, he played a spot during our rendering of 'Tin Roof Blues' like I've never heard before or since. It was an incredibly emotive solo, only twelve bars, but each note was picked out like a prospector finding gold nuggets in a stream. It took the whole band by surprise, not just me.

Ron had added a couple of pints of strong German beer to his intake of tablets, so once again he was about three feet off the ground! Afterwards I had tears in my eyes. I always thank the guys individually after every concert, and this time I was able to say, 'Ron, that's one of the most beautiful things I've ever heard.'

'Any time, Ken, any time,' was his rejoinder. But both of us knew that this sort of thing doesn't just happen any time, that he'd touched magic that night and that it was an abiding memory none of us would ever forget.

The band know they can come to me with their problems, and over the years I like to think I've been a shoulder to lean on. I'm no father confessor, but I hope I've been able to help now and again. However, some situations are beyond even my magic touch.

The scene: Melbourne, where we're playing gigs for a week. Our roadie Pete falls for a girl he meets in a bar, and persuades her to stay with us for what remains of the tour. They shack up together in a hotel and he stays with her in the room virtually all day for seven days, hardly putting his nose out of the door apart from doing the gig in the evening – then it's straight back into the sack. Pete has decided he is in love. Cupid's arrow has hit him fair and square. He orders bottle after bottle of champagne on room service, plus loads of delicacies off the menu, the whole bit. And puts it all on the bill. Our bill.

During this traumatic week, Pete has a birthday. He also has a family back home. His wife and kids ring up from their council house in Luton to wish him happy birthday.

Do you know what he says to his wife? 'Thanks for wishing me happy birthday, but I'm leaving you. I'm not coming back to England, I'm staying here. I'm in love.'

His wife rings my wife. Betty rings me. 'What's all this nonsense?'

I march down the hotel corridor and bang on his door.

'What the fuck's going on?' I demand of the tousled figure in a bathrobe who answers it.

'I'm not coming back, Kenny. I'm in love.'

'You've got to come back. You've got a return ticket.'

But no. Pete is adamant. He is going to take off into the outback with this girl, and start a new life. What can I do? In the end we leave without him.

Eventually he goes to the local agent, who validates his return ticket. Pete gets back to England six months later.

By chance we're playing at Luton the very weekend after he flies in. He comes to see us. By this time I've had his bill for £900. And we're talking thirty years ago, remember. I have to pay it. He'd also borrowed money off the boys which they never saw again. In my book, that made him a tea leaf – or thief in the Queen's English.

Out of the blue, he turns up in the bar during the interval. 'I want you to do me a favour, Kenny.'

'What's that?' I hitch my jaw back from waist level.

'I want you to give me a reference.'

'You're joking. After what you did to us! Where are you going to work?'

'Securicor!'

What's more, he got the job. Even without my reference.

CHAPTER TWELVE

CONCERNING
SATCHEL MOUTH

Mum died in December 1962. She was seventy-five. She had kidney failure, and eventually the hospital sent her home to 9 Oakwood Gardens to die in her own bed. In fact she died on a table, with the family gathered round. An explanation is due. She had gone into a coma for seven days. The table was a solid walnut table with thick legs. It was so big and heavy that we'd used it as an air-raid shelter in the Blitz, sleeping under it for protection with mattresses piled around.

This may sound strange, but we carried Mum out and laid her on it on a mattress so we could all gather round and talk to her. The bedroom was just too small. One weird thing was that, while she was in that coma for a week, there was no reaction when Dad or the others tried to talk to her. She just lay there with her eyes open, paralysed and unable to move or speak. We never knew whether she could hear us. Towards the end, I put my face close to her ear by the table and said quietly, 'Mum, if you can hear me, will you blink?'

And I saw a small flutter of her eyes. Astonishing. That's when we all started talking to her, and continued talking until she passed peacefully away a few hours later. I'm sure she heard every word.

Talking of the hereafter, this might be an appropriate moment to mention that on three separate occasions members of the audience came to see us arriving vertical and, alas, leaving horizontal. In short, they died on us.

Yes, three people have actually dropped off the perch during my concerts, which can be very off-putting. Two were in the middle of John Bennett's trombone solos. We would always leave this solo to the last song of the first set, immediately before the interval. The first time it happened was in Halifax. There was this old bloke suddenly getting out of his seat to dance madly about just below the stage to the strains of 'Ory's Creole Trombone', and all of a sudden he collapsed in a heap! They called the ambulance, but he was dead on arrival at the hospital. We stopped playing while they carried him off, then went on with the show.

Same scenario the second time, which happened at a club in Camberley. This old boy got up, felt a bit sprightly, and thought he'd have a go during the trombone solo again. Next thing we knew, he'd keeled over. I remember the tune we were playing: 'I Left My Love in Avalon'. As someone said afterwards, the poor beggar left *his* love in Camberley.

The third was only two years ago, in the Usher Hall in Edinburgh. It was a big concert, billed as the 'Three Bs: Barber, Bilk and Ball', starring Chris, Acker and Kenny in that order.

So we were on last, and were building up to our grand finale to finish the show. John Bennett (that man again — we call him the Macbeth of the group!) was just finishing his trombone solo, and we had about three more numbers left to play. This bloke just keeled over in the front row. There must have been close to 3,000 people there, the place was packed, and everyone had a view of the front row. They brought the medics in and tried to revive him in his seat while John hung on and finished the number, with us backing him up.

Then I had to step forward and say, 'I'm sorry, ladies and gentlemen, but we will have to leave the stage while a gentleman who has been taken ill is looked after.'

We trooped off stage, and hung around in the wings until the stage manager came up and said, 'Sorry to tell you, fellers, but he's gone.' The song had been 'Ole Man Mose is Dead', which didn't help.

After that I had to go back, and I remember saying, 'I'm awfully sorry, ladies and gentlemen, but the audience member I mentioned before is very seriously ill. Actually, I'm afraid he's died. We will stop the concert as a mark of respect.' I closed it down there and then, and you know what happened? Everybody stood up and applauded! I got a standing ovation for *not* playing!

In those circumstances it's always a difficult decision. You have to respect the dead, but if hundreds of people have paid a lot of money to hear a concert, do you just say sorry and give them their money back? Some of them have come from a long way away. But in this case the concert was close to the end, so it was the right thing to do.

I received a touching letter from this chap's widow. Apparently he was a doctor. She wrote, 'I want to tell you that he died at a moment of extreme happiness!' But it still gives you a shock, I don't mind admitting, standing there on the stage looking down at one of your audience expiring in front of you. Fortunately, it doesn't happen often: three in fifty years, and don't forget our fans are growing older the same way we are. They hear their favourite music from the days of their youth, the pulse starts racing, they start cavorting around, and momentarily they forget themselves. Then they keel over. Lights out!

We blame John Bennett for any sudden demise in our vicinity. John is well known amongst us for being accident prone. The accidents don't always involve him, but they happen around him. Apparently it started when he was at school, sitting in the back row of his class below a large framed picture. For no reason at all the picture just fell down, and his head went straight through it, so you could say that he'd been framed. He had to be taken to the carpentry shop to be released.

We have a standing joke. We'll see him staring at something and shout, 'John, don't stare at that!' He's giving it the evil eye. He has been offered contracts to go and play outside people's front doors. The musical assassin, looking for another hit! It's black humour, but it keeps us sane.

Another bizarre experience with someone pegging out while we were performing happened on a cruise liner. We've done a lot of cruises in our time, from the *Arcadia* in the sixties to the present-day *Canberra*, great liners with their own theatres where they put on top shows with international artistes.

This time, at least, it didn't happen in front of us, although this cadaver had been to our show every night, and laughed and applauded with the best of them.

It was in 1993, and the Jazzmen were on a month's cruise that took us across the Atlantic and around the Caribbean, a marvellous gig for all of us. Best of all, partners were included, so I took my second wife Michelle along and it was a wonderful five-star affair, with a state room for Michelle and myself, and picture windows with a view of the Atlantic rolling past beneath us.

This old fellow was in his nineties, the oldest passenger on the ship, and he had a nurse with him as a companion to look after him. We saw him at our concerts in the ship's theatre for the first week, then he just disappeared, and we didn't see him any more. Through the grapevine I learned that our oldest fan aboard ship had passed away.

A steward broke the news. 'Yes, Mr Ball, I'm afraid it's true.'

'What are you going to do with him?' I enquired.

'Well, we could give him a free burial at sea,' responded the steward, a man of the world who had seen it all. 'That's if his relatives request it. In this case his only companion is his nurse, so we have to take him home.'

'So where is he?'

'In the cold room. We keep him refrigerated, along with the other frozen goods. But kept away from the edibles, of course.'

'My God!' I was taken aback. But it made sense. The chap had to have a decent burial, after all.

Two days later, a message sounded over the tannoy. 'Would the chief electrician please come immediately to the cold room!' It turned out the refrigeration had gone off, and the body was starting to pong a bit. They try to keep these things quiet, and presumably they got the power going again, because we heard no more.

'Christ, man! It's enough to turn you vegetarian,' muttered Andy Cooper, when I confided the information to him.

That was a cruise to remember. Things happened on it that would have been fair game for a *Carry On* film. One chap I met had an ailment where his back muscles had gone, like a seizure, and he was bent over double, walking around face down so that all he could see was his feet. One night after dinner, Michelle and I bumped into him outside his cabin.

He peered round at us from waist height. 'Can you help me?'

'Sure,' I said. 'What's the matter?'

On reflection I could have chosen better words. It was pretty obvious what was the matter.

'I can't find the lock!' He waved his hand with his cabin key in it, scrabbling at the door above him.

'Of course. Allow me!'

I put the key in the lock, and pushed the door open.

'Thank you, Mr Ball. Er, it is Mr Ball, isn't it?'

'Call me Kenny,' I said gently. 'Good night. Sleep tight.'

A few days later we saw him again. Or rather, we didn't see him. I was in a crowd on the upper deck waiting to get into the lift to go down to the restaurant for lunch. We surged forward, and there was a clunk as the poor chap's head hit the mirror inside, and he collapsed in a heap on the floor. No one had seen him waiting patiently at the front. Luckily he was all right, and I was able to give him a wave when I saw his bandaged head in the front row that night.

This predicament is not as uncommon as it sounds. A drummer on the *Frank Skinner Show* named Ronnie Verrell suffered from the same condition. Not only was he a brilliant drummer, he also had a brilliant sense of humour which his ailment had not dimmed. Sadly, Ronnie is dead now. But a fellow musician in the band told me how they were once on an overseas tour in Bruges, and walking round the old city together.

His mate said, 'I tell you, Ronnie, this is a marvellous place. Look at these wonderful buildings.'

To which Ronnie, stooped like Quasimodo, replied, 'Bollocks to the buildings. All I can see is fucking dog shit!'

I don't allow myself to be superstitious about such things as members of the audience dying in the middle of gigs. If it happens, it happens. But performers *are* notoriously superstitious, whether they're actors, comedians or musicians. Peter Sellers, for instance, hated the colour green. The story goes that he once had an entire train sprayed red after it turned up green on the film *The Mouse that Roared*. My old mate Norman Wisdom actually kisses the door of his dressing room as he leaves to go on stage. All performers know about not whistling in dressing rooms – if you do you've got to go outside and turn round three times. But kissing the doors? That's a bit much. If I did that I'd be looking out of the corner of my eye for the men in white coats coming to take me away.

But I do confess to a couple of irrational impulses. I always put my left shoe on first, likewise my right leg into my trousers. Weird, or what? And magpies. This is a well-known superstition, and I'm afraid I am one of those poor souls who subscribes to it. I've got a pair of magpies in my garden, and whenever I see just one through the window I'm supposed to greet it with, 'Good morning, Mr Magpie.' So I do. I've changed it to, 'Good morning, Captain Birdseye.' If I see them both together, I say it twice! Daft, isn't it? But it keeps me busy. I'm giving the wretched birds a hearty hello all the time. So far, no reply.

In the early sixties we were rich and running. Four more hits made the top thirty in 1963 alone: 'Sukiyaki', 'Casablanca', 'Rondo' and 'Acapulco 1922'. At one point in that year I made the big mistake of shaving off my moustache. In a trip to the US with the band I had been referred to in the local New Orleans paper as 'looking like a cross between Errol Flynn and a fox'. I'm OK on Errol Flynn, not so sure about the fox. But at least the critic, one Jack Kneece, added, 'This reviewer thinks that Kenny Ball is the world's greatest trumpeter. He makes the lung-bursting little hunk of valves and metal almost glib, and held a note close to a full minute.' Jack, you are forgiven everything.

Maybe I thought it would make me look younger, in direct contrast to Bruce Forsyth who grew his moustache presumably for the same reason. In my case the *Daily Sketch* published before-and-after photographs with yours truly armed with a razor and a quizzical expression. The result was a deluge of protest letters that made me grow it again within a month!

The following year we recorded 'Hello, Dolly!' from the play which would later become a film directed by Gene Kelly, with an unforgettable performance from Barbra Streisand. I can't help wondering if I shouldn't have persuaded her to sing the theme song, with slightly different words as sent to our *Jazzette* magazine by one of our fans, shortly after we returned from a world trip. What do you think?

> Hello, Kenny! We're your fans, Kenny!
> It's so good to know you're playing hot and strong.
> Your band is fab, Kenny!
> You're king of jazz, Kenny!
> And people know you everywhere you go.
> When the band is playing,
> You have the room swaying,
> For you to play the favourite songs of long ago.
> So, take a bow, fellers!
> We'll get to see you somehow, fellers!
> Kenny, don't you go away again.

Now isn't that nice!

That song – Dolly, not Kenny – became a regular at our UK concerts, as well as at our overseas gigs which were now taking us out of the country with increasing frequency. As you will have gathered, it hadn't all been glamour and five-star treatment, though by now we were getting used to being handed that red boarding pass at the check-in desk which meant we were up front, flying first class with all the trimmings.

But the tours still pushed us to the limit. If it's Tuesday, where the heck are we? And strange things happen when you get overtired or overstretched. Like starting one song, and finishing it with another without realising it! There are some songs with similar character, chords, structure, even the tune. One time we were in Germany in 1968, and we had been travelling for days with very little sleep. We were dog tired, and in this particular concert hall in Leipzig we had downed a few beers in the interval. Curtain up on the second half. Out we go on stage, and start in with 'Big Butter and Egg Man'. All the band knows it. 'I want a big butter and egg man …' What it means I've never actually sussed out, though I can imagine what it *might* mean.

Halfway through, quite unaccountably, the song became 'Strutting with Some Barbecue', another jazz favourite which is in the same key and has a similar structure. We start with one song, and finish with another. How did it happen? We stared at one another as we came to the end of the barbecue, shaking our heads in genuine bewilderment and hoping the audience thought it was deliberate.

That same year I found out that Louis Armstrong did exactly the same thing with the same tunes, so we were in good company. How do I know? Because Satchmo told me so himself, when we were picked to be his support band on his UK concert tour. This was the big time.

This was the guy who had influenced me most in those early heady days. Louis Armstrong, born in Jane Alley, New Orleans, in 1901, was the king of the jazz castle. Satchmo was the shortened version of his affectionate nickname of Satchel Mouth. This legendary icon made hundreds of records, and between 1931 and 1960 featured in thirty-one films. On his death on 6 July 1971 they said of him, 'No one musician has contributed more to jazz.' In those few words is the kind of simple and moving tribute that speaks volumes.

But now here I am at the Hammersmith Odeon, a venue just below the flyover which has been a magnet for great artists since it changed from being a cinema to live music venue. The Jazzmen are the first half of the sell-out concert which happens to coincide with the great man's sixty-eighth birthday. We meet backstage, and I shake his big hand and wish him well. He spreads a beaming smile. 'Let me tell you, Kenny. When I wake up in the morning and look in the mirror and find myself staring back at myself … I just know it's going to be a good day!'

That first concert together at the Odeon set the shape of things to come, and sealed our friendship. As we played the first half to a crowd I suspected couldn't wait for the big man, I was aware of a movement on the side. Glancing to my right, I saw the impressive figure of Louis Armstrong standing there in the wings to hear how we sounded. We'd done a couple of numbers, and were into 'South Rampart Street Parade'.

And suddenly there's Louis strolling out on to the stage in his dressing gown to put his arms around me and give me a huge bear hug. He announces to the crowd, 'This man is a genius!' They roar their approval – well, who's going to argue? Then he ambles off again, and we don't see him until the second half.

At the end of the show we had our own surprise for him. I walked out with a huge birthday cake, candles flaming, followed by my band playing 'Happy Birthday'. Satchmo's own band joined in, and so did the entire theatre. They gave him an ovation that raised the rafters before we all stomped into the grand finale of 'When the Saints Go Marching In', with the audience cheering and clapping in unison.

That was one night in my life, and I suspect in all our lives, that I will never forget. It got his tour off to a good start. Over the next weeks I discovered that Satchmo never forgot a name, and he must have met a few people in his life. He knew all my boys by their first names, and never slipped up once.

He also had that presence – you knew when he was in a room. 'I love to see you guys coming up,' he said, and he was talking about us as a band making our way in the world. We were well established, and had hit records under our belts, but he saw our future beckoning even more rosily. Satchmo knew. Throughout the tour he sat in the wings and watched us every single night, the whole of our set.

At one theatre when we got into the lift after the first half to go up to our dressing rooms, Louis was with us. One of the roadies turned round in front of him, saw who he was, and said out loud, 'Fuck! This is like going up to heaven!' And that's how it felt.

Another insight into his character came the night Sir Max Aitken threw a party at the Savoy Grill for that birthday. We were invited. Louis insisted on being with the musicians, and of course our two bands were sitting together separated by an invisible wall from the VIP guests at the far side of the room. Satchmo excused himself from the toffs, came over and joined us, and wouldn't budge despite subtle hints from the host. 'Why, sure,' Louis would beam. He would walk back and dutifully shake everyone's hand, and then return to where he felt most at home.

Much later, I told him about the first time I heard one of his records, and what it taught me. Jazz is fun! The actual session was at a New York City Town Hall concert, though Louis had made loads of records before that. This one was such fun to listen to. They paid him $1,000 to play with a small band, and recorded it there in 1946. It was one of the best jazz records ever made, and apparently after only one rehearsal in the afternoon.

He nodded thoughtfully. 'Yeah, I remember that. You're right. Jazz should be fun.'

Music should convey happiness, and that's what Satchmo was all about. That's what the Jazzmen are all about. That's why I loved him. He had a sense of fun that poured out from his trumpet, and the people went away happy. You don't want to put your head in a gas oven after a good gig, do you?

CHAPTER THIRTEEN

TWO MARRIAGES END

My marriage lasted from 1952 until 1978, when I walked out. I knew it was going wrong. I was literally working every day of the week, and in between gigs I was doing TV interviews and radio shows, as well as making records. Over the years, counting it up now, we made seventy albums in addition to the hundreds of singles.

Betty was fully aware that she was a musician's wife. It was spelled out by Alan Freeman, a top DJ and a household name, when he met her backstage during one of our appearances on *Sunday Night at the London Palladium*. Alan said something very significant to her. We had made our first two hit records, and he was playing them all the time on his nightly show. Kenny Ball and the Jazzmen were filling the airwaves.

'You know, Betty,' he said, 'that I'm going to take your husband away from you?'

'I know,' she replied, 'and I don't like it.'

163

It was a stark prophecy, not intended unkindly, and with a woman's instinct Betty understood precisely what he meant. From a financial point of view things had got much better as my career took off. I paid off the mortgage, we got ourselves a better house, bigger cars and took care of the kids' education. Finally I had a mansion in Essex and a Rolls Royce in the drive. I was able to look after Betty's family – buy her disabled old mother a bungalow, things like that.

But in the end it wasn't enough. You can't buy time.

Once I was away with the band for three long months, touring the world without her. I found myself taking the winter sun on Bondi beach in Sydney, splashing around in the waves on Waikiki beach in Honolulu, strolling down Bourbon Street in New Orleans and through Manhattan in New York, living the good life between the shows. Without Betty.

We couldn't afford to bring wives or girlfriends with us. Fares were expensive, and hotel rooms, though usually more reasonable than in Britain, weren't cheap. And with one-night stands on the schedule, flying across continents from town to town, the pattern was something I don't think the girls would have enjoyed. Perhaps they would have done at first, but the gloss wears off as swiftly as lipstick. The routine had a relentless pattern about it. Up in the morning at seven, off to the airport, check in to a new hotel in a new town in a new country, and on stage for the next gig. What are the women going to do? Sit around a pool during the day, scour the shops, maybe see us play or more likely stay in their room and watch the local TV. Most crucially of all, they'll miss the kids.

A musician's life is completely different from any other profession. So even at home, conditions were strange and unreal for her: husband asleep in the daytime, working at night, my body clock way out. I was seldom home before midnight, often later, and wide awake. I'd crash out around two in the morning, then sleep through until noon. It doesn't bode well for family life.

I must say this for Betty: she did a fantastic job bringing up our children. She was a wonderful mother. I know it's the oldest story in show business, but it was truly pressure of work that destroyed our marriage.

Most of the time we got on well enough, especially on holidays together. But, as the years went by, we found we didn't have an awful lot to say to one another, and that *is* sad. I think maybe we'd met too young. And possibly married too young.

I also have to say that life was never exactly dull behind the lace curtains. As I have remarked already, she had a fiery temperament, which was good. We did have our arguments, and, like any family, some of them were spectacular. She actually threw cutlery and saucepans at me during some of our more heated moments, a gesture which tended to bring an argument to a swift close while she exited the room in tears and I reached for the dustpan and brush and mentally totted up the damage.

The worst row we had came when she found out about an affair I'd had with a girl called Rosemary. I don't know how Betty learned of it – maybe some careless remark overheard from the band. But I do know that I had to give up three jobs that week and stay home to placate her. Now that hurt! What a rotten swine I was.

My own temperament is entirely the opposite. In that department we were chalk and cheese. I hate rows. It takes me a long time to get steamed up over anything but, when the lid blows, everybody knows about it! It took me forty years to sack our drummer, who apparently disliked me for twenty years of them. That's the kind of bloke I am. I don't have a short fuse but, once it's lit, get ready to duck!

Ah, you'll want to know about the drummer. It's a good yarn, and like so much of my life is one that everyone says deserves to be written into a comedy film.

The band and I have always had huge fun together. We support each other, and there's no jealousy because I'm selling the band as well as myself. I've tried to bear in mind that, if I spot someone doing a bit of business that goes down incredibly well with an audience, I'll put the guy in the forefront. I won't hold him back. That's our whole success, and it's a source of personal satisfaction to me that so many of the boys have stuck with me for so long over the years.

Obviously there have been a few exceptions. It hasn't always been sweetness and light. But it was a surprise for me that there should have been a clash of personalities with Ron Bowden, the drummer who was with the Jazzmen for forty years.

There are always two sides to a coin. The way I saw it was that Ron had become increasingly disenchanted over the final years, and things started happening on the stage that I didn't like. He sat just behind me on the percussion stand, sheltered by a formidable arsenal of drums and cymbals. During the show I had to reach down and pick up my mute, which is like a bowler hat and goes over the end of the trumpet when I want to muffle the instrument and create particular sounds. I keep the mute just by the drum kit.

For several gigs Ron had been hitting his cymbals hard just when I bent down to pick up the mute. It was getting to be a bad habit, and he still persisted even after I asked him to stop. Finally, at a fortieth anniversary concert in Sonning when we were playing 'The Hawaiian War Chant', it happened again. The 'bowler' was just under the cymbal stand and, as I reached behind to grab hold of it, crash! Ron hit those cymbals so hard it deafened me. My head was ringing for the rest of the first set. You've seen

166

those Tom and Jerry cartoons where one of them bashes a pair of cymbals over the other, and his head vibrates like a tuning fork? Well, that was my head!

It sounds funny now, but at the time I was mad as hell. If it had happened once, OK. Bad timing. But this happened over and over again, and I knew it was deliberate. It wasn't even part of the number.

Ron was a good musician, so on professional grounds there was no way I could get rid of him. But I told him anyway: 'That's it. Piss off!' We faced each other like a pair of fighting cocks in the dressing room afterwards, and I had to shout because I couldn't hear myself speak!

Ron protested that it was rubbish to allege he was doing it deliberately, adding that if he wasn't enjoying himself he'd have quit a long time ago. Quite rightly, he pointed out that being with a band for that long is like a marriage. You have the odd row, but next day you kiss and make up. Well, I'm sorry, but I wasn't having it. It was kiss-off time.

The *News of the World* published the story under the headline: DRUMMED OUT! Ron took me to an industrial tribunal, backed by the Musicians' Union. He lost, but even so it cost me a lot of money. I paid him £1,100 I owed him for the rest of the dates under contract, and it was all very unfortunate. It's a shame it had to happen.

So you could say that made two marriages that ended in tears.

Ron today sadly suffers from rheumatoid arthritis, but, in his home in Greenford, Middlesex, he still keeps his original cymbals and snare drums as a memento of the years we shared together from 1959 to 1999. 'It's unusual for anyone to stay that long with one band,' he agrees, adding generously, and I hope accurately, 'but I had some crazy, wonderful times with the boys. Whatever happened, they're a great bunch.'

Betty and I came to the end of a chapter together, and went our own ways. I actually felt sorry for her, because she didn't have much of a life in the normal sense of a married woman, though in other ways she had a lot of fun. But too often she had to make her own life, go out with her own friends or to parties by herself while I was working.

She was thrown into the arms of other people, including one man in particular, an electrician named Ron. He worked from home, and when it all came out I thought, Good luck to them. The truth is that I just fell out of love with her. And do you know the odd thing? I never felt a twinge of jealousy, ever, which is strange. Not for her, not for the new boyfriend. So I was obviously out of love by then.

Maybe it was inevitable. All these years later I still provide alimony, still care if she's well or not. But to put things in perspective, as I left out of one door, Betty had the boyfriend virtually walking in through another!

I knew him well. He was the chap who had wired our house, and, when the cat was away, the mouse played! When our marriage broke up I sold our house in Hornchurch, and the pair of them immediately bought another place and moved in together. So Betty was never on the shelf. They had a long and happy relationship, fourteen years altogether, which only ended when Ron died in 1993.

When the crunch came, I walked out of the house with just one suitcase and my trumpet for company after a blazing row. It was the usual storm of accusations that goes with any separation, and it was probably me wanting out of the marriage because by that time I had known Michelle, who became my second wife, for six years and she was the new woman in my life.

When I stormed out of the family home I went to the only

place I could think of to doss down, apart from some hotel: one of the flats in Seven Kings that I owned. I wasn't in the right state of mind for a hotel at that time. Like Greta Garbo, though for different reasons, I wanted to be alone.

There was one problem: the place was virtually derelict. I'd had it gutted, and was in the process of renovating it throughout with a view to renting or selling it. So I walked in with my single suitcase, into an empty two-room flat with no gas or electricity, and no bed. All I had to sleep on was a sunlounger I managed to get hold of from somewhere, the fold-over kind you normally find around swimming pools. I didn't even have a camp bed to lay my weary head. All I had was a supply of candles for lighting, and a torch in case I tripped over in the night. There was no heating and the water was cold, but at least it was running and the plumbing worked.

In the six weeks that followed, my weight dropped from twelve stone to ten stone, and I got a stomach ulcer which doubled me up in agony and stopped me from eating. In our business we always have to watch out for stress anyway, but this took me right over the top. Another flat became vacant, and I decided to do it up and move into it, which eventually I managed to achieve.

The weird thing about all this was that I was at the peak of my career, and not a soul suspected I was living like a dosser. My feelings at that time were a maelstrom of mixed emotions churning around inside me, ranging from elation to despair and changing by the hour and often by the minute. Part of me was saying, OK, that's it. Another part was full of self-doubt. You shouldn't have done it, Kenny. If Betty wants you back desperately enough, you'll go to her, won't you? But she never phoned, never called.

The first time the phone rang in that bare flat, it was an old friend named Frank, calling to commiserate. At least I had a line to the outside world – I'd had the phone reconnected quickly as I needed it for the band. Frank had been the guy who bailed me out when I had some tax problems in the sixties and found myself owing the Inland Revenue £6,000. I happened to mention I owed the tax man some money, and Frank had said, 'Oh, how much?'

When I said, 'Six thousand quid!' his reply was, 'I've got that saved up if you want it.'

How's that for friendship? Frank is eighty-one now, and we still talk on the phone every week. I took him up on his offer, and paid him back within three months. But I'll never forget that single act of generosity, his whole life savings.

Betty kept the car. I paid for all the running repairs and petrol, and gave her a substantial weekly fee without even asking. Then the solicitors came into it, and we agreed alimony which I've kept up ever since. After twenty-odd years we have come to a mutually amicable situation: Betty phones up Michelle from time to time, and when I've been in hospital she has wanted to see me. I guess it's about as good as it can get.

CHAPTER FOURTEEN

MICHELLE

I met Michelle Wilde at Gosforth cricket club in Newcastle, and knew in that same instant that I wanted to marry her. I was hit by a veritable strike of lightning. A bolt from the blue. The earth moved. All the things that poets write their sonnets about and songs are written about happened to me in one split second.

Does that sound a bit naff? I suppose it does. I'd heard about things like this happening, and didn't believe a word of it. Until it happened to me.

I was literally struck dumb. She was twenty-seven, I was forty-two, so there was quite an age difference. Gosforth cricket club may not sound like the most romantic place to fall in love, but when I set eyes on Michelle it could have rained rose petals and I wouldn't have noticed.

It was the half-hour interval in our concert. The usual thing — a room packed with people, the band signing autographs and chatting to the fans. Time for a drink in the bar and a spot of chatting and pressing the flesh. Her mum, Violette Pertho, who is French and married to a Danish naval officer, apparently said, 'Come on, I'm going to get Kenny's autograph.'

And up she marched, a very fanciable lady I have to say, as I sat at a table with a pint of beer next to me and a pen ready and waiting. 'Can I have your autograph?'

I said, 'Yes, sure.'

Then she said, 'Oh, by the way, this is my daughter.'

That's when everything stopped still. To this day I can't remember any other face in the room. Voices faded away. It was like a thunderbolt. What struck me about Michelle was her voice, the absolute femininity in it, a girl–woman voice I'd call it, and after that, there was the blonde hair, eyes that looked blue but were actually on closer inspection grey-green. Wow! She was wearing a frock with a white top, not a lot of make-up, thank God, and looked stunning.

I can only say it was instant attraction both ways.

Michelle was a beautician who worked in Newcastle. She had been divorced eighteen months and had two kids, but that night her mum had said, 'Come on, girl, get a life, get out and enjoy yourself. It's time to move on.' Good advice, at least it was as far as I was concerned, or I wouldn't have met her darling daughter.

I signed the programme just as the bell rang for the second half. Above the hubbub of the audience heading back, I said urgently to Michelle, 'Where do you live?'

'I'm close by my mother, she lives about two miles away.'

'I'll give you both a lift afterwards,' I said. 'Wait for me out here.'

I could hardly wait to finish the second set. They were both there when I came out. I dropped Violette off first, then took Michelle on to her house. I gave her a goodnight kiss, nothing too passionate because I didn't want to frighten her off. Before we parted I'd invited her to see me at my next gig two days later in Redcar, which wasn't so far away.

'Do you fancy popping over there?'

'Maybe I will,' she said, with that lovely smile.

And she did. And when I played at Carlisle a week afterwards she was there again. After that it just blossomed. We fell in love, and there's nothing more I can say. Except that if anything I'm more in love with her now than I was then. In the words of the old song, love is so much lovelier the second time around. That's the way it is with us.

I've always respected women. I think that came from my mum, who drummed it into me at an early age. I can never understand how those coarse macho types score with the girls, though some of them seem to! Can someone please explain? On second thoughts, don't bother. But Michelle was the sort of person it was easy to respect, the sort of person that you open a door for, assist out of the car, pull up the chair for dinner and treat like a lady because that's what she is. As for me, shall we say that she's softened the Cockney in me, and I'm talking about my attitude as well as how I pronounce my vowels!

The other thing Michelle has done for me is to calm me down. I don't rush about like a blue-arsed fly the way I used to. We've grown so close, knowing each other's little idiosyncrasies, and we've got nothing to hide from each other. That's the way I've always been with the women I've known, remember: tell them the truth, then you don't have to lie. They either accept it or they walk away, which is the risk you have to take.

When I asked Michelle to marry me, I'd already told her all about my previous relationships. I said to her, 'Sooner or later, someone's going to turn up when I'm on tour who could prove, well, difficult. I'd rather you knew all about her before that happens. I don't want you to be embarrassed or upset.'

Sometimes I'd get the frosty face when an ex-girlfriend turned up, but not too often. Michelle was always pre-warned, and that meant pre-armed. Let's say she knew I wasn't a virgin! She knew I'd been a bad boy when I was younger. Out on the road with the band, I played the field as well as my trumpet. It went with the game.

Not any more, though. I've never looked at another woman since I met Michelle. The fact is, I've never been tempted. I'd sown my wild oats, and now was the right time to quit while I was ahead.

OK, when we met I was married. For my own situation, I have only myself to blame. I was on the road six or seven days a week, travelling all over the world. Betty had done a great job looking after the house and bringing up the kids without me. But my main concern before I made any move to end it was that all the children should be grown up and in work, so that they could take the break-up a bit better. But it was still a very stressful and distressing time, and not something I recommend to anyone. If a marriage is not working, and it's full of shouting and screaming, it's not an environment that's going to do the kids much good.

For six years after I met Michelle, I was living a double life. I'm not particularly proud of it, but that's the way it was. Michelle knew I had a wife. In fact we broke up a couple of times in those six years, because we were 300 miles apart and I could only see her when I travelled north. But eventually, in 1979, we started living together.

I got divorced in 1982 at the High Court in the Strand. Whatever you read and hear, I don't think there's any such thing as an amicable divorce. Our daughter Jane was very bitter.

Fortunately, she has since come round to becoming one of my best friends, and Michelle's, too. Time is a great healer. But it was a rough patch to go through, and not helped by the kind of headline that appeared in the *Sun* on 24 March 1984: I HATE DAD, SAYS KENNY BALL'S DAUGHTER. And below it, the strap line: JANE'S FURY OVER DIVORCE CASH ROW. That put it in a nutshell, and summed up the scenes on the steps of the High Court when an unseemly row erupted between us on the pavement.

It was a tense time for all of us. To put the whole thing in perspective, I had invested my earnings in property in Essex. Unfortunately, while we were sorting it all out, one of the people in Betty's camp became very vituperative and unpleasant. His actual words to me were, 'We want it all. We're going to put you into the gutter!' He told me as much, face to face, just the two of us in a very nasty meeting in a pub in Chigwell. I can still see him sitting there spelling it out.

I can get just as nasty if I have to. 'OK,' I retorted. 'You can bloody well try if you like!' He'd said the wrong thing. I'm one of those blokes who stands firm when someone gets my back up. And I say to myself, I'll show them!

The split had become a shouting match, as most divorces do. On the big day, everyone turned up at the High Court: Betty, her brother, our daughter, a clutch of lawyers (you know how they clutch at your wallet), and the press. Oh, my! Talk about fun and games. The *Sun* misreported a 'fracas' on the steps outside afterwards, quoting Jane as saying, 'I hate my dad – he's treated Mum like dirt. He used to call me his little girl, but I've called him more choice names since then. I used to love him, now I never want to see him again.'

They reported that she had struck me. She didn't, in fact; it was a shouting match on the pavement with a lot of finger-prodding, nothing more. These things get blown out of all proportion, and the way it read she'd landed a left hook on me worthy of Henry Cooper. Ridiculous! The story was so bad that my solicitor said, 'You've got to sue them!' Well, I did, and I got thirty grand, settled out of court.

As for the divorce settlement, my accountant gave a summary of my affairs, and stated how I had bought a nice bungalow for Betty's parents, and put it in my wife's name. That was all she was awarded. I was landed with the costs, around £70,000 which I had to meet. It meant selling a couple of properties to pay them off.

I had actually been heading for a property empire with my investments, but after that little episode we only had a few flats left, which didn't actually amount to too much. I got rid of them all later. Betty had a half-stake in Kenbet investments, and the judge agreed to my offer of £2,000 a year to buy her share in the firm.

In the end I made a clean break, apart from the monthly payments to my ex-wife. It all seems a long time ago, and a lot of murky water has passed under the bridge. We all suffered from it, in our own ways: Betty, myself, our daughters Gillian and Jane, and my son Keith. But the river's cleaned up now. My relationship with Jane, the youngest, is fine. It was quite horrible for some years, but we've been through it and out the other side. And while I'm working and earning a crust I'm not going to stop the payments. The kids keep me in touch with how Betty is getting on.

After the case, the atmosphere before the first show two nights later was terrible. I knew it would be, and I faced that concert with enormous trepidation. The venue was in Camberley, and there was tension in the dressing room. God knows what the audience were thinking as they filed into their seats. On my side of the curtain I downed a large brandy, and then another one. Stage fright? Too right! I was a bag of nerves, but for all the wrong reasons. This was nothing to do with my ability to play the trumpet or lead a band. This was personal.

The tabloids had just come out with the divorce stories. When I walked out there on the stage, I wanted the floor to open up under me. I must have swallowed half a bottle of brandy before I ventured out, and I just wonder what messages my body language sent out across the footlights. The price any star pays when the media circus turns on you is hard to take. It's the most God-awful thing to be called an absolute shithouse in print and, until you've been through it, you can never know.

So there I am, walking out on to the stage, mentally stripped naked apart from my precious trumpet as a security blanket, facing the lions, waiting for Caesar to give the thumb's down. Would they applaud, or boo me into the rafters? Or, worse, a polite silence?

No! At Camberley, on that first testing moment of truth after the scandal, the audience were marvellous. They were totally supportive. If they'd read the stories, they didn't hold it against me. They accepted it. Fans, I love you!

I would say it took about two weeks for me to be able to put it at the back of my mind, and tell myself, OK, Kenny, the headlines are only tomorrow's fish and chip wrappers. Life goes on. But I needed their support – oh, how I needed it.

That period would prove to be one of the truly low points of my life. Working five days a week helped. Michelle rang every day, and that gave me some comfort. I climbed out of it eventually and, four years after we moved in together, I married her.

First, I had to pop the question. Trust me to do it from Russia. With love. It was 1983, a grey November, and I was on tour. The band had reached St Petersburg and the days were gloomy and cloudy. The nights drew in early, shrouding the place like a dark blanket, and all in all it was a pretty depressing place.

In the early eighties, phone calls to the Soviet Union were a nightmare. You had to wait up to four hours to get through, and often the line was so bad you could hardly make out what the other person was saying. So Michelle sent me a tape, and I played it in my equally depressing hotel room, staring out of my window at the sombre square outside, and suddenly I had a lump in my throat.

Her youngest daughter Sophie was with her – she must have been twelve – and I could hear Sacha barking in the background. Sacha was our Border collie whom we originally wanted to name Satchmo until she turned out to be female. A gorgeous dog with a gentle nature, she died at the ripe old age of eighteen and now rests in my back garden, complete with a small headstone to mark our happy days together.

But now Sophie was saying, 'We all miss you, Daddy.' And then Michelle's voice, 'Darling, I miss you. We're sending you some vitamin C tablets because they'll keep up your energy and I know you can't get any in Russia.' Sometimes both of them were talking together.

I must have played that tape a dozen times, and my hotel room grew lonelier and emptier by the minute. Eventually I said to myself, That's it! I'm phoning them up, however long it takes.

Well, it took four hours, just as I knew it would. But I got through. Michelle picked up the phone. I said to her, 'Are you sitting down?'

'Yes,' she answered

'Will you marry me?'

There was a long pause, then she stuttered, 'Wh … why?'

'Because I love you, and I want to marry you,'

There was a pause. Then Michelle said, 'Oh, all right!' No fainting on the end of the phone, no weeping. I think she was

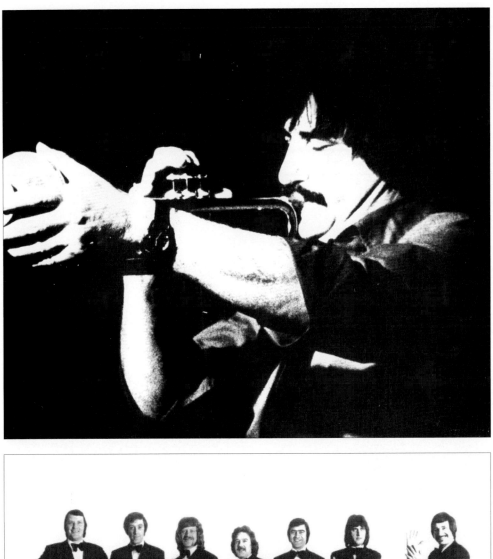

Top: Taking the spotlight for a solo.

Bottom: The Jazzmen in 1978. *From left*: Ron Bowden, Ted Baldwin, Vic Pitt, John Parker, John Bennett, Andy Cooper and my good self.

Meeting royalty. With the Queen Mother and *below* with Princess Margaret.

In the swing in the seventies.

Top: The *Jazzette* fanzine which has all the latest about me and the Jazzmen.

Bottom left: A program for one of our shows.

Bottom right: A flyer for the first of the Ball, Barber and Bilk shows.

Top: Lost in music on stage.

Bottom: Cards and real ale with the Jazzmen.

Top left: With Acker Bilk, right, and Chris Barber on the left.

Top right: With Phil Hoy, editor of the *Jazzette*.

Bottom left: Hall and Ball! The new double act. Me and my biographer William Hall.

Photo: Jean Pestell

Bottom right: John Benson, double bass player with the Jazzmen until 2002.

My marriage to Michelle in 1984 has brought me such great happiness.

Top: Fooling about with Michelle and the other love in my life.

Bottom: With family. Me, Dorothy (my dad's girlfriend), my dad Tim, Michelle and her mother Violette.

The line up of the Jazzmen until 2002. *Back row*: Me, John Benson, John Bennett, Andy Cooper. *Front row*: Nick Millward, Hugh Ledigo.

rather taken aback; let's amend that to totally stunned. We'd been together six years, remember, and it came right out of the blue.

Then she asked me, 'When?' I have to tell you that neither of us was very up for conversational callisthenics with that call.

'As soon as possible,' I said. 'I haven't got any gigs between Christmas and the New Year. Let's do it then.'

The problem was that at that time I was boracic. Lint, skint. I had spent £70,000 to pay off my debts, and I had no money in the purse. But, heck, we went ahead anyway. Michelle and I were married on 28 December 1983. I couldn't even hire a hall for the reception. But I had a bright idea: the house in Hornchurch where we were living had a double garage. Some friends we knew who were into catering offered to oblige for the wedding feast. I did the garages up myself, putting sheets along the walls and getting in the tables. We bought cheeses and patés and a load of drink, and decorated the whole place with balloons and decorations. The cars were relegated to the street.

We were married at Hornchurch Register Office. The reception in the garage was a wonderfully jolly and noisy affair, and I've still got pictures of Dad blowing the trumpet! We'd made a point of warning the neighbours, and they gave us their blessing – or went away for the night. The celebrations went on into the early hours.

The honeymoon had to wait three days. I was working on New Year's Eve in Harrogate, and that seemed ideal for it. The band were playing at the Majestic Hotel, which is where we all stayed, so at least I didn't have far to go after the show. I called up the manager from the wedding party, and asked him, 'Do you have a suite I can hire? I've just got married, and I want to spend my honeymoon there.'

'Of course. We can give you the bridal suite. How long do you want it for, Mr Ball?'

'Well, just one night …'

My mother-in-law came too, along with Michelle's two children from her first marriage, Sophie and Nicole. My lot stayed away. The manager had done us proud: loads of flowers in the suite and bottles of champagne, all on the house. Ma-in-law Violette had actually been the source of my meeting Michelle, remember, so I was quite happy to have her along to share the bubbly. Well, I owed her one. And if anyone's wondering, no, she didn't share the bedroom!

It was all wonderfully surreal. At least I managed to get one dance in with my new bride while the warm-up band was playing ahead of the Jazzmen. I always remember it: 'I Just Called to Say I Love You'.

Well, I had, hadn't I?

We had a good gig that New Year's Eve, and a lively audience who'd enjoyed a great feast as well as the music. We played until half past twelve, then the whole bunch of us trooped upstairs, opened the champagne and had a great party, with the entire band in attendance! I don't think the bridal suite had ever seen such a crowd. Bride and groom, mother-in-law, two kids and a bunch of Jazzmen plus a few hangers-on.

What a night, as a new year and a new life dawned for me.

CHAPTER FIFTEEN

OLLIE APPEARS

The popular BBC TV programme *Saturday Night at the Mill* was a winner for us, and a huge showcase for the Jazzmen. We were invited to be the resident band in 1975, and stayed for the next eight years. Based in Birmingham, and with a peak viewing time of ten o'clock on Saturday night, the show boasted audience figures up to nine million. What more could you ask? And, as it went out live, you never knew what was going to happen.

We got off to a great start with Norman Wisdom, a name I have mentioned before in these pages. In our second week, on a cold February weekend, little Norm was the guest of honour, and Wisdom can warm anyone up with his brilliant knockabout comedy. Bob Langley, the show's anchorman, had given Donny McLeod the job of interviewing him, but we all knew Norman would take over the moment he spied that camera running.

Sure enough, he bounced out to a roar of applause, which

rapidly turned to uncontrollable mirth as he went straight into overdrive, completely unaware that his fly buttons were undone, a state of undress which is every actor's nightmare. The camera, and the watching millions, could see virtually everything as he jigged around in his chair. Panic in the control box. We were taking it all in from our small stage in the centre, shaking our heads in disbelief. Hadn't he checked the mirror?

Apparently not. Out of camera range Bob Langley kept hissing, 'Trousers ... undone! *Trousers ... undone!*' and rolling his eyes significantly downwards. Somebody scrawled the same message on a big card, one of the 'idiot boards' they hold in reserve for emergencies. Norman just thought they were joking and went blithely on with his chat. And the more the audience laughed, the more manic the little chap became.

Finally it was time for him to sing. 'Don't Laugh at Me', of course, was the signature tune that became the title of his own autobiography when he first told his amazing rags-to-riches story. Laugh? We were in hysterics, but for all the wrong reasons. Norman stood up and strode over to the stage with his famous simian walk, at which point I couldn't contain myself any longer.

'Norman,' I said loudly. By now there was no point in whispering. 'I've got to tell you, your flies are undone!'

I'll say this for him – he took it on the chin. And what's more, he brought fresh waves of laughter, this time with him and not at him, when he responded, 'Well, Kenny, you know me. When I was in the Army I was flyweight champion!' And he sang his heart out as if nothing had happened.

Good for you, Norman. A number of viewers rang up, but very few complained. And Norman summed it up afterwards when he saw the predictable headlines: 'My office door was open, but you couldn't see the office boy!' Nice one, Norm.

Afterwards in the Green Room he still had us in stitches, even though his strongest drink was a cup of tea. The pair of us found we had something in common — pulling faces. For a trumpeter, or anyone who plays a wind instrument, this is actually very important. Your embouchure means using the face muscles and the lips. That's the one thing you must never lose — always keep those muscles around the lips alive and going strong. You exercise by doing what we call 'lip tricks', jumping octaves, working all your face muscles.

Funnily enough, the little feller told me a story once of how he used to practise pulling faces in the mirror for his act in quite a similar way. He was growing up in Deal, and had discovered the joys of facial contortions by rehearsing them in his upstairs bedroom. And he blows a mean trumpet, too!

'It really is quite easy. And the more you practise the more you can manipulate your skin into all sorts of monstrous-looking masks,' he said. 'In the end I could pull the most horrendous faces imaginable. One summer's day in Deal I was upstairs by myself, working out in my bedroom. Unknown to me, my mother had arranged for a window cleaner to go over the house.

'I was happily prancing around as the Hunchback of Notre Dame in front of the wardrobe mirror when I was aware of a movement behind me. I turned sharply, all twisted and horrible, and found myself glaring malevolently at another face peering through the window, a frightened bloke in a cloth cap. The poor chap was totally transfixed for a moment, before he let out a yell and vanished down the ladder and out of sight. He obviously thought there was a lunatic locked away. I heard the rattle of a bucket being kicked over, and then he was gone.

'Mum had to phone him and explain what was going on. "Tell him he scared the life out of me," said the cleaner. "I'll come back when he's gone."'

If unpredictability was the name of the game on *Saturday Night at the Mill*, then how can I leave out Spike Milligan? Crackpot, genius or maybe both, you never knew what he was going to say or do. Spike came on the show just once, and was his usual zany self. But talking to him in the Green Room afterwards, we really hit it off. He had been a trumpet player in his youth, which helped, and we found we had a great deal in common.

I broached the idea that he might compère a concert with us, and have a blow with me. 'OK,' Spike said. 'But can you give me some lessons? I'm a bit rusty.' I wrote some studies out for him, but sadly it never came to pass.

Oliver Reed holds the gold medal for creating the most havoc, and in his own inimitable way. Ollie happened one night early in 1980 and, believe me, Ollie always was a happening – like a volcano erupting. The idea was that he would come on with a fanfare from the Jazzmen at around half past ten, presumably with a film to promote, or some other topical peg on which to hang his hat for an interview.

Now as the world knew – but apparently not the brains at Pebble Mill – Ollie enjoyed a tipple, or six. What nobody had bothered to take into account was the fact that the bar opened in the Green Room at three o'clock in the afternoon, seven hours before the show went out at ten. Now for a serious drinker, that's a lot of imbibing time – and Ollie was a very serious drinker.

Yet nobody behind the scenes seemed to worry too much. We were frequently finding guests who couldn't hold their booze, either through nerves if they were an unknown or if they were celebrities who liked the sauce. So maybe those same powers that be had decided, What's another one? Well, they soon found out.

The audience were sitting in the studio, ready and waiting. They had been there since nine o'clock, and the warm-up man had done his bit to get everyone in the mood. I was stationed with the Jazzmen in our usual place on the small stage in the centre.

Ollie was supposed to come down the stairs, enter through glass doors to our right, cross in front of us and shake hands with Bob Langley, then plonk himself down in an armchair for the interview. We would see him in with 'There's No Business Like Show Business'. A voice would announce, 'Ladies and gentlemen – Oliver Reed!' We would play Ollie to the chair and fade out when he shook the proffered mitt. All nicely cut and dried.

So what happened? The red light came on, we struck up the familiar opening bars: 'There's *no* business like *show* business ...' And nothing moved. The doors stayed closed. No Ollie. So we kept going: 'Everything about it is *appealing* ...' This went on for about two minutes, by which time we were getting a bit irritated playing the same tune over and over again – particularly myself, as I was playing the melody on the trumpet.

We got through ten choruses – and still no Ollie.

I found out later what had happened from Michelle, who was watching from the floor with the stage manager, a small woman whose energy belied her size. Huge Ollie looms up beside her, pissed out of his head, and announces, 'I'm not going on!' He refuses to move, just stands there swaying glassy-eyed, and the woman can't budge him. She hisses to my wife, 'Michelle, please help me. *Get him on!*'

So the pair brace themselves behind the guest of honour, and charge him bodily in the back. Ollie goes windmilling down the stairs like a rocket, crashes through the doors as explosively as a genie out of a bottle, and announces grandly: 'I appear!'

Then he drops his trousers.

Can you imagine it? I must tell you that we all laughed like a drain, as Ollie stumbled through the interview and somehow made it without passing out.

Afterwards, of course, everyone tut-tutted with disapproval. But the fact is that we need characters like that on the box – rebels, roisterers, hell-raisers, call them what you like. It makes for dangerous TV, but great TV. These people are unpredictable, and they lift the ratings by thousands if viewers think they're going to get something unexpected, even if the late and much lamented Ollie tended to go over the top now and then. Now there *is* a hard act to follow.

In fact that same night Ollie turned up at a party at our hotel, and found the band chatting at the bar. We bought him a drink, then another. He bought several in return. And then some smart-arse appeared at his elbow and started giving him the verbals, trying to wind him up.

Finally Ollie put his face close to this clown's, and said very slowly and clearly, 'I'm talking to my friends here. If you want to cause trouble, come down to my manor and I'll kick shit out of you. Other than that, please go away!' And the other guy did. Ollie was holding back his temper, but I really thought he was going to explode.

When it comes to drink, I am reminded of pots and kettles. He who is without sin, let him pour the first pint down the sink. Put quite simply, it goes with the territory. And you're always in good company. A musician who doesn't touch the sauce is as rare as a rusty hub cap on a Rolls Royce. The ones that don't drink have usually given it up, rather than having been teetotal all their lives.

Me, I drank heavily. But I was never, ever near to losing control and becoming an alcoholic. Often I drank too much and paid for it next morning, but musicians normally sleep late and sleep it off. Twelve noon is the time I usually open one eye to check I'm still in the land of the living, and then I either get up or turn over for another hour's kip. You won't find me answering the phone before two in the afternoon, and my mobile stays switched off until then.

No drugs, either. I tried marijuana a couple of times. On the first occasion I lost my legs, and the second time was worse. To put it as politely as possible, I leaked both ends, and it was awful. The top half of me was throwing up, the bottom half remained close to the loo for two days. I thought about it, and decided, Hey, perhaps this isn't for me after all.

That first time was on a gig up in Scotland, some thirty-five years ago. The place was Alloa on the Forth River, but it was more good bye to drugs than 'allo-a, paradise'! We were in a boarding house, and our banjo player along the corridor had a joint. Back in our rooms, he called me in and offered me the soggy stub, so I tried it. I thought, Umm … this is OK! Then I got up to go to bed, and fell straight down on to my knees.

I had to crawl across the carpet, out into the passage and finally reach up to the door knob to get into my own room, still on my hands and knees. Then I passed out on the bed.

Next day I did some serious thinking. My main conclusion was: this is no bloody good. I've got children. I'm a responsible father. I've told them not to smoke grass or do any other drugs, and there's me crawling down the corridor because I literally can't stand up! What would they have thought of me if they'd seen me?

Another factor that put me off even experimenting with hard drugs was when I saw how much great talent in the business was being wasted. People were selling their lives for dope. The saxophone player Tubby Hayes, one of the true giants of jazz, was one. Phil Seamen, probably the greatest drummer who ever lived in this country, was another, and I saw for myself what it did to him.

I remember being at a jazz festival with Phil in Clacton. They provided us with chalets to stay in overnight, and I was occupying one with Phil and two other musicians. Before the gig I saw them with a teaspoon that had something in it which they were melting with a lighter to pour into a syringe. It wasn't white powder, the way you see it today in films, more of a liquid they were thinning down. Then they injected themselves.

Months later, on my *This is Your Life* show (which I will tell you about later), I saw the terrible effects. Phil had been a mate, though I hadn't seen him for some time. He was to be a surprise guest, but when they saw him they never actually asked him to appear on the show. He got into the party afterwards, though, and I was shocked at his appearance. He looked like a tramp. He'd lost most of his teeth. He was sitting down in the Green Room with a plate of coleslaw in front of him, and he was digging it out with his fingers and stuffing it into his mouth. Christ, it was awful.

Phil died shortly afterwards, and so did Tubby Hayes, chock full of heroin. What really shook me was that here were two of the finest jazz musicians ever born on God's earth, and look at the way they ended up.

The second time I tried drugs was at my home in Hornchurch. We had a few musicians and friends round, just an informal party. Someone gave me a black ball of marijuana, and said, 'Here, you want to be happy? Smoke some of this!' I scraped some off as he instructed, and put the shavings into a cigarette. Then I puffed away.

I said to Michelle, 'Well, this stuff doesn't affect me at all – and I'm happy anyway!' I started to get up, and it all happened. I was like a volcano erupting, covered in vomit and learning the meaning of the word 'incontinence' all at the same time. Michelle, bless her, somehow helped me up the stairs to the bathroom, and left me to clean myself up. There's devotion for you! I couldn't have made it alone, I was that bad.

Then she helped me into bed, and twelve hours later I came round. Twelve hours lost. Unbelievable. Never again! I've got the message loud and clear: drugs and Kenny Ball don't really hit it off.

I don't think any of my own band have been on drugs. Musicians drink, it goes with the game. We could drink the Atlantic dry. One trumpet player I knew couldn't go into a recording studio with less than half a bottle of Scotch inside him. He would play perfectly well. This guy was playing in the Teddy Foster band when he was suddenly overcome by an attack of conscience, and decided he'd stop drinking. He didn't have a drink all that day. He went to the pictures in the afternoon to get his mind off the gig ahead. When he walked on stage and opened the music in front of him, it was like he'd never seen it before! In the interval Teddy went to him, and said, 'Joe, are you all right? Are you ill? You need a drink!'

At least with the drink you know what you're getting. With drugs, they've got all these names like Colombian Brown or Paki Black, and you've no idea what you're putting into your veins or your lungs. But, with a gin and tonic, you know the score. So before I go on stage I might have two large G and Ts. And, when I come off, I'll have another two large G and Ts. You know your reaction, and, although there were times when I was aware that I was drinking too much, I never let it get the better of me so that I was out of control.

Now I don't drink at all during the day. Or smoke. I have no desire for either. But an hour before going on stage, I badly want a cigarette, and I badly want a drink. And, after the show, I'll enjoy both. But in the morning when I wake up, the idea is anathema. I'd be ill if I touched a drink or a cigarette.

Roy Castle is an object lesson in this: he was a good mate of mine, a great talent and a versatile musician. He could play almost any instrument. He also liked a tipple. Roy told me a story of how he flew to Las Vegas to do some shows, and was playing the great showcase hotel Caesar's Palace.

His dressing room is next door to a comedian and, as he emerges to begin his act, the comic calls out, 'Hey, Roy, like a drink?'

Roy replies, 'Thanks, but I never drink before I go on stage.'

The other guy's eyes bulge in disbelief. 'You mean you go on *alone?*'

That's a jokey story, but there's more than a grain – or grape – of truth in it, and we all know what he meant.

One time we were playing for the Scouts in Warwick in a school hall. The scoutmaster was a jolly soul, who took the band down to the pub in the interval and made sure they had plenty of booze. I stayed in the dressing room because I had some work to catch up on. Time went by. Twenty minutes … half an hour … forty minutes … and no sign of the team.

I was getting more and more steamed up, even going out to pace the empty stage clutching my trumpet and bowler-hat mute in frustration. What the hell were they doing? On the far side of the curtains I could hear the audience getting restless, although no one had started the slow handclap – yet.

I heard later that John, Vic Pitt, Andy and Ron Weatherburn had all been knocking it back with the scoutmaster in the public bar, oblivious to the passing of time, when someone suddenly said, 'Hey, fellers, I think we should be getting back. We've been here forty-five minutes!'

They raced back to find me on stage, fuming. The drapes were still drawn, with a boy scout on each side waiting to pull them back. The poor kids were looking petrified at the thunder on my brow. The guys marched out with their instruments, obviously fuelled up and looking anything but sheepish.

'Where the fuck have you been?' I snarled. I was so angry that when I saw them I lashed out with my foot and kicked the mute, which I always put ready beside the microphone. It sailed through the air, and hit the double bass. Vic kicked it back and the thing was sailing around the stage with each of us trying to get a kick in, when someone suddenly hissed, 'We're on!'

The scouts had pulled back the curtains – and the audience was treated to the sight of a bunch of enraged jazz players kicking the shit out of this inoffensive bowler, and growling imprecations at one another. They were staring at us open mouthed. What was that about 'be prepared'?

Afterwards, back in the pub, I joined in the laughter. You can't have time for sulking. Not in our profession. You're too close to each other. It never lasts, anyway.

One time we had what we call a 'band shout-up', when we were all pissed. Each and every one of us. It was the mid-seventies, and we had been at a four-day festival of some sort in Edinburgh, playing to 6,000 or 7,000 thousand people every night. We all wore biscuit-coloured mohair suits, and very smart and dapper we looked.

After this particular show we gathered in the VIP bar as usual, when someone started an argument. Apart from the band, there were only a couple of people in there with us at the time, but I tell you, that bar was wrecked! Andy put three pint pots through the glass cases where the drink was kept, which gives you an idea of the fracas. What started it? Don't ask me. Probably something very trivial and stupid, but Andy swears it was the banjo player at the time, Ted Baldwin, who kicked it off.

They used to wind each other up, so it's probably true. Andy would pull his leg: 'Banjo? Well, you've got to have something else going for you, so you might as well start an argument!'

Truth to tell, no actual punches were thrown. Nobody thumped anyone, but there was a lot of prodding in the chest with fingers, and threatening gestures. Fists up, but no contact – it was verbal but nasty. We were all telling the truth about each other – another mistake. Once something is said, it can never be unsaid. The row spilled out of the bar and continued into the dressing room. This is where drink was spilled on the floor and on ourselves. The biscuit-coloured suits turned a nasty shade of chocolate with patches with beer all over them.

Johnny Parker was our piano player at the time. He suffered from a form of paralysis which had left him with no feeling in one leg, and required him to use a walking stick. He coped with it incredibly bravely, and could play brilliantly.

At that point in the shout-up, Johnny was leaning against a radiator on the wall, and directing his wrath at me. 'You can't fucking tell me what to do,' he was shouting. 'Don't you dare call me that, you're worse …' and so on. In the middle of his tirade the radiator came away from the wall with an almighty crack, and took Johnny with it. He went rolling on the carpet, covered in beer, and found he couldn't get up. Water was spurting from both ends of the radiator, splashing the walls and soaking us.

All of a sudden Johnny rolled over and glared up at me from the carpet. He waved a finger. 'And another thing,' he began … and that did it! It completely finished the whole argument. The band was convulsed. We fell into each other's arms almost weeping with laughter.

As I say, it never lasts!

Both these episodes pale into insignificance when I think of the night no less than three of the Jazzmen toppled over – one of them actually falling off the stage. It had to be Andy! He's the joker in the pack, right? We were playing at a truly awful place in Carlisle

– I'll save our hosts the embarrassment of naming the venue but they have probably closed down now, or changed the name. There must have been 400 people in the crowd giving us a less than enthusiastic response.

The boys felt so miserable with the general conditions that when they trooped into the bar in the interval someone had the bright idea of forming the Down in one Club, effective immediately. That someone was Johnny Parker, bless his socks. I wasn't there to see it, having remained backstage to catch up on some work, or I might have put a stop to it, knowing the possible consequences of an overkill on the amber nectar.

The quartet involved were Andy, Johnny, Ted Baldwin the banjo player and Vic Pitt. They chose to drink shorts, and they made them doubles. Each man would make his choice, and the others would carry on in sequence: whisky, gin, vodka, brandy … whisky, gin, vodka, brandy. You get the picture? For some reason the interval extended to forty minutes, at the end of which the picture was distinctly blurred when the boys received the come-back call for the second half.

The first number had to be Andy doing his chicken act – and he tumbled off the stage, straight on to the floor. He was past caring by now, and totally unhurt. Not even a bruise. He lay there staring up at the stage, giggling, while I gave him the fish eye of disapproval. The others were killing themselves laughing, and suddenly it was like a domino effect. First Vic fell backwards, taking his bass with him. Then Johnny Parker fell off his piano stool. Unbelievable.

It's bad news to put on a performance like that, I know. But it was such a bloody awful gig that somehow it didn't seem to matter!

The strangest thing was that it went down better than anything we did all night. The crowd loved it! They fell about, too. I gave the gang a roasting afterwards, and told them, 'You're a bunch of assholes!'

'You're right, Kenny,' came the unrepentant chorus. 'We're a bunch of assholes!'

What can you say to that?

It's nothing new to fall off stage. I've seen other guys do it. Ron Weatherburn, our brilliant piano player, fell off his stool once. Other times he would simply join the audience. Those were the days when people left their seats in the second half to come and stand at the front, whooping and jiving, catching our eye and waving to us. Frequently we would troop back on stage to find the piano player missing. Instead, there was Ron down in the front with the fans, a pint in his hand, chatting animatedly to one and all.

'Oi!' I would call to him. 'What are you doing down there?

'Just talking, Kenny. Just talking.' A beaming smile, and he went on chatting until he felt ready to join us.

One more for the record. An open-air riverside concert by the Thames in Fulham, not far from the famous Craven Cottage soccer ground. There must have been 3,000 people there in Bishop's Park enjoying a beautiful summer's evening.

Showtime! We begin the introduction, intending to appear from the makeshift wings while the drummer, Ron Bowden, gives us a big roll to announce each name. But … nothing. No sound, no drum roll. I look around, and there's Ron lying on the stage with his head down underneath the drums. He's not dead – more like dead drunk. We'd been to a wedding that afternoon. Ron must have toasted the bride a few times too many.

Thinking desperately, I grab the microphone. 'Ladies and gentlemen, I'm sorry about this – it seems as if the drums are broke!'

At which point Ron's purple face appears from beneath the cymbals, and his voice rasps out, 'Jus' like the fuckin' drummer!'

It was in 1971 that I was awarded one of the ultimate accolades of show business: an appearance on *This is Your Life*. And no one was more surprised than I was to be nailed by a grinning Eamonn Andrews, dressed as a porter on the platform at King's Cross as I got off the InterCity from Glasgow. I was walking down the platform towards the exit, and the embarrassing thing was that I had a copy of a glossy men's magazine under my arm for all the world to see!

Eamonn came bustling up to me, keeping his face hidden under a peaked cap, then grabbed my suitcase, and before I could protest said, 'Good evening, Kenny Ball. This is your life!' It was a brilliant ambush, and caught me completely by surprise. At the studio I found not only celebrities like Joe Brown and Lonnie Donegan walking through the doors, but most of my family, too, even my old dad. All the Jazzmen were there, and they played 'When the Saints Go Marching In' with the whole audience clapping and stamping. My only regret is that I can't find a recording of the programme. If there ever were any, they've all gone.

The fun and games continued. We went on to a telethon in the early eighties, a twenty-four-hour marathon going out live to raise money for charity. We must have done a dozen pieces throughout the night, and were due to remain on call until six in the morning for our last appearance. Now that was a *long* night. We managed to arrive late, around eleven o'clock, but at least the drinks were flowing backstage in the Green Room.

Around three in the morning a guy named Tony came on, with a moustache which he was going to shave off for charity. Four of the boys stood behind the chair singing like a barber's shop quartet. I flourished a cut-throat razor, a real one, and at that time I wasn't too sure of my ability to use it after a night's drinking. This was live, remember, with no rehearsal. The boys started singing, 'We are poor little lambs who have lost our way … baa baa baa …' which was enough to put even Sweeney Todd off his stroke. 'We are little black sheep who have gone astray ...'

All of a sudden, the razor nicked this chap's nose. Oh, Christ! The blood starting flowing. All I could do was to keep my hand over the victim's nose, which was copiously dripping blood. 'Lord have mercy on such as we ...' The boys sang on, the moustache came off, and the man finally walked off, holding a handkerchief to his proboscis, and shaking his head.

Over the years we pushed out many albums, as well as hit singles. The above anecdotes bring to mind *Have a Drink on Me*, which sold like hot toddy, since we released it at Christmas. Another album entitled simply *Cheers!* kept the message bright and breezy, but included the haunting theme from *The Good, the Bad and the Ugly* and the menacing 'Mack the Knife'. Hit songs were headed by 'I Wanna Be Like You', from the *Jungle Book*; and on the album *Kenny Ball's Cotton Club* we played two personal favourites of mine, 'Minnie the Moocher' and the classic 'St Louis Blues'. Over the years I would record well over 500 songs, so it's hard to get them all down in date order. You'll find the titles at the end of the book.

We had our highs, but we also had our lows. In half a century, it's bound to happen. The trick is never to let anyone see that you're down. A remark by the millionaire Peter de Savary, who among his other ventures ran the swish St James's Club in Mayfair, impressed me no end. He once declared, 'I normally cycle to work. You can tell I'm in trouble when I arrive by Rolls Royce!' There's a lesson in there for all of us.

The Jazzmen had a bad patch in the early seventies. At one point we only had ten gigs in May in our order book. I had an urgent meeting with my agent at his office near Marble Arch. 'What's going on?' I demanded. 'What happened to May?'

He shrugged. 'Well, Kenny, you know how it is. You've been going for almost fifteen years now. That's the usual life for a band. I can't see you carrying on much longer.'

I stared at him across the desk. 'Are you kidding?'

'No,' he said. 'I'd advise you to give it up. Try gardening or something.'

'Thank you for your advice,' I replied. 'I'll think about it.'

I sat there facing him across the desk, and thought about it – for ten seconds. Then I said, 'I'm finding myself another agent. Good morning.' And walked out.

That kind of thing lights a fire under your feet. Faced with being made redundant, it would have been all too easy to panic. Instead I started up my own agency. I hired a secretary, and we opened an office in Shaftesbury Avenue. It was an entire first floor which I rented for a vast sum. It had four rooms and just three desks in it – one for her, one for an assistant, one for me. Despite the wall-to-wall carpet and the double-glazed windows, our voices tended to echo when we talked to each other. Dates for the Jazzmen trickled in, but it was hardly a tidal wave. The Kenny Ball Agency managed to book a number of acts, including the Band of the Royal Marines and other brass bands. I actually carried on for three years like that, until one day my bank manager called me up.

'I've got to tell you, Kenny. If you go on like this, paying out enormous rents, you'll be bankrupt in a month.'

So I packed it in, found another agent and went back to what I knew best, full time. The first job that came up was the *Morecambe and Wise Show*, and that did it. Our whole career got a fresh kick-start. That show was seen by millions every Saturday night, and even eclipsed the soaps.

Yes, that had been a low point, but I fought through it. Hand on heart, I never thought of giving up. Never, never, never! I would have been letting myself down, and more importantly letting the boys down too. The work started flooding in again.

Television kept us busy. We backed Michael Parkinson for sixteen weeks, and met a load of his celebrity guests. We took time off to get a tape done of John Inman singing 'Teddy Bears' Picnic'. But it was Morecambe and Wise who kept us busier than most. We did five series with them, and we wore a different-coloured jacket for each show. Eric was a great jazz fan, and introduced us with gags like: 'We've got Kenny Ball back with us again. I don't know why the heck they're here, but I've got an idea how they managed it. Kenny's found out where Ernie has buried his wallet, so we've got to give them a spot!'

These icons of mirth did their own warm-ups – not that the audiences needed any encouragement to laugh. All Eric had to do was shift his specs sideways, or pat little Ern on the cheeks, and the place dissolved into laughter. After they introduced us we kicked off the show, playing them in and playing them out, and occasionally taking part in a sketch.

Nothing would ever go wrong because that show was so tightly rehearsed. Well, next to nothing. Even the unforgettable Shirley Bassey sketch was meticulously planned, though it looked to all intents and purposes like a mishap when she lost her shoe and had to hobble down the stairs, still singing her heart out. I was there that night waiting to go on and it was hysterical, one of the funniest gags I've seen in my life. They did it all in one take. That's how professional everyone was on the show.

But the pair played one joke on us I won't forget. The idea was that the band would stand behind the grand piano, all of us wearing just a little pair of briefs so that the viewers would think, Strewth, they're not wearing any clothes! All people could see was naked chests and our bare feet under the piano. Eric and

Ernie would introduce us: 'Tonight, folks, we have a very permissive show!'

Filming started. The pair pointed over to our line-up – but unknown to us Eric had had the piano rigged. Someone pulled on a length of string, and the lid that had been protecting our modesty came crashing down. Wallop! Every man jack of us leaped out of our skins as if we'd been shot.

CHAPTER SIXTEEN

A RIGHT ROYAL
KNEES-UP

Prince Charles married his lady Diana in July 1981, and my present to them was to bring the band along to Buckingham Palace for the celebrations. At his invitation.

It happened this way: I had met Charles some months before at a charity function in Guildford. Prior to the entertainment, they served us a sumptuous dinner. I found myself seated opposite him at a long table below the stage, and sensed an immediate rapport. Our main topic of conversation was trumpets – Charles used to play in his younger days, though I somehow doubt if he has kept it up. Certainly there have been no reports of foot-stomping rhythm floating across the fields from Highgrove, but I know how much the heir to the throne likes his jazz. When we played it was very gratifying for each of the Jazzmen to see him applaud our solos.

Just before I excused myself to take to the stage, he leaned forward and said, 'Would you like to play at my wedding ball?' Or it might have been, 'Would you like to play at my wedding, Ball?'

I replied, 'Yes, sir. Sure. Make it my wedding present!'

'Oh, that will be very nice,' he said. 'Thank you very much.' So that's what we did.

That ball was some night. Unforgettable is an understatement to describe it. As far as we were concerned, we were treated like – well, like royalty. The royal household provided a well-stocked bar in a room for us to change in. While the guests tucked into their nosh upstairs, we were down in the kitchen being wined and dined before being summoned up to the investiture room for the musical shenanigans. High in a gallery at the far end sat the band of the Welsh Guards doing their thing when called upon, while a large gazebo had been erected in the middle of the room as our stage, so that the great and the good could dance around it.

The vision that caught my eye was Diana in a long red velvet dress which stood out like a beacon. I had never been near her before, but now I saw those electric blue eyes and the hypnotic effect they had when they fixed on you. And what a dancer that woman was! We started playing, and suddenly people were swirling past us like one of those grand Hollywood musicals they used to make. Every time I took the trumpet away from my face there was a tiara floating by – and everyone seemed to be waving at me. Were my flies undone? No, it was simply all those VIPs and heads of state having a wonderful time, and appreciating us.

We played in twenty-minute sets. When it came to our first break I wandered backstage, and found the Queen's loo was right there. I had to pay that a visit, didn't I? I reasoned that it was the only throne I'd get to sit on at the Palace, after all.

Back in our changing room, Prince Charles put his head round the door. He had lost his voice – it had been a long day – but managed to croak, 'How's it going, Ken?'

'Great, sir,' I told him.

'Are they feeding you well, and drinking you well?'

They certainly were. No expense spared, and the bubbly was flowing like tap water. 'Yes, sir, it's going great.'

'I think so, too,' he said. 'It's going absolutely fabulously. Please carry on.'

What I didn't like to tell him was that I was clutching a half-smoked fag behind my back. The Prince of Wales is known to be completely anti cigarettes, even if there weren't any of those annoying signs on the walls that say 'Thank You For Not Smoking'. But I'd been so nervous that I had to have a calming drag or two before I went out there to face the most intimidating audience of my life. In the end, of course, they were just like anyone else wanting to enjoy themselves.

The formal dancing went on until midnight. At one point Princess Margaret came up for a chat, during which she revealed that she had collected every one of our records. 'That's nice to hear,' was all I could muster for a lame response, but I meant it.

Then the Queen suddenly appeared by the podium. 'Would you and your band like to come down to the discotheque and have a dance?' she enquired.

'We certainly would, ma'am.'

And we certainly did. My stint was over. Now I could relax on one of the epic nights of my life. Through a glass darkly, and through a haze of gyrating bodies and flashing lights, I glimpsed the bearded figure of John Benson relinquishing his double bass to boogie with the monarch. That was one for John – and the rest of us – to dine out on.

Still mixing in rarefied circles, I found myself in the early eighties at the House of Commons with Margaret Thatcher, at that time riding high as prime minister during the Falklands War.

Someone produced a clarinet, and she posed with us in a photograph as if she were playing a tune. 'Just make out you're blowing it!' one of her aides exhorted her.

The stunt was purely for publicity, but I can now record that the PM actually managed to get a note out of it. She is a determined lady, even if it slightly backfired when Argentinian newspapers printed the picture with the caption, 'This is the sort of woman we are fighting!'

If this is a warts-and-all story, then the warts have to come with the wine and roses. And the worst episode of my entire career was the nightmare that every musician who spends his life blowing into a wind instrument must fear: when he loses his puff! Or gets 'Charlie-horse mouth', our expression for lip trouble.

It is the moment every horn player dreads. It happened to me in 1965.

It can occur in two ways. 'Lip lag', to borrow that jokey phrase from the Prince of Wales to me, can actually happen. This part of my anatomy is as important to me as sensitive fingers are to a pianist. Over the years of constant playing, a ridge of tough muscle forms around the mouth, making a perfect fit for the mouthpiece. The danger is that, if the muscles become strained because of overwork and lack of special practice scales, the lip goes. Suddenly, you're not playing with your old range and power.

As for the puff, I lost that too. The moment of truth came in Perth on our 1965 Australian tour. The place was packed. The song was 'Hello, Dolly!'. I tapped out the beat with my foot, lifted the trumpet to my mouth, blew – and nothing happened! I tried again, and just about managed to get some sort of sound to emerge.

But I knew that I'd really lost it when I got to the final stratospheric E above top C, the sound that normally sends a shiver through the whole theatre when I hit it. This time I missed it by a yard. Lips and lungs just weren't there for me when I needed them most.

I was aware of the band wincing around me. Bad, bad news! And the audience shuddered with embarrassment. Christ, I wanted the stage to swallow me up. Afterwards I tried to shrug it away as an off night. But suddenly those top notes became as hard to reach as the peak of Mount Everest.

I knew it wasn't a one-off, and I was right. The boys knew, too. I might just as well have been standing in front of them doing nothing. They had to cover for me when I was trying to perform my solos. There are few things sadder than a trumpet player who can't get more than a squawk out of his instrument. My confidence and humour hit an all-time low. Searching desperately around for ideas, the thought came to me that maybe I could double on bass or drums. Crazy, after my whole life had been devoted to the trumpet, but when you're running scared you claw after any solution, however unreal.

I even toyed with the idea of getting out of the business altogether, and finding a job on the petrol pumps! It was as bad as that. How I got through those early months I'll never know. One night at the Winter Gardens in Blackpool it was so bad that I stopped my solo on 'My Mother's Eyes', halted the band and started all over again. It was like being on stage without my trousers on, except that nobody was laughing.

It really hit home one night when I was taken ill at a gig, and unable to play the first hour. In the interval I went up to Ron Bowden. 'Well, what was it like playing without a trumpet?' I asked.

'Oh, much the same as usual,' came the reply. Cruel, but necessary. It made me realise how badly I was letting the band down.

Somehow we staggered on like this for five, repeat *five*, long years before I found the answer, and the cure. In any other band I would have been finished, out on my neck, and in all probability turned to drink and become a washed-up alcoholic. But we are no ordinary band. We're an extended family.

I tried to keep it secret, pulled myself together and went into a bone-breaking – some might say ball-breaking – training regime. I puffed endlessly into a trumpet mouthpiece to get my facial muscles back in shape. I ran for miles around the roads and heathland of Essex. I did fifty press-ups each morning. Why, I even gave up drinking and fags! Greater sacrifice hath no man, but still it did me no good.

I even took up yoga breathing, which basically teaches you to breathe in while you count to eight, slowly, then exhale out in short spurts. The beauty about this is that you can practise it at any time – when you're walking, or when you're in a train or waiting at a bus stop. It also increases your lung power and your puff.

When I finally got around to exploring this simple formula, I struck lucky. It coincided with a tour of New Zealand, the climax being a sell-out gig in Auckland attended by no less a personage than the magnificent Dame Kiri Te Kanawa. The stunningly beautiful and world-famous soprano came backstage afterwards and told me how much she had enjoyed the show.

Kiri – a Maori, whose English name actually is Janette – suddenly asked, 'How's your breathing, Kenny?'

I was taken aback. I'd really been trying to keep it a secret, but after all these months it was inevitable that someone would have guessed, or passed the word around the grapevine. People aren't stupid. Although I like to think I was putting a brave front on it, I was getting more depressed with every passing week.

'Not bad,' I said. 'I'll get by.'

'I hope so,' she said encouragingly. 'But if you have problems, try this out.' She put a hand on my chest. 'You know you only use two-thirds of your lungs when you breathe, don't you? That's a fact. Singing opera, I've been taught to breathe from my diaphragm, the lower stomach, and then at the end of the breath you draw in another two quick gulps, which fill another quarter of your lungs. As a normal person, you never fill them. It's also a terrific way to relax because it calms the central nervous system. Believe me.'

'I'll try it,' I promised.

I believed her. It made sense. From that moment I combined the Kiri method with the yoga method, and within three months I was back in top gear, blowing as hot and strong as I'd ever done.

Thanks, Kiri. I don't suppose I can ever repay you, but thanks again.

CHAPTER SEVENTEEN

BEHIND THE IRON
CURTAIN

The tours never let up. They weren't all caviar and champagne, that's for sure, even in Russia where you'd expect to find the odd tin of Beluga on offer. But when we first ventured in that direction it was at the height of the cold war, remember, and there was an iron curtain in the way.

Let's start with Romania, where we were treated like gods. Our first show was an eye-opener for me personally for three reasons. First off, the lady announcer was very beautiful. Her name was Erika, and she was actually a local TV star, recognised throughout the country. Secondly, she spoke Romanian, and I actually understood bits of it because in some ways it's close to French. One, two, three – un, deux, troy, as she pronounced it. Thirdly, I had a fling with her, which can't be bad in any language.

Erika actually took a fancy to John Bennett, who was so handsome it was quite painful for us lesser mortals to observe. I've already compared him to Elvis, but that's enough flattery for one night. The pair were inseparable for a few days, but then for some reason they decided enough was enough, and split up. She turned on me as first reserve, and since there was nobody else in the queue I was prepared to succumb to her advances. Prepared? She was gorgeous, and I was a willing slave.

'Lie back, Kenny!' We were out of town, in one of the provincial cities where the Jazzmen were due to play the next evening, and for the moment I had a chance to relax. Erika and I had indulged ourselves in a long, lazy dinner in a local restaurant, where the food seemed to be mainly pork and beans, washed down with heavy red wine. It wasn't three-star Michelin, but good enough for a hungry musician who was willing to ignore any sound effects on the morning after.

Now we were back in my room at the hotel, and Erika was kneeling at the foot of the bed, removing my shoes, then my socks, with a sensuality that made me feel as if she was the stripper, not me.

Then something happened I'd never experienced before with my sheltered upbringing: she was sucking on my bare toes, one by one, starting with the big one and moving down to the piglet. This little piggy … it was one of the sexiest things I'd ever had done to me in my life. I have to say that it was a one-off – for years afterwards I was frightened to ask anyone else to do it in case they thought I was some sort of pervert!

One toe led to another, and one thing led to another, and I played the concert next night with a mighty big smile on my face.

Romania was extremely primitive, and still is. We had a week in Bucharest, which left us with a mountain of memories, none of which would merit a mention in a travel brochure. During our week at the hotel we discovered the delights of sheatfish, pronounced the way it's spelled, which caused some mirth when we were ordering. They catch it in the Danube, and it's a large freshwater catfish, and extremely tasty.

The hotel was old fashioned and Gothic, with a lot of marble and mirrors and a wide curving staircase that led up from the foyer. One night we were outside on the terrace under the lights having a late supper of sheatfish soup and bread, when suddenly a black blizzard of enormous flying beetles hit us from nowhere. They came in a swarm, more than two inches long like flying cockroaches, banging into the walls of the hotel, falling into our drinks and even into our soup.

We made a precipitate withdrawal into the bar as the hailstorm continued outside, with kamikaze beetles squashing themselves like giant pockmarks on the French windows. I was bunking with my pal Dave the clarinet player, and we had been given a huge room two floors up with a marvellous view of the Dimbovita river, a four-poster bed each, ornate mirrors and antique furniture. But when we left the bar and made our way upstairs some time around one o'clock in the morning, we found Dave had left the windows open, and the place was alive with scaly intruders.

The bugs were everywhere – in the sheets, under the pillows, clinging to the bedside lamps, in the shower. Yuk! Flapping at them with towels didn't do any good, and it meant either stamping on them or picking them up and slinging them out of the window. I can't stand beetles anyway, but I didn't want a mess on the carpet so I gritted my teeth and scooped them up with my hands. Dave wasn't as bothered as me. He even kept one in a matchbox as a souvenir to show the folks back home – a Swan Vesta box because it was so big.

The final night in Bucharest produced a bizarre drama which we still talk about. We had to catch the midnight train after the concert in the capital, and headed off for the station, leaving our gear to follow in a van.

Our temporary roadie was Ivan, a middle-aged, serious man who was extremely conscientious and reliable. They had also assigned a PR lady to smooth our way. On the platform, amid the turmoil of passengers and luggage, she confidently told us, 'Get on the train! Your instruments will be all right. Leave it to me.' Fatal words, and I should have known better. But, OK, stupidly I left it to her.

Blissfully unaware of anything untoward going on outside the windows, we parked ourselves in the restaurant car for a late-night vodka session and a few hands of poker to unwind after the show, waiting for the train to move. What we failed to see or hear was Ivan arriving with our gear seconds before the train pulled out, driving his truck right up to the guard's van, screeching to a halt and single-handedly slinging the gear inside. Drum kit, double bass, everything was unceremoniously thrown in. Ivan was due to travel with us, but somehow the door of the guard's van slammed shut and he was left on the platform. Obviously a man who wasn't giving up in a hurry, he grabbed the outside of the last carriage and hung on.

You see that sort of thing in a James Bond movie, but not too often in real life. Ivan stayed like that for 30 miles, clinging to a handle like a leech. At times that train was going close to 90 miles per hour. Inside our car, the game was warming up: 'I'll raise you ten ... let's see you ... pass the vodka ... how's this for a flush ...'

All of a sudden the train pulled up with a squeal of brakes. There was a frantic rattling on the door, it opened with a rush of cold night air and Ivan half fell, half rolled in at our feet. He was white as a sheet and shaking like a leaf. We pulled him to his feet, sat him down with us and poured half a bottle of vodka down his throat.

'Christ, where have you been?'

He could only shake his head, and gulp more of the fiery fluid.

When the story finally came out, we toasted him in vodka, champagne and anything we could find on the wine list. We found out later that a signal man in his box had spotted Ivan hanging on to the train, and slammed the signals into red a mile down the line to stop the train. Now that's what I call devotion to duty, and we kept Ivan on with us for the rest of the tour. We owed him that at the very least.

Things happen on tour, often out of sheer boredom and the lure of the hotel bar. Now Dave liked a drink. One night at our Bucharest hotel he came staggering into the room. I was already in bed and fast asleep, as I'd had a long day. He got undressed, took a look at himself in one of the huge mirrors, didn't like what he saw and smashed his fist into it! There was glass all over the floor, and Dave swayed around the room in his bare feet, and bare everything, come to think of it, as I saw when I woke up.

'Dave, for Christ's sake, get into bed!' He stared at me uncomprehendingly, then swivelled round, fell flat on his face on the bed and passed out. Next morning it took him half an hour to get bits of glass out of his feet, while I made my apologies to the manager for the blood on the blankets and the broken mirror.

I understood. Like I say, it happens. You can be on the road for thirteen weeks with a different gig and a different hotel every week, and sometimes every night. You get jaded. It's inevitable. John Bennett used to call it the 'midweek blues'. The Jazzmen would stick together for the first month, eating together in various restaurants and drinking in the bars. But about five weeks into the tour I noticed how the guys would go off on their own in the evenings; the band would literally disintegrate socially and kind of turn inwards, not talking and laughing so much. We wouldn't even go to lunch together. And after a week – presto! The mood had lightened again, and we were back together.

A lot of it has to do with homesickness, especially for those with families and young kids they'd had to leave behind with their wives. It's a kind of mid-term crisis, a musical menopause! It must happen with cricketers too, I guess, on a long tour.

The boys chose their own company. John Bennett used to shack up with the drummer Ron Bowden. Then Ron moved on to share with one of my early roadies, a great guy named Pete Brown. It was a movable feast, never anything too formal.

The funny thing about Ron and Pete was that they used to bicker all the time. We would hear them arguing. 'You silly old fart, I'll smoke if I want to' or 'This place is like a bleeding incinerator, all your stuff everywhere.' We called them the Odd Couple, like the Jack Lemmon and Walter Matthau movie. But they were still the best of mates.

Being the boss of the group had its perks. Like getting the only single room available. But you could run into trouble with hotels, as I found out to my cost yet again on another early tour of Eastern Europe.

We had three gigs in Lithuania, and among our party was Pete the roadie, already mentioned, who was an unashamed serial womaniser. We used to pull his leg by saying that nothing in a skirt was safe, 'Not even a Scotsman in a kilt, laddie!' He was a terrific bloke, and a brilliant manager on the road, always thinking ahead.

The tour director escorting us around Lithuania was an attractive German-born blonde who could speak enough English to make herself understood. Pete didn't speak a word of Lithuanian, but he didn't need to. Eye contact and body language were enough to get the message across.

One morning Pete approached me at breakfast. 'Kenny, any chance of using your room tonight? I really fancy this bird, and I think she's got the hots for me too.'

'Sure,' I said. 'I'll be happy to oblige. Just leave a tip under the pillow in the morning.'

What none of us knew was that my room was wired. Someone, somewhere, was listening, and taping any sounds that came from it. No doubt they were expecting the usual phone calls, or maybe a business meeting. What they got instead were Pete and his new girlfriend going at it like rabbits, and the air filled with grunts, cries and creaking bedsprings as they made passionate love until dawn.

Next day the hotel manager greeted me in reception. 'I heard you had a good time last night, Mr Ball.'

'Yes, thank you,' I said, uncomprehending the gleam of appreciation in his eye. 'I had a nice dinner and a very good night's sleep.'

'Of course,' he said, with a knowing grin, before nodding and making his way back to the foyer. Very kind of him to be so solicitous, I thought to myself.

Of course, everyone thought it was me. The word went round, and my reputation as a stud was sealed for the duration of the tour.

The days of the cold war had an atmosphere all their own. The first time we set foot behind the iron curtain was both fascinating and unsettling, as we had no idea what we were in for. Our route was Holland, West Germany, East Germany, ending up on the far side of the menacing Berlin Wall and taking a month from start to finish.

The famous air corridor was operating at the time, to get over the Russian ban on travel. But since we had been invited by the East German government to play in their backyard, including East Berlin and Dresden, we had special passes to get our van through.

East Berlin was a disturbing experience, especially that first time in 1960 and in midwinter. With the cold war at its height, and everyone in a raincoat looking like a character out of a John Le Carré spy novel, going through Checkpoint Charlie was a spooky experience. There weren't many Western bands out there for a start, and the guards stamping their feet in the snow on the far side of the bridge viewed us with a mixture of suspicion and dislike. The decadent West? Here we come!

Someone had escaped over the Wall the previous week, and the tension in the air was almost palpable. Everyone was very edgy. 'Out!' It wasn't a request, it was an order. No one said 'please'. Two stony-faced guards had stopped us by the red barrier. Looking up, I saw an overhead railway behind a high steel-mesh fence, and the sinister shadows of guards on the vaulted ceilings.

Behind the obscene concrete barrier I glimpsed the *Vopos*, the East German police, patrolling with machine guns, their Alsatian guard dogs straining at the leash. In fact the leashes were attached by a ring to an overhead cable, so that the animals could run unhindered along the grass and reach the Wall itself, and any unfortunate fugitive trying to make the twelve-foot climb.

'Out!' The guard repeated the command, only more loudly, and this time both of them had their guns pointed at us.

I knew one or two of the boys had short fuses when it came to being ordered around by petty officialdom, especially military apparatchiks armed with lethal weapons, and I hastened to calm the situation. 'Remember, fellers, we're guests of the government,' I exhorted our small entourage. 'As long as we behave ourselves, we'll be OK. Just keep a smile stitched on your face, however painful.'

We managed it, just about, as we were herded into what looked like a garage, and left standing there while the soldiers searched the van. I don't know about you, but I'm always tempted to bleat like a sheep or moo like a cow when I'm shuffling along in a crowd. But now was most definitely not the time for sardonic humour.

Finally our passports were stamped, and we were through. It had taken an hour, since they had unlocked all our cases and unzipped our canvas instrument bags to root around inside. Welcome to East Berlin!

Our first concert was at the Congress Hall, a massive building with thousands of young fans going wild over us. They closed the place down a few years later, and demolished it because of asbestos. But on that night no one had any thoughts of the dangers lurking in the walls and ceilings. Even now it stands out as the best live concert we ever recorded.

Yet it started badly. Somehow we just couldn't seem to warm up. You get moments like that, and it can be highly disquieting until you get into your stride. Ron Weatherburn was doing a piano solo, and as usual the rest of us, apart from the drummer and the bass player, had strolled off into the wings to leave him in the spotlight.

Staring out at the packed hall, I muttered to Andy Cooper, 'We're not getting to them, are we?'

'No, we're not.'

'Tell you what,' I said. 'I'll do "Ain't Misbehavin'". See if that does the trick.'

It did. Someone had thoughtfully provided a couple of bottles of German brandy backstage. I passed them round, and we each took a large swig, went out and wowed them. Suddenly the band was steaming. The place went mad. Over the tumult I heard a voice, 'Bravo, Kenny! One more time!' To my grateful ears it sounded like Count Basie with a German accent.

Payment could be another problem. The method of settling our bill was that we received half the money in hard currency – sterling or dollars – and the rest in 'tap washers', the name we gave to their coins, which were useless anywhere else. The mark was hardly worth the price of a bus fare anyway, so we would find ourselves weighed down with literally hundreds of coins in our bulging pockets.

We had to spend the money there, which usually meant ending up with a load of cheap rubbish to bring home in our luggage. I've still got a set of saucepans which I have been meaning to throw away for thirty years! At least I found a couple of trumpets in a shop down a side street, made in Prague, and quality stuff they were. I've still got them.

CHAPTER EIGHTEEN

THE FAN CLUB'S
BRAVEST FAN

One of the most extraordinary events in the life and times of Kenny and the Jazzmen featured a gentleman named Hans-Jurgen Kruger. We met in Magdeburg in East Germany in 1968, when he came to one of our concerts and became an instant convert. As a qualified medical practitioner, Dr Kruger was greatly in demand in the German Democratic Republic in those tense and suffocating days on the far side of the iron curtain, and for him there was no way out. Unless ...

In his heart, as he confided to me later, he had wanted to escape to the West from the moment the first slab was laid on that monstrous edifice to cut one people off from another. But it was his meeting with me during the interval at the concert hall that apparently inspired him to risk his life to achieve this potentially deadly ambition.

The story of his great escape is charted over three separate volumes of *Jazzette*, and even now it makes scary reading. He became an old friend of the Kenny Ball Appreciation Society (German chapter!), and I was honoured to count him as a friend and a follower of the Jazzmen. He recalled:

> I was born in Magdeburg, educated at state schools, and thus I was on the best route to become an upright communist. At the age of thirty, having grown somewhat older and wiser, I became doubtful about whether the socialist system was right or not.
>
> We did not have the chance of freely expressing our opinions, nor was it possible to travel abroad to the West. More and more we were lacking in breathing freely.
>
> I suddenly had the idea to escape to the West, and I couldn't get it out of my mind. The problem was how to do it: the Berlin Wall had been built in 1961, and all other frontiers had been closed. I had relatives in West Germany, and several ways of escape were discussed a thousand times with a few hand-picked friends, and given up on.
>
> The State Security Service (STASI) had their ears everywhere and in every corner. One of the hardest things to bear was that anyone, the closest of friends or even one's own family, could have been a STASI informer. Therefore only a few trusted friends could know about the plan, and only where it was absolutely necessary.
>
> It was in 1968 after meeting Kenny Ball that I first came to think seriously about getting away. But it took another eleven years (until 1980) before I was able to

set foot upon the soil of free West Germany. During those years I made several attempts, sometimes alone without any assistance, sometimes with other people and with the help of different organisations. But they all failed within the planning phase before they could even be carried out in earnest.

I was travelling a lot in my holidays, and that way took my chances to have a look at the borders to the West, from Czechoslovakia down to Romania and Yugoslavia. Frequently I was thoroughly checked and noted down in written reports. Once in 1979 I was arrested in Hungary not far from the Yugoslav border.

The state police questioned me closely all night long. As they couldn't prove my intention to escape they had to let me go, but on condition that I left Hungary immediately. I was lucky they hadn't searched the boot of my car – in it were a map of Yugoslavia, a pair of Japanese binoculars and Yugoslav currency, all of which would have been enough to guarantee me a place in prison for several years. But fortune was on my side.

A close friend named Albert had already managed to get into West Berlin, and promised to help me. In the summer of 1980 I got a message in a coded letter telling me to be prepared and plan a holiday in Hungary. The countdown was on.

On Wednesday 5 June 1980, Albert rang me in the evening and told me he was waiting for me in Hungary. Phone calls of that kind were dangerous, and had to be encrypted – you could only drop hints since some STASI snooper was certain to overhear what you were talking about. I quickly packed the most necessary things, and when midnight came I was in my car on my way non-stop to Hungary.

The next afternoon I finally met up with Albert not far from the Yugoslav border. He introduced me to two locals, both looking as though they were well experienced in Mafia affairs and neither able to speak a single word in my language. We used our hands to converse in sign language.

Albert left for Yugoslavia where he would meet me in Zagreb. I got back in my car accompanied by these two dangerous-looking men, heading for Budapest. The next night they hid me in the coach of a passenger train standing in a siding in the main station. My hiding place was above the cover moulding in the ceiling, between dusty cables and vent pipes. There I lay in the dirt, propped on my knees and elbows. Movement was almost impossible, and I would have to stay like that for twenty-four hours. This was my prison, hot and airless, and I wondered if I would hold out. But I had to if I wanted my freedom.

It was around ten p.m. when invisible hands screwed the cover moulding into place beneath me, but the train did not leave for Zagreb until noon the next day, a journey which would take a further eight hours. Throughout this horror trip I was aware that there were passengers underneath, and I had to avoid any rustling or other movement that would have made dust fall through the air shafts.

The worst moment came when the customs officials checked over the train. They actually knocked at the cover moulding and examined it with their torches while I held my breath and froze like a statue. I'm sure my heart stopped for several seconds! But then they moved on and I could breathe again.

In Zagreb, my refugee smugglers came to set me free. Albert was waiting for me, and paid my companions DM10,000, around £4,000 in those days. From there we travelled together by train to Belgrade like normal passengers. At the German Embassy I obtained a provisional passport which was enough to get me into Austria and freedom.

Ten years later the doors were opened for everybody. I gained ten years that I wouldn't have missed for anything. I made my new home in West Berlin, and when I finally met up with Kenny Ball I embraced him like a long-lost brother. I became a member of the KBAS on the spot!

There's guts for you. When we did get together and I heard Hans-Jurgen's story first-hand, I felt a mixture of sadness for the plight of these people who have to take such risks, and pride in the human spirit that gives them the strength to go through with it. And I told him as much. Bully for you, my friend.

Mother Russia herself had her moments – ah, comrades, such memories!

In Moscow in the winter of 1983, John Bennett found himself being followed by the KGB. He first became aware of unwanted shadows on his trail when he set off from the Rossiya Hotel for a spot of sightseeing and a look in the shops.

He was examining what was on show in their famous

department store GUM near Red Square when he caught the reflection in the window of two men in raincoats. He wandered on, and on the next corner casually glanced over his shoulder. There they were, acting as unostentatiously as possible, 'but standing out like sore thumbs', he told us later.

Feeling in mischievous mood, John decided to lead them a dance, and darted off down side streets and in and out of shops. He even took a ride on the Metro, like that scene from *The French Connection* with Gene Hackman tailing the drugs baron. But they were better than Popeye Doyle, Hackman's memorable character. John couldn't lose them. They followed him for a whole morning, all the way across Moscow and back to the Rossiya Hotel again.

When he regaled us with the story later, we realised that probably all of us had agents on our tail, but only John was savvy enough to spot them.

We played in the hotel's large underground theatre. Tony Pitt was our guitarist in the band at the time. His speciality was a great solo of 'Hotcha Chornia'. Afterwards, as we signed autographs in the bar, a man came up and said, 'Mr Pitt, you have done a great guitar playing. You have it written down?'

Tony said, 'No, I don't read anything. I just make it up.'

The fan was astounded. 'You have to write it down. You can't just make it up.'

'Sure I can.'

'You mean you're a fake!' And off he stormed.

Tony turned to me. 'For once in my life,' he said, 'I can't think of a suitable reply.'

'Likewise,' I said.

John Bennett gives a vivid account of the dark side of the moon of a musician's tour when he regaled *Jazzette* fans with his

'Russian Journal'. I quote this excerpt, and expect sympathetic murmurs all round:

> It is half past four in the morning. Figures are stumbling about in the darkened corridor of our hotel. Suitcases are being whisked away by porters. To Moscow airport, bound for Minsk, still in darkness. Minsk sounds cold. Definitely thermal underwear territory, I would think.
>
> At the airport we grab cups of weird-looking coffee which tastes like digestive biscuits. There is a hold-up at the customs check, but soon we are through and shivering in the departure lounge which is grey and depressing, devoid of furniture, carpets, hope. It is as though we are being assembled for the Final Solution. Then the door opens and we shuffle out into the dawn and on to the plane. Grey is the colour of everything; even the dawn is grey.
>
> Minsk is grey too. It is like a Hollywood set supposed to resemble ancient Greece. All its pillared façades in pastel shades of ochre, beige and cream look as if they have been knocked up by a carpenter and cobbled together in a hurry like gigantic bits of Lego. We have been told that very little of Minsk was left standing after the war.
>
> We've picked up a few words of Russian. *Da* for yes, *niet* for no. Judging by what I've heard so far, *niet* gets my vote for most frequently used word. *Spaceba* is not part of a typewriter, it means thank you. *Biva* is Russian for beer. We have a local roadie named Igor who has a fondness for ale, which means we could nickname him 'Igor Biva'!

In our hotel I pour myself a large Grouse whisky, switch on the TV and for the rest of the evening watch a feature film about Robin Hood and his merry men triumphing over the Sheriff of Nottingham. It is only when the credits roll that I discover it was really the story of Lenin and the 1917 revolution!

Great stuff, John. I remember it well.

We attempted to break into the Russian market by sending Nikita Kruschev our record of 'Midnight in Moscow', with our compliments. Let's warm up the cold war, and do something to melt the hearts and minds of the populace, I say. On the flip side was 'Song of the Machine Gun Regiment', which we had recorded in East Berlin. How's that for a title? Perhaps that's why we never got a handwritten letter of thanks from the Soviet premier. But reports did filter back to us that it had become a favourite of the Russian army, whose soldiers played it regularly when relaxing in their barracks. Not 'Midnight in Moscow' – I'm talking about the 'Machine Gun Regiment'. Honest!

Later we made real inroads with 'Troika' and 'Russian Instrumental', and made further waves with our big-selling numbers. We must have found some kind of favour with the authorities, because none of our records was ever banned, and we were invited back several times even as the politicians rattled their sabres at one another.

'What about "Marching Through Georgia"?' a bright spark in the entourage enquired, after we recorded it in 1981.

'I think not,' I told him. 'Wrong continent.'

On that trip to Moscow we were guests of the British Embassy, no less. Dinner was included in the invite, and we would give them a special concert afterwards. There's no such thing as a free lunch, remember, and that goes for dinner too.

The ambassador, Sir Iain Sutherland, was an impressive figure in DJ and black tie who headed a line-up to welcome us under the chandeliers. 'Ah, Mr Ball. So glad to see you. Actually I've invited a few Russian musicians along for a little, er, jam session.'

'That's OK with me,' I said.

We sat down to a memorable dinner, with vodka and champagne flowing in equal measure, or so it seemed. The ambassador had invited all his counterparts in Moscow to the shindig, so we were in pretty high-grade company. They included an American lady who was particularly delightful and outspoken, with a choice turn of phrase. I gather she was representing the US Ambassador Mr Arthur Adair Hartman, though in all the flurry of handshakes and chatter I never did get her name.

After dinner we performed a few numbers in the Embassy ballroom, which went down extremely well. But suddenly I became aware of people sidling in through the big double doors and taking up their places along the side of the small stage, armed with tubular bells, banjos, accordions, guitars, trombones, even a drum kit. They stood watching while we played for half an hour, standing close by their instruments and applauding enthusiastically after every number.

Finally I became a bit uncomfortable. They were guests, too, even if they had arrived after the feast. Maybe it was time they joined in the action.

'Would you like to come up for a blow?' That's what we say in the business, though it does sound distinctly undiplomatic in the cold light of day. I swung my arm in one of those wide gestures that embraces everybody and nobody, then backed away as there was a mad rush for the stage. Our band was virtually bundled off,

227

and I counted more than fifty musicians milling about while I signalled to the boys to creep away for a much-needed reviver.

That's when the noise started. This whole bunch of itinerant musicians all began playing at once, no rehearsal, no band leader, none of them seeming to know each other – but they were all insistent on having a go. The result was horrendous. It was the most God-awful row I'd ever heard.

'Leave them to it!' I muttered, accepting a glass of champagne from a waiter by the window. 'They won't keep it up.'

Wrong. They kept it up for two hours, total chaos, with a relentless cacophony of different sounds and rhythms. All I can say from the expressions on the diplomats' faces was that this had to be one night they weren't expecting. I wasn't too sure if it was the best commercial for jazz there has ever been, but it was certainly the funniest. At the end we knew we'd been to some party!

As we were leaving, I found myself next to the American lady diplomat. Our host was with us. She turned round to him, and I heard her utter the memorable words, 'How the bloody hell are we going to top that!'

CHAPTER NINETEEN

STREWTH! IT'S KENNY BILK!

It still happens. On a tour down under, guess what one announcer said to a packed concert hall in Melbourne? 'Ladies and gentlemen, will you please welcome Kenny Bilk and his Jazzmen!' Here we go again. And we'd only been going to Australia for about forty years! I thought of coming on and shouting, 'The name's Ball. *Acker* Ball!' But I resisted the temptation. It happens all the time, Acker and I being mistaken for one another. Don't ask me why, because studying the mugshots we don't look anything like each other. And we never, ever wear the same kind of outfits. Acker makes his statement in bowler hat and gaudy waistcoats, while I go for smart jackets of varying hues, and trousers with a knife-edge crease.

Acker gets asked to play his big hit 'Midnight in Moscow' while I'm asked for 'Stranger on the Shore'. That's OK. I'm not losing any sleep over it, and neither I suspect is my old chum. If anyone requests it at a gig, of course I'll play it – my way. We recorded it too, didn't we? Whether Acker returns the compliment I can't say for sure, but we do often appear together on the circuit as 'The Three Bs: Barber, Bilk and Ball', so maybe we'll do a duet one day.

But right now here we are back in Oz, playing in Sydney for Expo 88, and 20,000 people are cheering us on out there under the stars by the beach. We're on a stage under a canopy set in a half dome, as if someone has circumcised the Opera House. A wonderful night, and the adrenaline is pumping.

Other matters in Sydney stir our interest, and maybe our loins, and I'm not talking about the notorious King's Cross area. I'm talking about the nude parties that seem to be the current thing in this city. My first hint of this intriguing new fad is an elegant card left in the pigeon hole of our hotel, edged in gold, with the teasing invitation in embossed letters: 'Drink, eat – and drown!'

Investigating this intriguing phenomenon, I am reliably informed that the parties always take place round a pool in someone's house. This one is no exception. 'You'll be expected to take off your clothes and leave them at the door as you go in, mate,' my informant tells me.

Well, OK then. As long as the rest of the Jazzmen are there to back me up.

It's a nice house in a middle-class area. A manservant (clothed) answers the door. We are shown to a ground-floor room on the right, where sure enough there are piles of clothes lying on the carpet around the walls. 'Please join the guests when you are ready!' Jeeves retires discreetly, leaving us to discard our clothes with a certain amount of trepidation, piling them defensively in the far corner. Exploring further, we locate the kitchen and help ourselves to wine and beer from the table.

'Kenny, look out there!' Andy nudges me in my naked ribs.

I follow his gaze, through a picture window and out to a floodlit terrace beside a swimming pool in the garden.

'Christ!' There must have been some thirty people standing around drinking, chatting and laughing. No qualms, no embarrassment. No clothes. It reminded me of a nudists' convention – not that I've ever been to one, I should add hastily.

'Anybody who gets a hard-on is disqualified!' The voice comes in heavy Aussie tones from a middle-aged man with iron-grey hair and a ready smile – our host, whom I'd better call Bruce. 'We don't wish to hear, "Is that for me to hang my hat on, or are you just pleased to see me?" You'll be asked to leave – or dive into the pool to get rid of it. And the pool isn't heated.' He laughed a jolly, rough-hewn Australian laugh. Obviously a humorist.

I would love to say it all erupted into a massive Roman-style orgy, and maybe it did. If so, yours truly and his Jazzmen weren't there to see it. We downed a few beers, then quietly slipped back to the front room, scrambled into our clothes and left. We didn't even make our excuses. 'I found that all really rather boring,' Andy remarked in the cab back to the hotel. 'Most of those women would look a jolly sight sexier in clothes, anyway.'

There were nods and mutters of affirmation. 'I tell you what,' I said. 'I think it's because none of us fancied a swim.'

Andy Cooper caused us some alarm when he actually spent a night in the nick in Sydney for, would you believe, using foul language. 'In *Australia*, Andy?' I couldn't take it in when he appeared unshaven at the airport to catch an early morning flight to Melbourne by a whisker after we'd played a sell-out concert at Sydney Town Hall.

'Yeah.' He looked despondent and hung-over. Actually he looked like death warmed up. 'Have you ever heard anything so hypocritical in your life? Every other word these beggars use is 4X. How can they know what foul language is?'

The story came out. Andy had been led astray by a gentleman named Don de Silva, a musician and a great mate of the group, who had taken him on the razzle the previous night. 'It was about three in the morning. We'd done the gig, I was wide awake, we'd been to the yacht club and closed that up for the night. Don suddenly said, "I feel hungry. Do you fancy a nice meat pie?"

'"At three in the morning?" I asked. "Where are you going to get a fucking meat pie at this time of night?"

'"Come with me," he said. "I'll show you."

'We ended up at a pie stall in Potts Point, down by the wharf. Apparently it's a very well-known all-night spot, run by a charming Australian lady. Delicious pies and a mug of tea were all we wanted. We were chatting, and a few choice words came out in the course of conversation, but with no malice intended. We probably weren't even aware of it.

'All of a sudden I felt a large hand on my collar, and looked round to see the biggest copper ever. He said, "I'll teach you to swear in front of a fucking lady. You're under arrest, you Pommie bastard." And I was straight into the Black Maria!

'We were due to fly out at eight the following morning, right?' True enough, we were. Andy's eyed bulged with the indignity of what had been inflicted upon him. 'They put me in a cage – an actual cage – in King's Cross nick, bare foot and no belt round my trousers, a filthy cell filled with druggies and beggars.

'The cage was like something out of a Hollywood film. I asked for a cigarette, and the desk sergeant said, "No, you fucking cannot. Shut your mouth!"

'At which point I lost my rag, and rather foolishly said, "Why don't you give Australia back to the fucking Abbos?"'

How to win friends and influence people, Andy. Nice try. What then?

'He came to the cage, and whack! He poleaxed me with the back of his hand through the bars. I was laid out on the floor for a few seconds, and when I recovered I said to myself, Cooper, you've really cracked it this time, you and your big mouth.

'My friend put up $250 bail. That got me out, and we just made it to the airport. Big mouth Pom, that was me! I'm going to have the charge sheet framed.'

Just another episode in the life and times of a Jazzman!

The world was our oyster. We had a passport to all points of the compass. Not every gig was a pearl, in fact some gave us a distinct ache in the guts when I think back on them. One such was in the Middle East, which is not everyone's cup of tea. Somehow we had been contracted to give two concerts on a small island in the middle of the Persian Gulf, half an hour's drive from Abu Dhabi and connected by a bridge from the shore. The place was close to an oil refinery, run like an army base to keep some semblance of order.

The problem with this part of the planet is that bureaucracy is the name of the game, and they just love their form-filling. The more they can push that pen, the happier they are. Everything has to be signed and counter-signed, and you can have twenty signatures before anything happens.

We flew to Dubai to catch a connecting local flight along the coast. The travel agent who met us was named Dave, an English guy in his forties sporting a briefcase and a worried frown, who informed us that there was a heap of paperwork to get through before we could board the second plane. It was something to do with our instruments, which had obviously aroused great suspicion with the officials. Permits needed. Documents to be produced. Is that a machine gun in your guitar case, mister?

Poor Dave aged visibly as he scurried from desk to desk, and aged more rapidly when we missed the flight by ten minutes. That meant a minibus through the desert, close to 200 miles in scorching heat, with the first gig due to start at ten o'clock that night. I won't go into the sordid details, but let's just say the climactic moment was when the bus became stuck in the mud in the middle of a vast flyblown acreage of nothingness, just scrub and sand, and we had to push it out ourselves.

'Shades of the Green Goddess,' John Bennett muttered to me, as we heaved and sweated and finally got her out of the mire.

We made it to our destination with half an hour to go before curtain up, to find there was no curtain anyway, and they were still laying out a makeshift stage for us, hammering boards together on top of a hotel swimming pool. The Jazzmen, exhausted, ravenous and thirsty, were not happy.

Dave had been forced to race to Abu Dhabi airport to recover some vital papers which had unaccountably gone by air, and rejoined us looking as if he would soon be in need of a Zimmer frame.

As we gathered in a miserable group by the open reception area, a dragonfly suddenly buzzed past us like a tiny dive-bomber. As it swooped past and away into the night, someone remarked knowingly, 'Funny thing about dragonflies. Did you know that they're born, procreate and die in a lifespan of only twenty-four hours?'

There was a pregnant pause while we digested this snippet of vital information. Then our haggard tour guide brushed the last speck of sand off his creased tropical suit, and said, 'Well, I hope he has a better fucking day than I just had!' Give that man a medal!

We made a return trip to Dubai a couple of years later, and fell foul of the religious fundamentalists. It was actually New Year's Eve, a celebration they don't recognise too much in that part of the world. We were playing a concert at a five-star hotel, and giving them a spot of seasonal music to bring some cheer into the lives of the ex-pats who might be missing their homeland.

I couldn't help noticing some swarthy faces and scowling expressions from the sidelines, but thought no more about it until we belted out 'We Shall Not Be Moved', actually played and sung as a solo by our double bassist John Benson, with the rest of the boys marching in for the grand finale.

This contains the well-known line 'Jesus is my saviour ...', and it produced a tense moment when the scowlers came up to the stage and revealed themselves as political police who had been stationed along the walls to watch the show and report back to their masters.

'What's all this about Jesus is my saviour?' demanded the leader unpleasantly. 'You're not singing religious songs, are you?'

I could only think of one reply on the spur of the moment. 'Oh, no. It's about food and sustenance. It's *cheeses* is my saviour!'

And, do you know, they swallowed it.

Whenever and wherever I travel, I do TV chat shows and radio interviews. Any publicity is good publicity, that's the Kenny Ball motto, and I look forward to a load of fun and banter with the presenters. But it isn't often that you go on a programme where the host has a loaded gun on the desk beside him.

It happened to me in Florida, which is not that surprising, I suppose, considering the American gun culture. During one of our tours my schedule included a late-night appearance on a local Miami radio show. I didn't mind the late hour – I always say I'm at my best after midnight.

This was timed for two in the morning – obviously a programme for insomniacs – at a studio down near the docks. A cab picked me up at the hotel, courtesy of the radio station. As I was driven through the dark empty streets it started to look a little spooky. The only people in sight seemed to be groups of young black guys hanging around street corners, and I had no idea of the kind of area to which I was heading. We finally stopped outside some tall iron gates, with a uniformed guard inside carrying a shotgun across his chest.

'What is this – Alcatraz?' I asked, attempting one of my wittier remarks to lighten the air. The thought occurred to me that I wouldn't want to walk home, or for us to break down on the way back.

The cab driver shook his head. 'Close,' was all he said, as I was checked over and finally allowed through.

I had also been warned about the host. 'Steve is the rudest, most aggressive interviewer in the entire state,' said the PR man who was handling our publicity for the tour. 'I thought you should know. To put it bluntly, he'll tear the arse off you! You don't have to do it if you don't want to. But he's got a huge audience. A lot of folks will be listening.'

At that hour? 'Oh, I'll do it,' I said. 'What's he going to do – shoot me?'

I remembered this jokey remark when I was escorted into the small studio, ushered into a seat across from the host and handed a set of earphones to put on. I glimpsed a young, unsmiling figure talking rapidly into the microphone suspended in front of him. But then my eye was caught by something else. There was a gleaming revolver on the desk by his elbow that looked like something out of *Dirty Harry*, and I promptly forgot about everything else except the need to keep on the right side of the host.

236

A commercial break. Steve leaned across the desk. 'Hi,' he said. 'Welcome to Miami.' I glanced down at the gun. In the hundreds of times I'd been interviewed over the years, this had to be a first.

'Er, what's that? Is it for if you don't like your guests?'

He followed my look. 'Oh, that. No, it's for protection.'

'Against *me*? I play the trumpet. I've left the violin case in the car.'

He laughed at that one. 'This is for real. I've had a few death threats recently, and I've got to take them seriously. This place is like Fort Knox now. It has to be.'

The red light was still off. 'Who's threatening you?'

'Anyone … everyone … It's the kind of show I do. I'm rude to people. But it seems I overstepped the mark last week, and insulted someone with friends in low places. They've taken exception to my remarks. So I have my peacemaker by me here, just in case. And it's loaded.'

Red light on. Steve turned from pussycat into predator in one seamless move. 'So,' he began, without preamble, glowering at me. 'Tonight I have with me for you night owls out there a limey called Kenny Ball, all the way from London, England. So you're some kind of a jazz musician, right?'

I kept my smile intact. 'I'm trying to be,' I said. 'I'm working on it.'

He interrupted. 'OK, I'm sure you are. So who are your favourite jazz musicians, then?'

'Well,' I said. 'The one who started me off was Bunny Berigan.'

Steve's eyes widened suddenly. 'Bunny Berigan? How come you know all about him?'

I said, 'I've got all his records.' It was true. I had.

His face brightened like the sun suddenly emerging from behind a dark cloud. 'You're kidding,' he said. 'He's my favourite trumpeter!'

From that moment I couldn't do a thing wrong. I was on the

air, live and bubbling, for almost an hour as the night ticked away. I took a few calls from the night owls somewhere out there in the Florida darkness, but mainly Steve and I talked jazz.

I was quite sorry when it was over. He grinned, shook my hand warmly and said, 'Come back and see us again, Kenny. Any time.'

'Next time I'll bring my own gun,' I promised.

Invitations poured in from all corners of the globe. The Land of the Rising Sun was an eye-opener, a whole new bowl of rice for the Jazzmen, and on our first experience of Japan in 1965 we felt as if we had stepped into an alien culture as our luxury coach took us from the airport into the heart of Tokyo. We went out on the strength of two major hits in Japan – 'Sukiyaki' and 'The March of the Siamese Children' – and were greeted like gods, with much bowing and formality.

I did my homework, and studied the niceties of behaviour. On the plane over I had filled the boys in with some useful tips from a leaflet. '"If someone presents you with a business card, which they will all the time, scrutinise it carefully at once before you put it away. And never write on it. Handkerchiefs are seen as disgusting. If you must blow your nose in public, use a tissue and throw it away at once. It is rude to point your chopsticks at someone, and to leave them in the rice bowl during a meal."

'And you'll like this one, fellers. "Pouring a drink for yourself is also impolite."'

That's where I lost them.

First we had to get over the initial shock of our introductory concert, a sell-out in a huge auditorium amid the skyscrapers of downtown Tokyo. In those days Japanese audiences used to be almost unnervingly polite, sitting in total silence until the end of the first half before putting their hands together, and following the same procedure until the grand finale at the close. That was when their enthusiasm poured out, and the applause could go on for up to five minutes.

This meant that each number was concluded in a monastic hush. Apparently it was a sign of respect, but if we hadn't been warned beforehand we might have packed our bags after the first song and stolen off into the night. Now they've learned our western ways, and every rock concert is a riot.

There were occasional glitches with the language. 'Give it crutch,' was a favourite saying of the band – I wonder why – and became adopted as a slogan by our entourage. On our second tour in 1972, we had two Japanese roadies assigned to us, who proved happy and willing workers, helping us with our gear as we journeyed from the North Island to the South. From Sapporo and Otaru in the North Island down to Kyoto, Osaka and Yokohama in the South, via the formidable bulk of Mount Fuji, their holy mountain, we got a wonderful reception and bags of publicity wherever we set foot.

I had noticed the two roadies eyeing me curiously as I gave the band the usual clarion call before our first gig. 'Right, boys, get on the stage and give it crutch!'

'What you say?' one of them asked, puzzled.

When I explained, he brightened. 'Ah, you teach us, please?'

So we taught them. But even after two patient weeks, all they could come up with was a shout of, 'Go on stage! Give fuck crutch!' They never got it right.

The first time I ever saw and heard karaoke was on that trip, and it was absolutely hilarious. The Japanese as a nation are not good drinkers. They get ratted out of their brains on Scotch, and they think they're singing like Sinatra. Drink, of course, can lead to trouble and, even though I always instruct the boys to look the other way wherever possible, sometimes provocation can take things a step too far.

As happened in Miyazake, a coastal town on the South Island. Surprise, surprise, our footsteps took us in the direction of a drinking club late at night after we'd played the concert. Up to now the populace had been incredibly polite and gracious, but perhaps it was too much to expect it to last. A Japanese businessman sitting at the bar watched us come in, and I could see he was the worse for wear.

All of a sudden he stood up in front of his stool, and made a flying motion with his hand, then yelled out: 'Rrrrrrraaagh! Japanese air force! Plince of Wales battleship: POW!'

There was an uncomfortable silence. Then Johnny Parker, our pianist at the time, looked across at him and said, 'Boom! Hiroshima!' Johnny never took any stick from anyone, despite that gammy leg of his.

That was our cue to leave in a hurry. We were hustled out by the bouncers before World War III broke out, and pushed into taxis. 'Hotel, quick!'

It's the whisky that does it.

CHAPTER TWENTY

AN INTERLUDE
WITH HUMPH

The legendary Humphrey Lyttelton teams up with Kenny Ball regularly in Giants of Jazz *concerts around the country. They once performed twenty-nine gigs together in thirty-one days.*

I've known Kenny since before he was with Sid Phillips. We go back that far. It was in the early fifties on those mammoth concerts, fifteen bands on one show with ten-minutes' playing time each. Everybody seemed to end with 'When the Saints Go Marching In' and a drum solo. It could become quite boring! But Kenny Ball, you can always tell it's him by the ebullience and the enthusiasm. He's indestructible.

I love his humour. He's also a very kind man. We'd be signing autographs in the foyer afterwards and, if Kenny spotted someone in a wheelchair, he'd be over there talking to them. He'd make a point of it. That person would leave feeling happier.

As for rivalry between bands, there's none whatsoever between any of us. And upstaging? It doesn't happen. We're ships that pass in the night, touring bands. We meet at festivals, and the bus pulls out afterwards and we go our separate ways. I still find it fun. OK, I'm a ham! Maybe we all are. Anybody who goes on stage for fifty-four years as we've done must have a strong element of ham in their make-up!

It's also enjoying the music, getting together with musicians you've known for a long time. And it's a funny thing: we talk about 'Dr Footlights' in the theatre. It means that when the guys are ill or have flu or something they still go on – and they get better! Over the years I've very often arrived at a theatre and thought, The last thing I want is to go out there on that stage. But as soon as you step out, it's marvellous.

It's not so much that you want adulation from an audience. It's just wonderful to be able to communicate with a thousand people. You feel the warmth coming back to you.

Like Kenny, the day I wake up not looking forward to it is the day I'll stay in bed – for ever.

CHAPTER TWENTY-ONE

ONE FOR
THE ROADIE

Roadies are a breed apart, and a law unto themselves. They come from nowhere, offer their services, and if you pick a bad one they can vanish into the night without so much as a farewell handshake. But we need them. Every gig is a potential disaster area because so much can go wrong, and I can't afford someone who turns a drama into a crisis.

The first thing I look for in a roadie is a driving licence. Hopefully a clean driving licence. He needs to be an organiser, able to sort things out at a moment's notice and deal with the things I shouldn't have to bother with.

I've been through a lot of roadies over the years. I started with Arthur, then Bill. At the time of writing the Jazzmen have two roadies, Rob Millson and Sid Appleton, and they're both brilliant. Between the pair of them they sort everything out. You'll see them out there on the stage before each concert, usually wearing black, setting up the instruments and checking everything is in place.

Rob has been with us for ten years, which is something of a record. He's absolutely smashing, as honest as the day is long, and a terrific driver. Rob is the diplomat of the outfit, in charge of the important task of getting the cheque at the end of the night – with a bit of luck and a following wind – before we head off in the band bus home or to the next gig.

They're all characters. We had a roadie we dubbed 'Harpic', because we said he was clean round the bend. His real name was Harry Isaacs, and eventually he became Mayor of St Ives, so he must have done something right. He was a good guy, the type who could get things sorted. Every time I play down there in Cornwall we meet up for a pint and reminisce about the old days. When we met, Harry was one of the original hippies of the sixties. He liked a drink, too. On one occasion we were on a fortnight's cruise out of Cannes, all the way down to Greece and back, playing for our supper and having a great time mingling with both the passengers and the crew.

On the second day out, Harry was invited down to the crew's quarters for a session. He got terribly drunk, and finally was sick in the loo. His false teeth went down the pan, and ended up in the bottom of the Mediterranean. Good old Harpic, living up to his name. 'Sorry, Harpic. We can't stop the ship for you,' I said when he staggered up to me, flashing his gums. 'But you know the old saying?'

'Wha's that?'

'Nothing dentured, nothing gained!'

Poor Harry had to endure the next two weeks without his molars.

Normally he was a man of the utmost patience. But he did whinge one time when I had a new Jaguar and gave him the job of running it in. I didn't think it was a lot to ask, but Harry moaned and groaned, and even wrote a piece in *Jazzette*, as follows: 'I often get called upon to do some wacky things. But the daftest of them all had to be when Kenny gave me the job of running in his Jaguar. For three days I drove that car up and down the M1 at a steady thirty miles per hour – for sixteen hours a day. I used to think Jaguars were great cars. Now I hate the sight of them!'

'Listen, Harpic,' I told him. 'You're a roadie. The M1 is a road. Where's the problem?'

You have to look after your own, even if he proves to be a dubious character. One guy we had named Joe gave me a lot of grief. One of the roadie's jobs is to take care of the band bus, and at that time we had a large white Mercedes vehicle which Joe kept outside his house in north London when we weren't using it. The trouble was, he lived in a parking zone, and chalked up a massive amount of fines at something like £10 a day. He ignored them all, until the bill stood at several hundred pounds and the law finally caught up with him, in the form of the local council.

Joe appeared at Marylebone Magistrates' Court, and to his horror was given three months in Pentonville nick. They allowed him one phone call from the cells. Out of the blue I heard a panicky voice shouting down the line, 'Kenny! I'm going to jail.'

'Do not pass Go!' I rejoined, feeling jocular.

'No, this is serious. I'm going down for three months. You've got to get me out.'

'How much?' I demanded.

'Three hundred quid! In cash. Now.'

I shot off to the bank, grabbed the money and hurtled round to the court. As I drove up to the entrance, no kidding, I spotted my roadie being hustled into the back of a blue prison van. I leaped out and banged on the window.

'Get him out! *Get him out*!' I hollered. 'I've got the money!' I waved a bundle of notes to prove it.

Today I suspect they would have driven off regardless. But somehow, after a lot of cajoling and form-filling, we got him out of there. On the steps of the court, Joe shook my hand. 'Thanks, Kenny. You're ace,' he said.

I never saw him again.

Another guy we had was an American, a huge fellow who weighed more than 20 stone. He was *big*. When he walked into a room, the room shrank. I put my usual first question to him. 'Do you have a driving licence?'

'Sure, sir,' he said, and foolishly I never asked to see it.

His first job was a gig we had in Herne Bay. We meet up in central London, and we're off on the M2 down towards Ramsgate. Our man is driving all over the place, ending up on the forbidden hard shoulder which he stuck to all the way down. God knows how the police didn't pull us in.

'You should be out there,' I shouted from the passenger seat, gesturing at the main highway.

'Why?' he retorted. 'I'm doing OK here.'

He had no licence, of course. And no idea of the Highway Code, either. Mr America lasted two weeks, and was fired before he got us all killed.

Roadies also have to link up with security to guard our backs and make sure we're safe if anyone becomes obnoxious, which I must say is thankfully rare. But it does happen, usually because some drunk gets the impression we're flirting with his girlfriend.

Over the years, I can honestly say there have only been three incidents where violence flared and things got ugly. One was when we played in an open-air concert in Battersea Park. It was in the late eighties. Afterwards we went for a drink at a pub half a mile away before being driven home. I was standing at the bar nursing a gin and tonic, chatting to people who had been in the audience.

The conversation was the usual kind of thing. Me: 'Did you have a good time?' Them: 'Yes thanks, Kenny … great night …' Or words to that effect.

All of a sudden this guy came flying across the room, and smacked me right in the kisser. The punch knocked me down, and nearly out. Through a dim haze I heard him snarl, 'Stop looking at my girlfriend!'

Well, I had my wife Michelle with me for a start, so I wasn't aware that I was looking at anybody else. In fact I hadn't even noticed him, or his girlfriend. I thought of saying, 'The last thing I want to look at is your girlfriend, mate!' but I deemed that unwise in the circumstances.

As he towered over me the first chair hit him in the back. A second bounced off his head. Then all hell broke out, everybody piling in for a brawl that was straight out of a Wild West film. Chairs were smashed, tables went over, bottles went through the windows and bodies rolled across the floor. All that was missing was John Wayne.

It was a total riot. I stayed down, with my hands over my head, until I saw a space and crawled through it to grab Michelle and duck out through the rear door by the Gents. The roadies who would normally have been watching my back were outside, stowing the gear away for the drive home. We got out of there, and I was driven off with a headache and a nagging thought that I should have slugged him back. But, when you're a celebrity, you can't afford to lose your rag. The consequences just aren't worth it, however strong the temptation.

The other time was at a place called Ashington, up near the coast north of Newcastle. Some obnoxious oik had been getting stoned in the bar of the theatre where we'd been performing, and was waiting for me when I came out after the show to mingle with the customers and sign autographs.

For no apparent reason this guy started baiting me. His voice rose drunkenly over the crowd. 'I suppose you think that, because you're famous, you're good. Well, you're not! You're no fucking good at all!'

Since he wasn't joking, I squared up to him, eyeball to eyeball. 'Listen, mate. All I'm doing is playing the trumpet, trying to earn a living. Have you got a problem with that?'

His girlfriend was trying to calm him down, and Michelle was doing the same for me. Basically, he was pissed. He took a swing at me, but luckily the two girls got in the way – so you could say I was saved by the belles!

Michelle shouted for the roadies. Sid and Rob came rushing up, grabbed the drunk, and dragged him off me as he tried to get at me again. Then they marched him to the door and gave him the bum's rush into the street.

'Sorry about that, Michelle.' The other girl had disappeared.

'It could have been nasty, Kenny. What brought it on?'

'I've no idea, love,' I said wearily. 'It goes with the game.'

But, thank goodness, not too often.

The final incident took place in Bradford – and this time I actually left the stage to go down into the audience and thump somebody! Now this is a *mad* thing to do, and I broke every rule in the book by doing it. There must have been 2,000 people who saw me do it, too, because the place was stuffed to the rafters.

A bloke in the stalls had been heckling me, but not in the normal way, which I can handle. All entertainers have their ways of dealing with hecklers. The secret is to be jokey enough to shut them up, but not too inflammatory to wind them up further. Above all, you've got to win over the rest of the audience.

My usual riposte is 'Why aren't you sitting over by the wall? That's plastered as well.' Or 'The last time I saw a mouth like that, it had a hook in it!' And a rather nice one, addressed to the audience in general at the expense of the noisy interrupter, 'Aren't they delightful at that age?'

This time the heckler was just too loud, too obnoxious and wouldn't stop. His voice even rose above the applause after one of my trumpet solos. 'What a load of fucking shit you are!'

Finally I couldn't take any more.

I strode down the steps off the stage, marched up the aisle to his seat, grabbed hold of him by his shirt and swore at him. I admit it: I totally lost it. I had my trumpet in one hand and a fistful of shirt in the other. To put it mildly, I questioned his parentage in no uncertain manner, and suggested he embarked upon reproduction and travel in two short words, the second being 'off'!

OK, it was a stupid thing to do. The unwritten rule says an entertainer should never ever charge down into the audience, whatever the provocation. Luckily the roadies were hot on my heels and took the situation in hand before it got worse.

'Get back on stage, Kenny!' Rob, ever the diplomat, kept his cool. 'And you,' he said to the heckler, 'out!' Two against one, and the oik did as he was told. He may have been pissed, but he wasn't so far gone not to know when discretion was the better part of Dutch courage. One less in the audience for the rest of the night.

So roadies are essential to the smooth running of the outfit. The final part of our team, and an integral one, is Heather Lewis, my super-efficient PA, secretary and secret weapon. Behind the scenes she organises everything, takes care of all the bookings and date sheets, and generally keeps me in order. Actually her husband Ray Lewis, who is retired now, was a professional soccer referee, and was in charge of that terrible Liverpool–Nottingham Forest match the Hillsborough disaster occured. He stopped the match. It affected him so badly he left the game shortly after.

If we're doing up to sixteen gigs a month, we need all the details set out like a military operation: venues, times of starting, contact points to pick up the band bus, emergency numbers, all the hundred and one things nobody ever thinks about. A tall brunette with a lovely warm personality, Heather used to work for a theatrical agent until he retired. That's when I had the sense to step in and ask her if she'd like to work for me full time. I'm delighted that she said yes. That was fifteen years ago, and she has been with me ever since. She's also a fan of the band and, most important of all, she thinks I'm wonderful!

CHAPTER TWENTY-TWO

FOOTBALL CRAZY

I've been involved in some crazy ideas, but none more fanciful than the time I was invited to cut an LP of football anthems in 1998. The plan originated from Peter Clayton, a millionaire who loved swing and jazz. Out of the blue he arranged a meeting, and said, 'I'd like to combine my enthusiasm for jazz and soccer with an album: *Kenny Ball Plays Football Anthems.*'

His scheme was to put us into the middle of a big stadium, fill it with supporters from sixteen top soccer sides and get the crowd to sing along to their team's anthem. I'm a keen soccer fan myself. I have fond memories of a hilarious incident only four years ago when two pubs were competing for the Kenny Ball Cup which I present every year to Sunday league sides in the North. This particular game was being played at Seaton Carew, County Durham, and was abandoned after fierce winds and driving hail swept over the pitch and obscured most of it. The players could hardly see in front of their faces, and were doing their best to play with their backs turned to keep the hail out of their eyes.

Finally, sixty-five minutes into the match with the Touchdown pub trailing Wingate 2–3, the referee called it off. Everyone trooped from the pitch, apart from one chap who missed the decision and valiantly went on with his job – a linesman named Peter Rhoden who continued to run the line for a full five minutes before he realised he was the only one on the field!

So, when Peter Clayton came to me with his football anthem project, I said, 'It's a fantastic idea – but no way! I'd love to, but I can't. Forty thousand supporters? How are you going to get them all to sing in the right key, at the right time and with the right words? Would the crowd know one anthem from another – and would they care? They'll simply try to upstage each other. Can you imagine "You'll Never Walk Alone" from the Liverpool fans being drowned out by the Chelsea lot giving tongue to "Blue is the Colour"? It will be mayhem on the terraces! I'm sorry …'

Peter wasn't at all happy, and went away to think about it. Two days later he was back on the phone. 'I've cracked it,' he said. 'I've booked the Treorchy Male Voice Choir in Swansea. They're very famous, ninety strong, and they'll do it if you will.'

Now that's a lot of voice, and I went for the idea straight away. Now we were in business. I got Hugh Ledigo to write all the arrangements, sixteen numbers in all. A number of teams had recorded their own songs at that time, so it wasn't hard to find the words.

He had to write the band parts in such a way that they would support the choir, but also with sections where you could hear the Kenny Ball sound doing its own thing. It was a constant juggling act. The only thing I can swear to is that we never used the words 'The referee's a wanker!' Or, if we did, I wasn't aware of it!

Finally we laid down the entire thing over three days in a studio without the choir. We took the result down to Swansea and recorded these wonderful male voices over the tapes. It was great. It was so good that our entrepreneur friend insisted on reinstating arena sounds as if it was a stadium background.

Personally, I think that spoiled it – but he got what he wanted. He was the paymaster, and that's what went into the shops. He brought the commentator Brian Moore in to talk about every team that was represented. He even dug out archive material of all the teams, which was inserted as well like an information package on a soccer programme.

You have to take your hat off to him for an ambitious idea. But it didn't sell very well. In fact, in 2002 it was reissued without the sound effects under the title *Singalonga Kenny*, which did bring some more funds into the coffers.

I suspect that when you have a choir singing 'Maybe It's Because I'm a Londoner' in broad Welsh accents it doesn't always have the desired effect. But where would you be without enthusiasts – especially rich ones?

CHAPTER TWENTY-THREE

SWINGING ON

Swinging on through the nineties and into the twenty-first century, we can now call on a repertoire of more than 500 numbers that the band all know. If we need a last-minute replacement musician, because of illness perhaps, we may have to rehearse. But ninety per cent of the time we can talk it through. We don't necessarily have to go out on stage and play, even with a new face debuting. Most musicians in the Dixieland and mainstream area know the tunes anyhow. People don't realise how talented some of these people are – their whole life is their music, it's what they live for.

Sometimes I'll freshen everybody up by running through their solo with them on stage. A song like 'The March of the Siamese Children', which was a number-one hit for us, is actually fairly complicated and needs an occasional look without an audience to get the details spot on again.

The way I run the band has always been to keep everything as friendly as possible. I make a point of thanking each member of the group after every show. If I've got a comment or criticism, I'll present it tactfully. 'May I just say that, when you do so-and-so, would you mind doing it this way instead of that … how do you feel about it?' We change the solos once every year, and work it all out amicably.

Everybody is sensitive. Especially musicians, who obviously have to have a temperament to play jazz. For me, encouragement works better than bullying. Some band leaders can be real bastards. Benny Goodman was notorious: they used to say he had 'the evil eye', meaning that he never missed a trick, and would make people's lives a misery if they got it wrong.

The trumpet is a demanding mistress. You have to look after her, spoil her a little and be totally dedicated to her if you want to get full satisfaction and great results. Actually it's one of the hardest instruments to play. I've learned over the years just how demanding it can be. I practise two hours every day, starting at five in the afternoon, but I still believe you never master the instrument. Never. It's there as a challenge for the rest of your life. You can play great and it's a wonderful feeling. But you never conquer it.

Undoubtedly it's one of the loudest too. So you have to have supreme confidence if you want to be the leader and hold the whole thing together. You can get over making a mistake on a clarinet or a trombone, or even a piano or the drums. But if you make a mistake on the trumpet everybody says, 'Oh, shit. He's no good!'

There was a trumpet player called Bert Ezzard, a lovely chap, who gave me a piece of advice once. I said to him, 'What happens if you make a mistake, Bert, and hit a duff note when you're playing solo?'

He replied, 'You wait a couple of bars, then go back and make the same mistake again. Everyone will think, Now *there's* a modern jazz player!'

So now, every time I crack a note, I go back two bars later and do it again!

I clean my trumpet every night, washing it out with plain warm water. With soapy water you'll wash the oil off the valves. If you drink, alcohol goes in, and it's like an acid that permeates in and hits the third valve first, so it takes all the oil off your third valve, which then has a tendency to stick first. The third valve is actually the furthest one away, but your puff goes straight through to it first, then back round to the first and second. Sounds complicated, but really it isn't.

What I use is a special trumpet oil, very fine and thin. It's also highly poisonous. You mustn't get it into your mouth, or even on your mouthpiece. If you get it in your mouth it'll kill you. The one thing you don't do is use anything like olive oil or three-in-one.

On the downside, I've had a few bouts of illness in recent years, including a couple of spells in hospital which always makes me fret. I just hate being incapacitated. Medically speaking, I did relinquish my spleen to the surgeons, but without going into the boring details they took bits out of me in one operation, then sewed them back again in another. Now I'm right as rain.

And to those fans who heard about it and sent me get-well messages and flowers, my own message now is that Kenny did get well again, and bless you all for your thoughts and kind words. I'm only sorry that I had to miss some dates and disappoint you, but I know that Andy did a marvellous job by standing in for me and keeping the show running.

My lovely lady Michelle also went through the wringer. Poor girl, she was diagnosed with lumbarloctomy (I think that's the word for it), which is as unpleasant as it sounds. In layman's terms, the jelly substance between the vertebrae in her spine collapsed. I have never seen anyone in such agony, and I only wish I could somehow have taken the pain away from her.

That was around 1985, and in the end she went to fourteen different treatment centres before they were able to mend it. A scanner found that her spinal cord was actually twisted. The doctors were marvellous. They solved it by fusing the vertebrae together, and in all that time Michelle faced it with such stoicism and bravery that my heart bled for her. Sometimes you just feel so helpless when someone you love is suffering like that.

Michelle showed her own fighting spirit in December 2003 when she came through a bad fall at our converted farmhouse near Stansted after suffering broken ribs and more damage to her back. She spent Christmas in intensive care, and saw 2004 in from a hospital bed – but she could still manage a smile and a joke as I sat by her bedside holding her hand and telling her how much I loved her. There's a woman with supreme courage.

And the future? There's always a new song to find, a new interpretation of a golden oldie to stir the blood. My personal challenge is that, even when I know someone's done a great rendering of a record, I'll have a stab at it – like Bing Crosby's version of 'Samantha' or Sinatra's 'My Way'.

But I admit there are some that can't be repeated, like Louis Armstrong's solos when he was in his twenties, with his Hot Fives and Hot Sevens. You just can't improve on something like that. 'Potato Head Blues', 'Cornet Chop Suey', 'Wild Man Blues': those performances have become part of jazz history. So you can't do much better than the top man. If someone requests one of those tunes, I try to play it with the same swing, but I know I won't better it.

But, if jazz wants to survive, it must look to the new generation. There are plenty of talented youngsters around. I just hope they're 'full of beans and tram tickets' like my dad, and like me. I tell aspiring young jazz enthusiasts, 'Look at the music. Look at the tune. After you've learned it, throw away the music sheets and play it your own way!' In other words, put your own stamp on it.

My mission in life is to set people's feet tapping. When you're winning over an audience, their feet are tapping and they probably don't even know it! That's the way I've always been, and the way I'll always be until, like Humph, the day comes when I don't get out of bed in the morning. Perish the thought! That will never happen, because we won't let it! Music is in our blood, and jazz keeps us young at heart and youthful in spirit.

Why, only last December, Princess Anne walked across the dance floor after we'd been playing our hearts out at a charity bash, and said, 'Thank you for that, Kenny. You look so young!' For that, ma'am, I thank *you*.

Now for my final blast. I bid farewell in the only way I know how, as I have always done in my regular *Jazzette* letters to all those wonderful and loyal fans who have stuck with me through the years.

Ready? Here we go …

HAVE A BALL!

SONG LIST

Songs are listed in alphabetical order, with the years of their release listed alongside.

55 Days to Peking	63	All Of Me	73
900 Miles	64	All Through The Night	70
1919 March/Rag	60, 61, 90	Alligator Crawl	71
1999	68	Am I Blue	63
10,000 Years Ago	70, 72	Amen	78
		American Patrol	61
A		Anchors Aweigh	64
Acapulco	63, 72, 79, 92, 97	And I Love Her	98
		Annie's Song	79, 84
Ace In The Hole	68, 95	April Showers	73
After You've Gone	81, 89	Arcadia Stomp	62
Ain't It Hard	64	Arthur's Theme	87
Ain't Misbehavin'	68, 71, 77, 78, 89, 97, 99	As Time Goes By	87
		At A Georgia Camp Meeting	99
Ain't Nobody Here But Us Chickens	99	At The Jazz Band Ball	63, 65, 68 72, 77 90
Alabama Jubilee	64		
Alexander's Ragtime Band	62, 81	Auf Weidersehn	83

261

Compiled by Phil Hoy

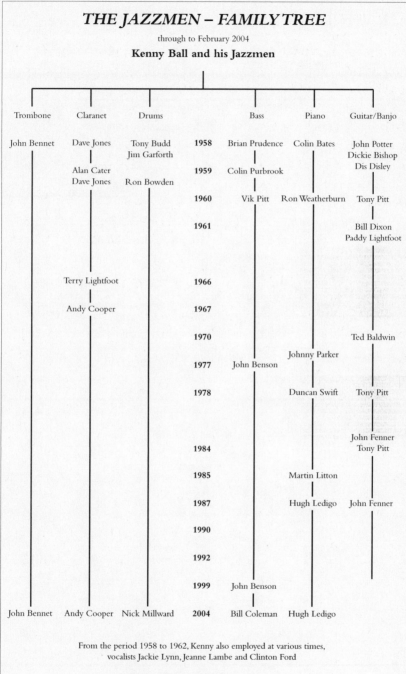

THE JAZZMEN – FAMILY TREE

through to February 2004

Kenny Ball and his Jazzmen

	Trombone	Claranet	Drums		Bass	Piano	Guitar/Banjo
1958	John Bennet	Dave Jones	Tony Budd / Jim Garforth		Brian Prudence	Colin Bates	John Potter / Dickie Bishop / Dis Disley
1959		Alan Cater / Dave Jones	Ron Bowden		Colin Purbrook		
1960					Vik Pitt	Ron Weatherburn	Tony Pitt
1961							Bill Dixon / Paddy Lightfoot
1966		Terry Lightfoot					
1967		Andy Cooper					
1970							Ted Baldwin
1977					John Benson	Johnny Parker	
1978						Duncan Swift	Tony Pitt
1984							John Fenner / Tony Pitt
1985						Martin Litton	
1987						Hugh Ledigo	John Fenner
1990							
1992							
1999					John Benson		
2004	John Bennet	Andy Cooper	Nick Millward		Bill Coleman	Hugh Ledigo	

From the period 1958 to 1962, Kenny also employed at various times,
vocalists Jackie Lynn, Jeanne Lambe and Clinton Ford

Kenny Ball and his Jazzmen